SEARCHING *for* HOPE

SEARCHING

for

HOPE

★ ★ ★

LIFE AT A

FAILING SCHOOL

IN THE HEART

OF AMERICA

★ ★ ★

MATTHEW TULLY

Indiana University Press
Bloomington & Indianapolis

This book is a publication of

Indiana University Press
601 North Morton Street
Bloomington, Indiana 47404-3797 USA

iupress.indiana.edu

Telephone orders   800-842-6796
Fax orders   812-855-7931

⊖ The paper used in this publication meets
the minimum requirements of the American
National Standard for Information
Sciences—Permanence of Paper for Printed
Library Materials, ANSI Z39.48-1992.

Manufactured in the
United States of America

Library of Congress Cataloging-in-
Publication Data

Tully, Matthew.
  Searching for hope : life at a failing school in
the heart of America / Matthew Tully.
    p. cm.
  ISBN 978-0-253-00593-9 (cloth : alk. paper)
— ISBN 978-0-253-00597-7 (eb)
  1. Emmerich Manual High School
(Indianapolis, Ind.) 2. Children with social
disabilities—Education (Secondary)—
Indiana—Indianapolis. I. Title.
  LD7501.I4646T85 2012
  373.772'52—DC23

                                    2011047610

1 2 3 4 5   16 15 14 13 12

TO VALERIE,
the greatest thing that has ever
happened to me; and

TO REID,
the greatest thing that has ever
happened to us.

CONTENTS

ACKNOWLEDGMENTS *ix*

PROLOGUE *xi*

1 WHY ARE YOU HERE? *1*

2 I NEVER WOULD HAVE THOUGHT HE WOULD BE A DANDELION. *10*

3 CAN YOU BELIEVE THIS? *15*

4 WE DO A GOOD JOB WITH THE KIDS WHO SHOW UP. *24*

5 I HATE THIS SCHOOL. *32*

6 GO TO CLASS, ZACH. *40*

7 WE'RE NOT GOING TO BE AVERAGE HERE. *68*

8 WHERE'S THE SCHOOL SPIRIT? *80*

9 I DON'T LIKE BEING CALLED STUPID. *87*

10 YOU HAVE TO CRAWL FIRST. *100*

11 WE'RE DROPPING OUT. *113*

12 I GET HIT ALL THE TIME. *124*

13 WE JUST COULDN'T GET ANYTHING STARTED. *131*

14 WHAT'S GONNA HAPPEN, MR. GRISMORE? *137*

15 COULD YOU IMAGINE IF WE FILLED THE HOUSE? *144*

16 IT FEELS LIKE I'M A SOMEBODY. *150*

17 I USED TO BE BAD. *161*

18 I KNEW I DIDN'T WANT THAT. *169*

19 THERE'S NOBODY THAT CAN'T DO SOMETHING. *175*

20 IT NEVER STOPS AROUND HERE. *185*

21 I LIKE TO SOLVE PROBLEMS. *193*

22 I'M THE KID WHO DOESN'T EXIST. *201*

23 TROUBLE FOLLOWS ME. *211*

24 I'M WILLING TO RUN THESE SCHOOLS. *218*

25 NOW I KNOW WHY I'M TALL. *227*

26 WOW, THIS IS AMAZING! *236*

27 WE'VE ACTED LIKE THIS IS OKAY. *243*

28 YOU ARE SURVIVORS. *248*

EPILOGUE *256*

Illustrations follow page 52.

Manual High School's leaders, teachers, students, and parents provided me with rare and sweeping access to the school for nearly ten months. That access included the ability to sit in on extremely sensitive meetings in the offices of the principal, dean, social worker, police officers and others. Because of the nature of certain stories, I have changed the names of a small number of students.

ACKNOWLEDGMENTS

This book is the result of more than two years of support and assistance from family, friends, colleagues, sources, and readers of the *Indianapolis Star*. To everyone who played a part—and there are so many who did that I cannot name them all—you have my deepest appreciation.

Most fundamentally, this book would not have been possible without the nearly complete access I was given to Emmerich Manual High School during the 2009/2010 school year. For that, I thank Indianapolis Public Schools superintendent Eugene White, former Manual principal Richard Grismore, and former dean Terry Hoover. I would also like to offer my gratitude to all of the teachers, staff, students, and parents who tolerated the sometimes-pesky presence of a newspaper columnist for nearly ten months. Thank you for sharing your stories, thoughts, praise, complaints, and, most of all, your time.

I am fortunate to have now spent several years working for a pair of wonderful editors at the *Star*, Dennis Ryerson and Tim Swarens, who allowed me the luxury of writing thirty-four columns on one high school and championed my series every step of the way. Tim and Dennis, I couldn't have done this without your expert guidance and support.

I would like to pay a particular tribute to Danese Kenon, a talented photojournalist whose images always make my words look better, and to Andy Murphy, who worked hard to find a publisher for this book. Thanks also to the following people who provided insight into the book's subject matter or agreed to read and critique various drafts of the manuscript: Suzanne Anthony, John Barrow, Scott Elliott, Jill Haughawout, Darolyn Jones, Cathy Knapp, Tammy Laughner, Daniel Lee, Spencer Lloyd, Jay Mathews, Kathleen O'Malley, Brendan O'Shaughnessy, Julie Steck, Brent Walls, Charles Walls, and Vickie Winslow. I greatly appreciate the effort and support of the staff at Indiana University Press and the methodical and caring work of copyeditor Jill R. Hughes.

I was moved many times by the reaction to my series from readers of the Indianapolis Star. It's easy to be cynical these days. But you weren't, and your support and heartwarming response to my columns week after week turned a project I had haphazardly undertaken into the professional highlight of my life. You strengthened my lifelong love affair with newspapers and made a difference in the lives of many Manual High School students.

Most important, I would like to thank my wife, Valerie, who pushed me to write this book, and my son, Reid, who in the first months of his life allowed me to read chapter after chapter to him while he played with his toys. I love you both.

PROLOGUE

The third week of the 2009/2010 school year was coming to a merciful end. It had been a week full of problems, headaches, and disasters. But that's pretty much how every week is at Manual High School. Administrators were frustrated that hundreds of students still hadn't shown up for school, or had shown up but immediately stopped coming, or were only coming occasionally. Day after day, teachers complained about students who cursed at them in the hallways, strolled into class late and left early, or threw fits that disrupted their classrooms. A few students in this school of about nine hundred had already been arrested or expelled for dealing drugs, having sex in a locker room, or threatening teachers. "Something's in the air this year," Terry Hoover, the school's tough-talking dean of discipline, told me that Friday morning. "I can already feel it."

I had been at the school every day for the past three weeks, working on a series of columns for my newspaper, the *Indianapolis Star*, about the struggles and challenges facing failing urban schools. Manual was one of several such schools in Indianapolis, riding a graduation rate of only 39 percent, test scores that showed far more students failing than passing, and a poverty problem that cruelly gripped most of the students who walked through the halls.

My embedment into Manual had been highly successful so far. At least that's what I thought on that hot Friday afternoon as I stood on the steps overlooking the school's courtyard and watched as hundreds of students raced to waiting school buses. I had written two front-page columns so far—one that exposed many of the problems that held the school back, from discipline and drugs to apathy and academic failure, and another that told of the struggles the school faced just to get kids to show up in the first place.

The columns received a tremendous response from readers. Through dozens of e-mails and phone calls, they had told me they'd had no idea that the things I was writing about actually occurred in schools in the mild-mannered city of Indianapolis. They cringed at the tales of burned-out teachers and the stories of students with profound personal problems. They were outraged and saddened by what they read and called for sweeping changes to the way schools are run. I was excited about the reaction and the work I'd done. It's not easy to get complete access to a school, access that includes the ability to sit in on meetings with social workers and school police that are normally held behind closed doors, but I'd been given that access.

Soon, though, before the first buses would roll away from the school that Friday afternoon, I would learn that I hadn't yet come close to painting a full picture of what Manual was all about. My columns had exposed some of what was going on at the surface—in the classrooms, in the offices, and even in the small room that housed the four-person school police unit. But I hadn't gotten to the heart of the school—in other words, the emotion and stories of the students, teachers, administrators, and others who made up Manual High School. Not yet.

Emmerich Manual High School wraps around a grassy, tree-covered courtyard on three sides like a horseshoe. With sidewalks crisscrossing it and sculptures and plaques dotting it, the courtyard is the kind of idyllic setting you might find in many of the wealthier school districts within Indianapolis and its suburbs. It's one of the nicest spots on the grounds of Manual, or anywhere else on the gritty near south side of Indianapolis that houses the school. But I had learned that students entered the courtyard only during those few minutes at the beginning and end of the school day as they made their way to and from the parking lot.

It wasn't always that way. For decades the courtyard served as a shortcut between one wing of the building and another or as a hangout during lunch periods. It was clearly designed to be a gathering place for students. That idea died more than a year before my arrival at Manual after a fight in which one student pulled a gun on another. School police had enough trouble patrolling the halls of the three-story brick building, along with its many nooks and crannies, without having to worry about the courtyard. By the time I wandered into the school, the courtyard was no longer open to students during the school day. It was instead another depressing reminder of what Manual used to be.

I was as tired as the teachers when that third week came to an end. Spending seven hours a day in a school was something I hadn't done since my senior year of high school twenty-two years earlier. To be honest, I hadn't even done it much back then. Either way, I'd forgotten how draining a day in a school could be, and the constant drama at Manual could particularly soak the energy out of a person. It's not easy to listen to a fourteen-year-old girl tell administrators that another student was teasing her because she'd been the victim of a rape, or to watch a fourteen-year-old boy cry on his way to jail for drug possession, or to wonder if a student whose mother has kicked her out of her house would find a place to stay. A day at Manual often left me drained.

Meanwhile, my first column—provocatively headlined "Can This School Succeed?"—had irritated quite a few people in the school. While many teachers appreciated the idea that others in the community were finally able to see what they faced every day, many students, and even a few educators, complained that I was there to sensationally criticize their school. I wasn't, of course. Rather, I'd gone out of my way to write about the school's positives in that first column. I had written about teachers, students, and programs that impressed me. But the negatives had clearly dominated both the column and everyone's attention. And let's be real: when your school's graduation rate is 39 percent, and when it has a few dozen arrests each year, and when the halls are never quiet or empty, there are simply more negatives than positives. My columns had to reflect that balance. That's what I said to myself every time I received a dirty look in the hallway or heard the occasional student complain.

"I hate reporters," one student in the welding class said as I talked with his teacher one day.

"There's the dude who thinks we're all stupid and poor," another said.

Of course, I didn't think that. But I had written an extremely tough column about the school and some of its teachers and students. I had put the school's flaws and deep-seated problems on the front page of the local newspaper, the largest paper in the state. I had written about the low incomes and family troubles that haunted many students. I had turned Manual into a glaring example of the many failing schools across Indianapolis and the country. So I understood the young man's point.

As the students walked to their buses that Friday afternoon, they laughed and teased one another. Some walked alone; others were in large groups. One boy shouted at another, telling him to call that afternoon. Girls and boys held hands. For all the problems these students faced, I thought, for all the heartbreaking stories I'd already heard, they looked like nothing other than typical American teenagers at the end of another school day. They were full of potential. For too many, it was potential that might never be tapped. But it was potential nonetheless.

As the students boarded their buses, I stood chatting with Sgt. John Barrow, head of the school police force. I had spent much of my time in the previous days wandering the halls with Barrow, who seemed to know everyone, and everyone's story, and was in many ways my guide into the school's inner workings. It helped that he was constantly cracking jokes, a trait that livened up more than a few mundane hours. "Would you two please stop that before I throw up?" Barrow shouted at two students who'd begun making out in the courtyard.

As Barrow continued to gently tease the students, I noticed two girls standing ten feet from me. They weren't just standing; they were plotting. And they were about to give me a lesson about their school and, ultimately, change the direction of the series I was undertaking, a series of columns my editors had titled "The Manual Project." The girls were nervous and clearly looking at me. One nearly pushed the other in my direction, urging her to "Go talk to him." She did. I was happy.

By that point I'd had many conversations with students, but most were relatively quick and all had been initiated by me. It wasn't always easy to get to know teenagers who, in many cases, had become guarded by many years of disappointments. And even though numerous students had already shared personal details about their struggles, my conversations with them had failed to penetrate that first layer of their story—the layer they were comfortable sharing. My project would be fine, but forgettable, if I failed to dig deeper into the school and the people in it.

"Can I talk to you for a minute?" the girl said as she approached.

"Absolutely."

She introduced herself. Her name was Allison Tomlinson. She was a seventeen-year-old senior with curly brown hair, wearing glasses and with an extremely serious look on her face. Her friend, another seventeen-year-old senior, was Kelly Leatherbury. She looked just as serious and stood to Allison's side. "We're wondering," Allison said bluntly. "Are you going to write about the kids who are trying to do the right thing at Manual?"

Her question struck me like a punch to the gut. The tone of her voice was somewhere between hurt and scolding. In essence, it reinforced the notion that a series about a struggling urban high school couldn't be only about test scores, graduation rates, arrests, and expulsions. It couldn't turn the positive stories into little more than footnotes and sidebars. For it to be successful, I would have to work even harder—and I had already worked pretty hard those first three weeks—to learn about the people within the school. Allison's question also told me that there were people in this school who took its reputation to heart, who feared that criticism of Manual was a criticism of them, who genuinely saw me as someone whose work could influence what people thought of them and where they could go in life.

Obviously the problems at the school had to be chronicled. Ignoring and sugarcoating them would be the same as forgiving and accepting them. Doing so would give readers little reason to demand change and would do little to put pressure on school leaders. It would be unfair to the many students and teachers throughout the city who deserve better schools. Still, the heart of schools like Manual can only be found in the students and teachers and other employees who are, as Allison said that Friday afternoon, doing the right thing.

I told Allison I had to write tough columns about her school's problems. I said some of the columns might make the school look bad. But I promised to do as much as I could to tell the other side of the story and to write about the people who were doing the right thing. I asked if I could start with her and her friend. She agreed and we made plans to meet in the school library the following Monday.

"I just want people to see that there are kids at Manual who really care," Allison said.

"I do too," I said.

Then two remarkable girls walked away. At that point I had known them for only a minute. But they had already changed the way I looked at Manual, and in doing so they had turned my series into a project unlike any I had ever worked on.

SEARCHING *for* HOPE

1

* * *

WHY ARE YOU HERE?

It was August 12, 2009, the first day of the school year, and I was already late. My plan was to walk through the front doors of Manual High School by 7:00 AM so that I could be there thirty minutes before the morning bell. I wanted to see what the students looked like as they entered the school and officially ended their summer vacations. Were they excited? Were they depressed? What did they have to say about the next nine months of their lives? But as I raced to the school, the clock in my nine-year-old Honda Accord showed that I was several minutes behind schedule. Just like when I was in high school, I thought to myself. Late as always.

My drive took me through the pride of Indianapolis, its compact but thriving downtown, and by the many office buildings that house the capital city's top lawyers and lobbyists. I drove past Conseco Fieldhouse, home to the NBA's Indiana Pacers, and then past the headquarters of the city's largest and most important employer, the pharmaceutical giant Eli Lilly and Company. Finally I entered the city's near south side. Just three minutes from downtown, the community is full of old and intermittently abandoned homes, depressed neighborhoods, and the occasional graffiti-scarred building or empty lot. The area used to be vibrant—long ago, that is. These days it's not the city's worst neighborhood. It doesn't have the worst crime rate. The neighborhood actually has many residents who still care, and other parts of the city have seen worse deterioration. But the neighborhood is hurting. In many ways it's just hanging on.

Manual High School was once the gem of the near south side; it was a school known for its sports programs, its curriculum, and the city and civic leaders it produced. Four decades ago it was the dream destination of many young education students eager to launch a teaching career. Four decades ago families were proud to send their children to Manual. That was a long time ago.

On this morning Manual was beginning another academic year with its reputation firmly in place as one of the state's worst-performing schools. There were few signs to suggest a turnaround would be coming, even though the state was finally beginning to demand one. Manual's failures were so entrenched and profound that it was one of twenty-three Indiana schools the state was threatening to take over. Like many once-stellar city schools from coast to coast, Manual's glory was found largely in its distant past.

By a bit after seven o'clock the parking lot was filling with cars and buses, and students who lived nearby were wandering onto the grounds from different directions. A few students stood on a median in the middle of Madison Avenue, waiting to cross the sometimes-busy street that runs in front of the school. They were easy to spot in their mandated uniforms of khaki or black slacks and red, white, or black shirts. The students laughed and talked with one another, and as I approached the school I wondered how teenagers from one of the city's most poverty-ridden areas would react to a balding, reserved thirty-nine-year-old journalist bugging them for information about their school, their lives, their dreams, their futures, and their struggles. It would be a challenge. But I had spent a career bugging people for information, and I'd been in tougher locales than this, so I wasn't too worried.

The entryway just beyond Manual's front doors was quiet when I walked in. I didn't see anyone in the hallways that ran to my left and right. The library in front of me was empty. The main office was still. Where was everyone? "You look lost," a husky voice declared. I turned and saw Jill Haughawout, one of Manual's veteran teachers. Tall, blonde, and loud, she asked me if I needed help. I said I did and asked why the school was so quiet. "It's never quiet here," she said. "The noise is just somewhere else. The action's in the gym today. Follow me." I did as ordered, making small talk with Haughawout as the heels she later told me she rarely wore clicked on the school's hard floors. She said the students were in the gym getting their schedules and other paperwork.

Haughawout led me into the belly of the school, past classrooms, the nurse's office, a county health department office, and the athletic department. I noticed how empty the walls were, with the exception of the occasional flyer seeking players for the football team. Many of the glass-enclosed trophy cases throughout the school were empty. Nothing on the walls announced or celebrated the new school year.

Haughawout's heels continued to click, echoing through the otherwise quiet halls. "So you're a reporter?" she asked.

"A columnist," I said, offering unnecessary clarification.

"And why are you here?"

That was a question I would hear over and over during the school year. From skeptical teachers. From students. From the janitors, cops, and secretaries. Schools like Manual typically live in obscurity, and nobody at the school seemed to understand why anyone would care about its inner workings. I could appreciate their concern. Most people don't come to work or school and find a journalist prowling the halls, standing to the side taking notes, asking pesky questions, and treating occasions they considered perfectly mundane as newsworthy.

I told Haughawout I wanted to learn more about education at the ground level, about the causes of the low graduation rate and test scores that plague so many American schools. I said I picked Manual because I'd heard it wasn't as chaotic as some other local schools and that it had exhibited signs of hope. I thought it would provide more complex column material than the many other schools in town that were known for their Wild West ways. Then I asked her how she felt about the new school year.

She smiled, looked at me as if I were an idiot, and sighed. "Actually, I'm a little nervous," she said. "This is my sixteenth year. I don't know why I'm nervous. But I am. I had trouble sleeping last night."

I asked if that was typical. It wasn't. There was something unique about this nervousness. There was something about this upcoming school year that was nagging at her. It was a nervousness she felt but couldn't explain. In reality, though, there was plenty to be nervous about.

The state had zeroed in on Manual, and there were many questions about the future of its staff and administration. There was also the nervous stomachache that must come, I thought, from knowing that so many of the students a school is supposed to educate will fall by the wayside, giving up on their education and any real chance at opportunity. Then there were the massive daily challenges and hassles teachers such as Haughawout face each time they step in front of a classroom full of students at schools like Manual.

We kept walking. Manual is a big building. Built in the mid-1950s for more than 2,000 students, enrollment has declined dramatically along with the surrounding neighborhood's population and economic fortunes. The school would claim about 950 students this year. Even that number, though, was inflated by a district that was desperate for funding.

"Well, here you are," Haughawout said as we arrived at the doors to the Manual gymnasium. I took a deep breath and wished myself luck as we walked in.

Opening the doors to the gym reminded me of the scene in *The Wizard of Oz* in which Dorothy walks out of her black-and-white farmhouse and into the colorful Land of Oz. The silent hallway gave way to a loud roar of voices. Dozens of students milled about. More sat on the gym bleachers. Students gathered, hugging and catching up. I stopped by the doors and watched it all.

Before I had much time to take in the scene, however, Haughawout led me across the busy gym floor and introduced me to Richard "Rocky" Grismore, the school's perpetually overwhelmed fifty-six-year-old principal. Wearing a shirt and tie, a black mustache, and glasses, Grismore stood handing out class schedules and quickly shot down my attempt at small talk. He was far too busy for that and instead asked me in his gravelly voice to help him hand out cards. But before I had a chance to do so, another teacher showed up and took her place alongside Grismore. So I pulled out my notebook.

As Grismore worked, offering friendly greetings to the students, I asked why he was dealing with registration issues on the first day of school. "It's the parents," he said. The school had offered three days of preregistration a week earlier, but only about a quarter of the expected student population had come out for that. "That's a sign," Grismore said, "of how hard it is to get parents involved around here." Even on this day he expected only about three-quarters of his students to show. It happens every year when the district kicks off its school year in mid-August.

"We have a lot of people here on the south side who don't believe school should start until after Labor Day," he said. "So they just don't send their kids here for the first two or three weeks."

"What?" I asked. "Some parents think they get to decide when the school year begins? Can't you do something about that?"

For the second time that day, I received a look that made clear I didn't know anything about Manual High School. Grismore's eyes peered over his glasses, his lips pursed as he seemed to ponder just how big an idiot I was. Instead, he told me I was welcome to spend as much time as I wanted at his school. It was an offer he would regret more than once during the school year, but he never rescinded it.

While Grismore returned to his duties, I leaned against the wall and took in the students. Unlike at many big-city public schools, a majority of Manual's students, roughly two-thirds, were white. About a quarter were black. And the rest came from Indianapolis' growing Hispanic community. For the most part, white students mingled with other white students. Black kids talked with other black kids. And the Hispanic students in particular huddled together.

Their voices, along with those of teachers and other school employees, contributed at first to a loud collective hum. But it didn't take long for one voice to emerge above the rest. It came from Larry Whiteman, a veteran teacher who stood in the middle of the gym floor with a tired frown on his face. He spoke into a microphone, though with his deep voice and gruff demeanor, he didn't need one. "Tuck in your shirts," he told one student after another. "Pull up your pants. Come on, pull 'em up. People, let's do this right. Tuck in those shirts. Pull up those pants."

With his left hand tucked into the pocket of his tan pants, Whiteman scoured the room and spotted a student who appeared to be in violation of every one of the rules in the district's dress code. "Young man," Whiteman said in his monotone way, "pull up your pants, tighten your belt, take your hat off, and tuck in your shirt. Other than that, you're doing a pretty good job."

The student halfheartedly began to tuck in his long black shirt as he walked away. Whiteman shook his head, a head that featured a ring of white hair around a bald top. He barely moved his tall, heavy body from its spot in the middle of the floor as he scanned the room looking for students to scold. They were everywhere. The dress code was now in its third year. But many students continued to struggle with the concept of rules. Many came from homes with few rules, after all, a disconnect that caused a never-ending tug and pull between the student population and the school's adults.

Whiteman continued to bark orders, looking and sounding as if he were impersonating Gen. George S. Patton—or at least George C. Scott's impersonation of him. "Tuck in your shirt," he barked into the microphone.

I walked over and introduced myself. Whiteman didn't seem impressed. Still, he talked. He told me he'd been at Manual for twenty years and was now in charge of running the thriving in-school-suspension program. He assured me there was plenty to write about but demanded I tell my readers what was really going on in the school rather than writing puff pieces and simply carrying water for the district. He said he'd rarely seen stories that accurately portrayed life in a school like his.

"Pull up your pants," he told a student.

"So," I asked, "what's Manual like?"

And for the third time that morning, I received a look that suggested I was an idiot. Nonetheless, the question produced an answer. "It's like triage here," he said. "That's what people need to know. Some of these students are going to die." He was talking about an academic death, mind you. "Some you can save. But some you can't. I think we spend too much time with the ones who are dying and not enough time with the kids in the middle that we can save."

I had been at the school for only a few minutes. But I was already hearing a teacher argue that some of the kids in desperate need of an education should be abandoned. If that's what the teachers are saying, I thought, what chance do these kids have?

Whiteman spotted a kid in need of a scolding, and I said good-bye. I would have many more conversations with him throughout the year, conversations that would make clear he was just as frustrated and burned out but not nearly as coldhearted as he sounded that morning.

As he got back to work, I stood in the gym observing and for a while simply watched a scene that was comically inept, a process so inefficiently organized that only a government entity could have designed it. For instance, each student had to stand in separate long lines—one for a schedule and one for a lunch voucher and textbook voucher—rather than one combined line. I wondered if I was the only one puzzled by the lines for class schedules, which were based on the first letter of each student's last name. Lines with popular letters had more than thirty students. Others at times had none. But the teachers at the head of the empty lines sat bored rather than help colleagues who faced a backlog of students. This was just the start of the confusion. For more than a week after opening day, students would wander to the office to get conflicts and mistakes in their schedules corrected, missing class after class as they waited for help. For all the inherent problems facing schools like Manual, I would notice many times throughout the year that any solutions were hampered by a mind-boggling inability to put efficient processes in place. The lost class time for students was staggering.

The students, not surprisingly, didn't seem to mind. They laughed and relaxed that morning. And as eight o'clock arrived, I headed their way, into the mass of teenagers, hoping to get to know a few of them.

Three senior girls sat on the wooden gym bleachers. They whispered to one another and shot blank stares my way when I sat down next to them. They looked tough, like many of the students at Manual. But once we began to talk, they began to smile. They all laughed when I asked whether they were looking forward to graduation. "We hope to graduate," they said, before quickly warning me that a diploma at the end of the school year wasn't guaranteed, because they had fallen behind in past years. One of the girls, Rachel Tucker, told me about her job at Burger King and her hope—a very common one, I would discover—to be a veterinarian. That was just a dream, she said, that at seventeen she had already begun to abandon. She said she couldn't afford to go to Purdue, home to the state's only veterinary school, and her grades weren't good enough anyway. Maybe she would attend one of the local for-profit trade schools and eventually get a job as a veterinarian's assistant. At least she'd be able to work with animals.

At a table nearby, school staffers handed out book rental bills. Most of the students came from low-income families and received vouchers to cover most or all of their fees. "John, did you have free book rental last year?" a bookkeeper asked one student, trying to figure out if he was eligible.

"I think so," he said, looking confused. "I don't know."

"Well, how about lunch? Did you have free lunch?"

"Yeah, I did."

He received a form to take home to his mother. I noticed that staffers who gave students forms and applications to take home always told the students to have their mothers sign them. It was reflexive. They had learned not to assume the presence of a father.

Chelsea McKinney was next in line. The sixteen-year-old stood on the wooden gym floor with her right hand on her side. She wore black pants and a white polo shirt over her pregnant frame. When I said hello, she flashed a slight but sweet smile. Her due date was seventeen days away. But she wanted to stay in school as long as possible—unlike the hundreds of other students who hadn't shown up that day. "My mom and dad just want me to finish school and graduate," she said. "I don't have to get a job and move out or anything like that. I'm lucky."

Chelsea told me she wanted to be a social worker one day. Along with veterinarian and csi technician, that was the most common career path girls at the school mentioned. I understood why they wanted to be vets and crime scene investigators. One dealt with pets, and the other had been glamorized by television. But social worker?

Chelsea said she'd been through a lot and would like to help young people who faced similar problems. I would later realize that for many students the most important relationship they'd ever had with a professional was with a social worker. They hadn't been exposed to expansive worlds of opportunity or a wide range of interesting jobs, like so many other teenagers. They didn't live in neighborhoods where Mr. Johnston down the block was a banker and Mrs. Smith was a lawyer. They didn't have uncles who owned their own businesses or aunts who worked for Fortune 500 companies. But at some point they'd met a social worker. A social worker had helped them. One had helped Chelsea. She wanted to return the favor.

I'd come to Manual to get a firsthand look at a struggling American school and to learn more about the nation's dropout epidemic. I wanted to get a better understanding of what was going on in schools that had been labeled "dropout factories." At Manual nearly six out of every ten students in recent years had failed to graduate within four years. Many never did. That's part of a broader epidemic that should be considered a national emergency but simply is not. Sure, you might not die from dropping out. But for most dropouts, dreams and opportunities do die the day they stop coming to school.

It didn't take long to bump into my first example of the problem. Her name was Mary. Sitting stone-faced on the first row of gym bleachers, Mary was tall, dark-haired, friendly, and overweight. Technically she was a senior. But she'd stopped coming to school the previous year and lacked the credits a senior should have. She'd come to school that morning with her mother, a city park worker also named Mary, with a plan to at least consider giving school another try. But before attending her first class, before catching up with any of her classmates or former teachers, and before even making it out of the gym, Mary decided not to stick around. Her reason was simple: she didn't like the school's dress code, because it required her to tuck in her shirt. She was fat, she bluntly told me, and tucking in only exacerbated the problem.

Mr. Whiteman's microphone-enhanced voice had targeted her and made clear there would be no leniency to a dress code the district bosses took more seriously than attendance rates. "It's a really good school," Mary said. "I like it here. But the teachers are really strict about the dress code. If you don't tuck in your shirt, they send you home." They wouldn't have to. Ultimately, Mary decided, an education wasn't worth looking fat. She was leaving voluntarily. I turned to her mom, asking how she felt about her daughter's decision. "I don't know how to keep her here," she said. "She doesn't want to stay."

I thought about the difference in attitude between Chelsea and Mary. One was nearly nine months pregnant, her stomach stretching her white shirt but her mind focused on receiving at least another week or two of education before giving birth. The other wasn't able to get past the idea—a terrifying one for a teenager—of fellow students judging her as she walked down the hall.

I wondered why Mary's mother didn't demand her daughter stay and why she couldn't convince her how much easier life would be with at least a high school diploma. That showed how much I didn't know. I would learn often throughout the school year that dropping out came with brutal ease at Manual High School, as it does at schools throughout the nation, and that for many families and students, tragically, there was little value placed on education.

2

* * *

I NEVER WOULD HAVE THOUGHT
HE WOULD BE A DANDELION.

Sgt. John Barrow and I were walking down a hallway midway through third period of the school year's first Friday when he got a call about a group of students who had been caught in the upstairs gym. The seven boys were skipping class and acting suspicious, another officer announced over the police radio. The day before, two students had been expelled for having oral sex in a nearby locker room. But the voice on the radio made clear to Barrow that he wouldn't make it through this first week without a much bigger mess. "Let's go," he said.

Barrow had just finished giving me the first of many lessons he would deliver throughout the school year, lessons learned from more than a dozen years spent patrolling the halls of Indianapolis Public Schools (IPS). He called this one the "Dandelion Theory." It's based on the idea that you sometimes have to pluck out one troublemaking student so that the others can thrive. "I want my grass to be perfectly green," said Barrow, an army veteran with a shaved head and a huge smile. "That means I want every kid in here to graduate and be happy. But if there is one dandelion, I can't ignore it. I have to pull it out, or before long we'll have a lawn full of weeds. It's like cancer. Trouble spreads if you don't watch out for it and do something about it."

As Barrow talked, I nodded and took notes. In just three days at the school he had become one of my favorite human beings on the planet. He'd grown up in Indianapolis, playing football at another local high school, and returned to his hometown after thirteen years in the army. Tall and stocky, with a loud laugh and a friendly voice that could turn deadly serious when necessary, he gave much more to the job than was required. When things were calm, he spent nearly every minute trying to build relationships with Manual's students. He knew many of them needed a friend and a role model, someone to talk with. He also knew that many of the kids would one day be in trouble and that any goodwill built up today could pay off later. His mission was a serious one. But his methods were often deceptively lighthearted. He was in a constant verbal jousting match with many of the students.

"Hi, Erin," he said to a girl earlier that morning. "Welcome back. What's this, your sixth year?" She smiled, waved him off like a pesky big brother, and kept walking to class. More students passed by. "How's your brother?" Barrow asked one. "Tell him I said hello." He recognized a girl who'd been a constant troublemaker the previous school year. "Just once I want to see you carrying a book," he said, loudly. "Just once. Please. Will you please do that for me? Once?"

Success at Manual is about small victories. So a bit later Barrow broke into a big smile when the same girl walked by him and cleared her throat to get his attention. "You've got a book in your hand," he shouted, even louder this time. "Hallelujah!"

Then he spotted another student and quickly got serious. Barrow had heard that the boy wouldn't be playing football despite being a good player the previous year. The coach of the school's desperately undermanned team had asked Barrow to check on the boy, knowing they'd built a relationship the previous year.

"Son, why aren't you playing this year?"

"I don't have my court hearing until September 10," the boy said. "I have early curfew till then. I can't practice late or play late."

The boy walked away, and Barrow shook his head as he returned to work. As he moved down the hall, students said hello and reached out to shake his hand. Each time, he offered them an elbow bump instead. He was a big, tough guy with army training and a gun at his side. But he was terrified of the germs on so many unwashed hands. He wasn't, though, the least bit hesitant to interact with them. Once, as we talked, I told him he seemed to know not only all of the students' names but also something about their lives. Who they'd dated last year. The name of a sibling. A problem they'd had in the past or were still dealing with. And when he didn't recognize a student, he would ask their name. "Don't worry," he'd tell the inevitably nervous teenager, "you're not in trouble." Then Barrow would introduce himself and make clear he was available if they needed anything.

"This job, it's not about arresting, busting, and cuffing," he said. "It's about relationships. Anything you can do to build a relationship with these kids helps. I can't save the world. I know that. But if you can get through to one or two kids a year, that's a lot. That means something." I nodded and thought how lucky the school was to have someone such as Barrow, someone eager to help the students wandering the halls, someone desperate to help any kid he could. And, I often thought throughout the year, if every adult in the building shared the same sense of urgency, the same drive to pull students out of their circumstances, Manual would likely be a better place.

Unfortunately, the job sometimes *is* about arresting, busting, and cuffing. The seven students who had been caught skipping that Friday morning, all boys and most with blond, Eminem-style buzz cuts, waited in the main office. They had been separated into two rooms. Barrow walked into one and told the four students there that this would be the right time to confess if they had anything in their pockets. "We're going to find it either way," he said, "but you'll be in a lot more trouble if we're surprised." He sounded serious but respectful. He told everyone to just be calm. Searches of the first few boys turned up lighters, cigarettes, and change. But before long, before he could be searched, one of the students in the second room confessed. He had a bag of marijuana in his pocket, and he could tell by the searches that there was no chance it would survive a police search. Other officers took the boy into the police force's cramped office and called Barrow in to deal with the first arrest of the school year.

The boy, a sophomore named Jacob, had lost the south-side toughness he'd brought to school with him that morning. He breathed hard and held back tears. He wore long black shorts and a black short-sleeved shirt, the kind a 1950s service station worker would wear. He had a tattoo of his initials on his calf, just above his Air Jordans. During a search of his pockets, officers pulled out a black wallet decorated with a Transformers logo. He sat under an antidrug poster with the picture of a high school athlete and the words "The only thing I light up is the scoreboard."

Barrow walked into the room, looked at Jacob, and shook his head. "Third day of school, man," he said. "On the third day of school. Really?" He paused and stared at the boy for a few seconds. "I'm sad about this, because you're one of my favorite kids."

Jacob slumped, his head nearly in his knees and his hands cuffed behind him. He sniffled constantly, trying to hold in tears. A small radio Barrow kept tuned to an African American talk station played a preacher giving a sermon. Then Barrow gave his own. He told Jacob he would be processed and sent to the county's juvenile detention facility on the north side of the city.

"You're going to lose your sophomore year here," he said. "But they're going to provide you with an education if you want one." He told Jacob about a program for students who had been expelled. He urged him to take advantage of it. He also told him to give up the lame defense he'd given to other officers—his insistence that he didn't realize the pot was in his pocket until he got to school and that someone might have put it there. "You have the right to a hearing," Barrow said. "But that 'I didn't know it was in my pocket,' that's not going to fly. That's not going to help you. Please, don't insult our intelligence."

As Barrow talked, Principal Grismore, who had just learned of the arrest, peeked in. He saw Jacob, a student he'd spent plenty of time trying to help the previous school year, sitting in handcuffs. Grismore began to talk but stopped. He shook his head slowly, looked at Barrow, and then walked away. Barrow, meanwhile, walked over to the office phone. He asked Jacob if his mom would be surprised to learn he was smoking pot. "She don't like me doing it," he said. "But she knows I do. And she ain't home anyway."

"Who's at home today?"

"My stepdad," Jacob said, a tear finally breaking free and streaming down his cheek.

He leaned down, trying to hide his face, before looking over and noticing I was taking notes. He asked who I was, and his sad look turned into a worried one when I said I wrote for the local paper. After being quizzed, I told him I wouldn't be using his last name, because he was a minor. Barrow dialed the phone. "You know this is going to be a tough phone call, don't you?" he said. Jacob nodded.

Barrow, who had also worked hard the previous year to help Jacob, clearly hated this moment. He told the teenager he had no choice, that there had to be zero tolerance for drugs at the school. "I know you feel bad right now," he said. "But you can learn from this." As the phone rang, Barrow turned to me and returned to his earlier theory. "I never would have thought he would be a dandelion."

Later, as the day's first lunch period began, Barrow returned to the crowded halls, walking them like a beat cop and joking with as many students as possible. "I saw you looking at her, son," Barrow shouted at one boy he passed. "That's okay. Just keep your eyes in your head."

But between the jokes he got serious. He talked about Jacob and the future he had put at risk. He talked about the constant stream of class-skipping students, the kids sleeping in class, and the parents who ignored the school's pleas for help. A girl walked by, looking nervous as she headed away from the lunchroom. Barrow stopped her and asked where she was going. She talked so fast I caught only a few of her words.

"I'm going to class," she said. "I messed up. I thought this was my lunch period. I swear to God."

"Okay, calm down," said Barrow, a deeply religious man. "Just get to class. And don't swear to God. You have to know him first."

Just like any other beat cop, Barrow built routines into his day. People he always stopped by to see and places he always visited. One of them was Room 118. "This is where I go for my peace and serenity," he said that day as we walked into a class for children with the most severe learning disabilities. "With all the madness in the building, this is where I go to come and rest."

We walked in. One sixteen-year-old student crawled on the ground, making loud and incomprehensible noises. Others sat at a table playing a game. A boy with severe autism named Barry waved when Barrow checked in on him. Two teachers ate their lunches as Barrow said hello to a girl named Lindsay.

"When's the baby due?" he asked.

"September 15."

A few minutes later Barrow said good-bye to the students and headed to the lunchroom to check on the students there. Everything in the lunchroom this day was calm. The rules had been tightened in the past year or so after a visiting district official complained about the noise. Barrow and I stood near the doorway, looking at the students. They sat in groups and they sat alone. Many laughed and talked, and others ate quietly, some reading and others just thinking. Boys and girls dined together like they were on dates. A girl named Jammyra Weekly, a senior with a big personality who seemed to run the school, nodded at Barrow as she talked with a few fellow college-bound friends.

"Look at this," Barrow said. "Look at these kids. They're just kids like anywhere else. This is IPS. This is it. Everything is fine here." I looked at him skeptically, and he paused for a few seconds. "Well, it's not always fine," he said. "But it's not as bad as the hype."

3

★ ★ ★

CAN YOU BELIEVE THIS?

The yelling spilled out of Dean Terry Hoover's office on a mid-August morning. A battle-tested veteran of tough schools, Hoover had been Manual's dean for seven years, her most recent stint in a three-decade education career. Her office was constantly filled with the sound of classic rock, the kind she had listened to in college. Her massive Hummer, parked in a spot in front of the school, could be seen through her office window.

Hoover's office was ground zero for many of Manual's most fundamental problems. It was filled daily with students headed toward suspension, expulsion, or some other penalty. It was home to many of the school's most delicate conversations—conversations about anything from a student's mental illness to past abuse. Some students, particularly girls, stopped by to talk about problems they were having with friends, enemies, or parents. Although the conversations often ended with Hoover sternly warning the girls about their behavior, many were open to the tough talk. They might not have taken her advice, but they smiled knowingly when she told them not to believe anything a boy said and to "keep an aspirin between your knees at all times."

The school day on this morning was an hour old, and "Another One Bites the Dust" by Queen was playing on Hoover's radio. She hadn't yet been able to slip away to the gas station across the street to fill her forty-four-ounce plastic cup with its daily soda. A constant stream of students had already been through her office. And now she was dealing with one of their parents, a woman named Tammy, whose son, who had run away several times, had been sent home for a dress code violation without her being told. Tammy was furious. The fury could be heard several offices away.

I walked into the room and Hoover invited me to sit down. Without asking who I was, and frustrated with Hoover, the angry mom turned to me and started complaining about the school's nitpicky administrators. As she talked, Hoover shook her head and sighed. It was a dramatic display that the mother sitting in front of her didn't appreciate. "Anytime you send kids home, you're denying them an education," the mother said.

I had already learned that Hoover didn't like being lectured to—not by students and not by their parents. She was the dean and, she often said, she wasn't there to make friends. Her job was to tell you what you needed to hear. "Where's your accountability?" she asked. "Where's your child's accountability? We have rules here. We have them for a reason. We've gone over this with him over and over. And," she said, looking straight at the thirty-something woman, "the problem isn't confined to the fifteen-year-old student. You know the rules too."

"I'm a single parent," Tammy shot back. "I can't just get up and leave my job in the middle of the day."

"Then hold your child accountable. You need to talk to your child."

Hoover looked down at her desk and sighed heavily once again as the boy's mother stormed out of the office, her lingering and unsatisfied complaints filling the halls for a few more seconds. It was the start of another day at Manual.

I spent the first several days of the school year doing just what I did that morning: observing. Without even requiring me to wear a pass or a badge, the school had opened its doors wide. I walked into classes and grabbed a seat at the back of the room. I sat in empty chairs in the corner of the dean's office, the principal's office, or the social worker's office. I checked out football practices, wandered through the lunchroom, and walked the halls with Barrow. I was trying to get a sense of the people at the school and to get them used to seeing me around. I was also trying to get used to it myself, used to the strange feeling of walking down a high school hallway with hundreds of people not even half my age. At first nobody seemed to mind, or care. Most of the teachers welcomed me into their classes, and students rarely cleaned up their language or halted their conversations because of my presence. Time and again, I had to correct people who mistook me for a substitute or a parent.

Meanwhile, it hadn't taken me long to come to the conclusion that despite all the problems and challenges—or perhaps because of them—there were few places more interesting than an urban high school. And per capita there were few places filled with more interesting characters. Everywhere I went in the school, I saw potential columns I wanted to write and stories I wanted to tell. The school's monumental issues jumped out at me as if they were falling off the walls. I was entertained by it all, sometimes feeling as if I were walking through a movie based on a gritty urban school. The dialogue was wonderful. "You be trippin'," a boy told Principal Grismore one day after he told the student to hurry to class. "No, I don't be trippin'," Grismore said.

After years of covering government bodies, it was fun to hang around a new place filled with new people. I had spent nearly two decades interviewing politicians and others in the political universe. In essence, I'd spent years dealing with people whose jobs at least in part required them to deal with the media—governors, mayors, senators, lobbyists, and others. So I was enjoying the prospect of spending what I initially thought would be at most several weeks talking with people who didn't come armed with talking points and agendas.

At first, I just watched. A fifty-three-year-old teacher named Rich Haton led the first class I observed. A tall man with eyes that bugged out, shaggy gray hair, and an equally shaggy beard, he spent the year working with about twenty special education students. It took me about two minutes to understand how committed to the job Haton was. That was clear by the way he talked to his students and the speed with which he walked through the halls in search of the next student to help. There was also urgency in his voice when he complained to me about the folly of district, state, and federal policies that don't take into account what his students face.

One day he pointed at his students with affection. He told me each was a wonderful individual, filled with creativity and sincerity. But he asked why they were forced to take standardized tests that they were certain to fail. He railed against the one-size-fits-all mentality that grips too many schools and too many education bosses.

Haton was quirky. In his personal life he attended gaming conventions, and I laughed one day when he told me he'd once come to school dressed as a hippie to teach his class about the 1960s. Looking at him, with that unruly hair and beard, and the first two or three of his shirt buttons unfastened, I wondered why he thought he needed to dress differently to look like a hippie.

That first class included only five students, all relatively high functioning students with mild learning disabilities. One of the girls was friendly and diligent but struggled to learn. She came across as dazed, but after meeting her only once she always waved and said hello when I passed her in the halls. One boy never spoke and rarely looked up from his desk. Another smiled constantly. He stood up when he saw me, walked over, and offered a formal handshake. The class gave Haton time to help the students with any homework they had and to assess where they were academically. "If you have a project you're working on or homework you need help on, I can stay after school to help you anytime," he told them. "You just have to let me know ahead of time and we'll work it out."

When a student looked discouraged, Haton cheered him up by insisting that he and the other students could achieve more than they thought they could. Trying to keep the class engaged, he taught the students how to do a Dracula accent and then offered a lecture to a girl who had answered one of his points with a dismissive "Whatever."

"If you're going to say, 'Whatever,' you need to say it like a Valley girl," he said, in his own Valley girl impression. "You need to flip your hair and say it like this: '*What-ever.*'"

The girl smiled and then quietly tried her own Valley girl impersonation. "*What-ever,*" she said.

Haton congratulated her and then put the students to work, asking them to write ten sentences explaining what they liked about their favorite restaurant. As they worked, he sat at his desk and talked to me about what he had learned in his four years at Manual, four years that followed a stint as an addictions counselor in a state prison. "The only thing anyone ever hears about IPS is that the test scores are horrible," he said. "I even have friends who come up to me and say, 'What are you guys doing over there?' But that's not all that happens over here. There are some bad teachers here. But there aren't many. Most of us want to and are willing to do whatever it takes to get these kids ready."

He kept talking, and I kept scribbling his words into my notebook. "People need to think a little more about the problems the kids in this school have and the issues they have to deal with day in and day out. There are a lot of social issues and a lot of home drama. There are a lot of things, a lot of factors that go into a school being successful. People want to say it's the kids. Or the parents. Or the teachers. Or the system. It's not that easy. There's no one factor that can turn everything around. Americans want quick fixes and easy solutions. Sorry, there isn't one when it comes to education. All you can do," he added, "is put every ounce of energy you have into helping every student you can." I walked out of Haton's class inspired. With teachers like that, I thought, a school like Manual actually has a chance.

And then later, as I sat in one of the school's math classes, I found the other side of the story. The class was led by one of the school's most veteran teachers, a thirty-fourth-year educator who had clearly given up long before I walked through the door. When she talked to students, she did so with a voice that screamed of boredom. She plodded through the day's curriculum, going over math equations on the overhead screen without stopping to explain the problems or asking students to provide the answers. During the first class, I observed several students talking with one another, ignoring the teacher. On another occasion, of eighteen students in the class, only four paid attention. The others slept, talked, or texted, violating school rules.

Their teacher moved slowly because of her age, but I couldn't understand her complete lack of interest in communicating with the students. At one point a school announcement noted that school superintendent Eugene White would be stopping by soon to meet with students. "Well, aren't we lucky?" she said sarcastically. Then, as two students slept at their desks, she went through a list of to-do items on a worksheet the school had provided, not looking at her students as she talked. "Number one. Warmly greet students," she said, finally looking up at her students with a frown. "Do you feel warmly greeted?"

In this and other classes I observed, the teacher started the class late and wrapped things up early, teaching for maybe thirty of the allotted forty-five minutes. As students waited for the class to end one day, she sat at her desk, not blinking when a young girl loudly called another a bitch. I walked out of the class stunned. She didn't even try, I thought. And that's with a journalist sitting in the back of the room taking notes.

The class was an example of the low expectations that can be found at many schools and a reminder that the lack of a top-notch teacher in every classroom is crushing low-performing schools nationwide. Despite all the evidence, too many people in too many districts—from parents to students and from taxpayers to district leaders—fail to demand more from schools or buy in to the concept that a fantastic teacher can pull more out of even the most challenging student population. The Brookings Institution, in its widely read Hamilton Project, argued that point effectively. "Ultimately," it wrote, "the success of U.S. public education depends upon the skills of the 3.1 million teachers managing classrooms in elementary and secondary schools around the country. Everything else—educational standards, testing, class size, greater accountability—is background, intended to support the crucial interactions between teachers and students." It didn't take me long during my stay at Manual to embrace the report's argument that "Without the right people standing in front of the classroom, school reform is a futile exercise."

I included a description of the bad class in my first column, not mentioning the teacher by name but writing about "an uninterested teacher who dryly plodded through her class plan, not bothering to wake a student asleep at his desk or to stop others who were talking to friends." I also noted with frustration that her seniority left her safely ensconced at Manual while younger and more energetic teachers faced the possibility of layoffs year after year because of the district's union policies and budget problems.

Then something interesting happened. More than once, students approached me to tell me they knew which teacher I had referred to in my column. In the school's sole calculus class, which included only eight students, two girls told me they'd had her as freshmen and had fallen behind in math because of it. They told me of friends who never recovered from algebra classes in which they were not engaged. They told me they often had no idea if they were doing their assignments correctly, because the teacher would only check to see that they had done the work rather than check to make sure it was correct. The girls said the classes were so out of control that the students who wanted to learn had trouble doing so. Their statements reminded me of the many reports I'd read about the damage one teacher can do. That was a particular problem in a class like algebra, a class that is a gateway to higher-level math classes.

With each visit to a Manual class or office, I learned more about the problems and challenges facing the school. And every time I walked through the halls, I sensed this was a school on the edge. It wasn't in chaos, but if school police and administrators let their guard down for even an hour or two, Manual would descend into that. During class periods the halls were constantly peppered with students. Police were on a nonstop mission to chase down class-skipping students or respond to the latest problem a teacher was having with an angry or even violent student. The administrative offices, meanwhile, were filled with heartbreak.

"Well, I made it five whole days before I had to call Child Protective Services [CPS]." The words came early in the second week of the year from Barbara Lyon, Manual's overworked social worker. She was sitting in her office with a therapist from a local mental health center who worked in the school a few days a week. Lyon had called CPS that morning after a school nurse found a nasty burn on the biceps of a student. The boy had given many conflicting explanations for the burn, which was the size and shape of an old car's cigarette lighter. School officials wondered whether the burn had been the result of abuse or perhaps a gang initiation. "Can you believe this?" Lyon said to me.

But few things surprised her anymore. And nothing did that day as she and the therapist went over the cases of thirteen of Manual's students. The cases were sweeping in scope. They ranged from self-mutilation to homelessness, to psychotic symptoms, to traumatic brain injury, to schizophrenia. One student had just been released from a state mental hospital after a two-year stay. Others were struggling to raise their own children. In many cases, the two women told me, the parents of the students had as many problems as the students themselves.

"It would be great if we could look at everyone walking into this building and say the goal was to help them graduate with honors and get into college," Lyon said, shaking her head. "But that's not the case. With some students we just want to be able to help prepare them to live independently—to be able to cook, ride the bus, and file for Medicaid. For some of these kids, it's amazing they even get up in the morning. They have so much going against them."

I told myself to think about that the next time Manual's test scores were released. What I was learning didn't excuse the school's paltry graduation rate or the failure rate among students. But the words of Lyon and others did provide necessary context to the complicated issue that is failing urban schools.

The next day I sat in Lyon's office as she met with a case manager from an organization that works with students who are homeless or at risk of homelessness. According to a National Association of School Psychologists' report, roughly 1.4 million school-age children are homeless at some point during the typical calendar year. Other estimates put the number at closer to 900,000. Either way, it is clear that these students drop out in huge numbers, and those who do go to school predominantly attend poverty-filled schools like Manual. Some of the students are homeless along with a parent, but many are on their own, kicked out of their homes or having left in frustration. All are forced to find places to sleep, turning their education into a secondary concern. The case manager told Lyon to alert teachers to the signs of homelessness: dirty shoes and backpacks, hunger, sleeping in class.

The two then met with a seventeen-year-old student named Erika who had recently moved to Indianapolis from Texas. She had a thirteen-month-old baby and had bounced around since returning to the city, living at times with her stepdad. Her story was convoluted, as if she didn't want to share all of it. She struggled to identify other people she had lived with and wasn't clear about where she would be staying in the coming weeks. Lyon suspected she had enrolled in school to secure certain government benefits but had no intention of attending on a regular basis. She asked Erika to return to her office in the coming days to check in and so that they could discuss any issues the girl was having. She wished the young student luck as the door closed behind her, and then she shook her head, smiling a smile that had nothing but frustration and sadness behind it. It was sadness that anyone charged with dealing with Manual's social problems would feel. "Every person has a unique situation," Lyon said. "There are just so many barriers in the lives these people have. It's heartbreaking what so many of these kids have to deal with at such a young age."

One floor up Rachel Lape was starting her second year as Manual's English as a Second Language (ESL) teacher. Young and eager, Lape was nonetheless already dispirited by the disorganized way Manual was run, the acceptance of something far short of mediocrity, and the lack of collaboration among the staff. She complained that administrators never visited her class to gauge her progress as a teacher and that many teachers at the school seemed to have given up. She longed for the camaraderie she had felt as a teacher at the local suburban school she had left for Manual with the idealistic goal of changing the world. Later in the year, she told me that she was being pulled down by the indifference among many teachers in the building and was giving her students and her job less than she ever could have imagined. During that first week, though, she was energized.

Lape's classes included thirty-five Hispanic students whose English reading and writing skills were lacking. Some would eventually move full time into regular classes while others would continue to struggle with the basics of English. Engaging and full of smiles, Lape talked with deep affection about her students. When I first approached her to ask if I could observe her class, she said that would be fine. But then she warned me that I'd better not write anything that might hurt her students. She didn't want anything to get in the way of the connection she was trying to build with them. "If they like you, they'll do anything for you," she said. "That's the key to everything, building a connection with them."

On one of the first mornings of the school year Lape sat on a desk talking with six students. One of the two girls in the room was pregnant. The four boys were constantly tapping one another on the shoulders to joke in Spanish about something. But Lape continued to pull them back in with a smile and a firm, "Boys." I looked around the room and saw a poster Lape had put up. "Everyone smiles in the same language," it said.

On another day early in the school year, Lape was disappointed to see that only four of her seven students had made it to class. Three boys—among the students she would later call "my little gangsters" because of the trouble they got into outside of school—were missing.

"Where are your partners?" she asked a boy.

"I don't know," he said.

"Why don't you call them in the morning from now on and tell them to come to school?" Lape suggested. "I think that would be a great idea."

During the class I met one of Lape's newest students. Her name was Casey, and she had just moved from the Dominican Republic. She was struggling to better learn a new language. "I understand everything," she said. "But I can't always say what I'm thinking."

"But you're improving every day," Lape told her with another smile.

Time and again, teachers and school staffers, the people at the ground level, urged me to get to know their students and to avoid simplicity in my writing. They had spent years listening to and reading generic criticism of the school district. They acknowledged that much of the criticism was valid, self-inflicted, and deserved. But it was also superficial and based on a lack of understanding of the issues students bring with them to school every day. They were issues that plague many of America's schools and deserve a sustained nationwide attack. The issues do not excuse failure. Instead, they are the best argument around for radical reform and infusions of both urgency and resources. The issues are staggering in scope, and even while sitting in a school in America's heartland, I was quickly getting a lesson in them.

4

★ ★ ★

WE DO A GOOD JOB
WITH THE KIDS WHO SHOW UP.

At Manual many of the students don't show up often enough to get left behind. I'd been at the school for less than a week but had already discovered that its most vexing problem was also the most fundamental: there was a basic inability to get students to walk through the front doors. Teachers repeatedly told me about leading classes that were missing half of their students. They complained about students who showed up once or twice a week, or students who walked out of or into a class midway through a lesson. Then they told me about the many students who simply never made it to school. Not for a month. Not for a week. Not for a day. And not for a single class. It happened every year, they said. It got worse as the school year went on, with many students—freshmen and sophomores in particular—disappearing. The missing kids were faded memories, their empty desks symbols of another generation of dropouts who would be forced to find a way in the world without even the most basic education.

Principal Grismore and other school district leaders worried most about this problem at the start of the year. That's because state funding for schools is based on the number of kids who have registered and shown up at least once during the first month of the year. It doesn't matter if the students come again or if a student ignores the building from October through May. Or if they learned anything. As long as a student shows up once early in the year, Indianapolis Public Schools can count on another seventy-five hundred dollars in state funding. So, Grismore told me, he spent about a third of his time in the early weeks of the school year dealing with the problem of missing students. He kept a running list of "no shows" and farmed out the task of calling homes to teachers and other staffers. As the school year began, he was shooting for 946 students. Anything less than 946 could result in one teacher being transferred to another school. It wouldn't be easy. The number 946 was roughly 200 students more than had shown up during the school year's first days.

The tenth day of the school year was a warm Tuesday. It was August 25 and the end of summer was four weeks away. Temperatures were blistering and the days long. The state fair, an annual rite of summer, had just wrapped up. But at Manual students were starting to settle into their school-year routines—the students who had shown up, that is. The first week's attendance rate hovered near 81 percent. But in reality the problem was even worse than it sounded. The roster of absent students didn't include the many students who had not yet enrolled and not yet shown up for their first day of school. And thanks to a convoluted government accounting policy, a student could be counted as present for the full day even if he or she missed half of the day's classes.

As the morning bell rang, Grismore raced from room to room, dealing with everything from upcoming student photos, to ongoing problems with class schedules, to a parent who was on the phone complaining that her child had been assigned to a pair of advanced placement classes. In a school marred by profound academic failure, the mother was worried that her child couldn't handle the work and would see her grades slip. At the same time, Grismore was preparing to head out in the neighborhoods surrounding Manual in hope of rounding up a student or two who hadn't yet appeared. It was clearly a show. He had a columnist on the premises, so why not impress the district bosses, who wanted to see as many seventy-five-hundred-dollar additions to the bottom line as possible?

A few staffers who'd heard that Grismore was going to take me on his hunt for students complained, calling his effort a public relations ploy. They said the school didn't take absenteeism seriously, as evidenced by the lack of a formal attendance policy. The issue was at the center of a constant struggle between the principal and teachers who argued he wasn't giving them leverage to hold over students who skipped classes. I didn't really care. I just wanted to see how the parents of absent students responded to the presence on their doorstep of the school principal. And who knows? Maybe some publicity would persuade a few parents to send their children to school. Some, after all, might not even know the year had begun. I remembered standing on the front porch of an apartment building in one of the city's most crime-ridden neighborhoods two years earlier with a worker from a local social services agency. The worker asked the mother of three children if she needed anything for the upcoming school year. In response the mother asked when classes began, not aware that the first bell of the school year was less than thirty-six hours away. So getting the word out wasn't a bad idea.

Roughly an hour into the school day, Grismore and I headed to the parking lot. As we stepped past the school's front doors, three girls walked in. "Good morning, ladies," Grismore said as we raced by them. "You're late." He shuffled through a handful of papers, including directions printed from MapQuest.com, and tossed some trash into the backseat when we got to his messy gray Audi Quattro. And we were off.

Heading east into a gritty industrial section of the south side, Grismore told me about his life. He'd been a teacher and administrator in the district for thirty-six years and had been at Manual for the past five. He lived with his wife in the suburbs just west of Indianapolis; he's one of the many district employees who sent their children to better schools elsewhere. Grismore, whose son now attended Purdue University, said his nickname came from his father's fondness for Rocky Marciano. The boxer, he said, had won a big match just after he'd been born. That fight sealed his nickname.

Then he said the first week of the year had gone well. Really? I wasn't sure how Manual's first week could be considered a success. So I asked about the arrest, the expulsions, the poor attendance, and the many students who had been sent home for dress code violations and other infractions. I didn't even mention the general dysfunction that had led to many students' missing classes because of scheduling snafus or the apathy that hung heavy in many classrooms. "It was chaotic at first," Grismore said. "But it smoothed out by the end." He said the expulsions and other punishments had sent word to the students that administrators were serious about the rules. Ultimately, it wasn't such a bad thing that the early problems had occurred. Everyone was now on notice. Anyway, the early hiccups were to be expected after the long summer break, he added.

A day earlier I had watched a frustrated Grismore address the school's junior class in the newly refurbished main auditorium. Many of the students wouldn't listen. Some laughed and talked loudly as the principal tried to go through the rules. An occasional obscenity pierced the room. Several students sat bored, their eyes closed and their heads tilted toward the ceiling. I couldn't blame them. Grismore was moving in a businesslike manner through a laundry list of policies and procedures, doing nothing to inspire the kids at the start of the school year.

I liked Grismore. He clearly cared about children, particularly those with learning disabilities whom he'd spent years teaching. But he'd been in the bureaucratic system for so long that he had been turned into a manager. His goal was to avoid trouble from district headquarters and to make sure the trains were running on time. He wasn't the bold, outspoken, energetic principal that a school like Manual seemed to need—one desperate to change the expectations at a school that had little. So he lost control of the auditorium, despite the presence of a police officer and teachers who were trying to quiet the crowd. "I was hoping you all would be role models for the underclassmen," Grismore finally said in frustration. "It appears to me that this won't be the case, because you don't know how to act in this situation."

As the students filed out, Grismore worried about an upcoming meeting with students and Superintendent White. The last thing he needed was a complaint from the district boss, or from another district official he mockingly called the "accountability guru" because she seemed to live to criticize school administrators for the behavior of their students.

During our drive Grismore talked about the frustration of not being able to spend much time on improving the quality of education at the school. Most of his time was spent dealing with the students' home and social problems, or with discipline problems and district directives. That week he was dealing with issues related to a transgender student. There were bathroom and locker room questions, and he wanted to make sure the student was safe. He also had to make sure girls who would be giving birth during the school year had access to in-home computer-based classes. The previous spring eighteen of the school's girls had been pregnant. But at least they showed up occasionally. The students on his list that morning had not. Most had come to school sporadically the previous year and were at the top of the list of students most likely to drop out.

After driving for a few miles, we turned onto a street that led to a string of small apartment complexes. As Grismore looked at the directions, his Audi slammed into a deep, rain-filled pothole. This is the life, I thought, of an Indianapolis Public Schools principal. After taking a wrong turn, Grismore stopped the car, figured out where he was, and pointed to an apartment building across the street. It was the rattiest of the bunch, with torn window screens and trash strewn in the small lawn out front. A beat-up car sat nearby.

Although a light was on, and though a curtain on the first floor briefly moved, nobody answered Grismore's knocks. A man walking by said he didn't know the family who lived there. So we left, heading toward another neighborhood, another apartment, and another missing student. This time a woman answered, opening the door just wide enough to see us. A TV played in the background. Grismore introduced himself—an introduction that the woman didn't seem the least bit interested in—and then asked if she could explain why her son hadn't yet made it to school. "What do you mean?" she said.

Grismore explained that this was the tenth day of the school year and her son had not yet attended one class. "He's getting behind," he said. "It's going to be hard to catch up if he misses many more days."

As the principal talked, the woman's expressionless eyes wandered. She looked past him outside. "I don't know what to tell you," she said. "He's left for school every morning. So I don't know what's going on with that."

Grismore looked surprised. He repeated the boy's name just to make sure he was at the right house. Then he asked if the boy was bringing schoolbooks home with him.

"He's got a backpack, that's all I know."

Grismore asked her to look through it when her son returned home. She said she would try. But when asked if a school employee could check in later, she apologetically said she didn't have a phone.

I'd already heard many teachers talk about the disturbing apathy toward education among many Manual families. It was sadly becoming clear to me. That was probably what surprised me most during my early days at the school—this feeling that in parts of Indianapolis, and in many parts of America, the message that education is valuable hadn't yet sunk in. I later compared the attitude to brushing your teeth. Even people who don't brush must know that they should. At Manual I assumed even families whose children didn't go to school knew they should. But I was starting to get the sense that the problem was deeper than I realized. Some families, it seemed, had not accepted the value of a high school diploma.

Apathy, I thought, now that's a tough one. I thought about my own past, how I'd been a lackluster student in my high school years and had missed dozens of school days. I thought about living my first decade in Gary, Indiana, in neighborhoods just as gritty as these. Like many of these kids, I grew up barely knowing my dad, living with an alcoholic stepfather, and occasionally getting into trouble. That would help me in many of my conversations with students. But the problems that Manual children faced, and the challenges that stood planted in their way, were deeper than anything I could imagine. Despite not always being a dedicated student, it was hard for me to comprehend the idea that some kids believed a high school diploma was optional and that life wasn't full of big opportunities.

A few minutes after our encounter with the missing boy's mother, Grismore and I were standing in front of a cute yellow house with a manicured lawn less than a half a mile from Manual. It was just after 9:30 AM when a young man, who appeared to be quite stoned, answered the door. Grismore was looking for the boy's sister, Abigail, a seventeen-year-old who should have been starting her sophomore year. The boy rubbed his eyes and yawned. "I don't think she's planning to return," he said.

"She's not?" Grismore asked.

"Not that I know of," he said. "I think she's gonna get her GED or something."

Grismore seemed genuinely bothered and wrote down the family's phone number. He asked the boy to have his sister call him and said he'd like to talk to her about the school's Opportunity Center program, which helps students who have fallen behind catch up. Most of the work is done on computers, at the students' own pace, and away from traditional classroom settings that just don't work for some. The program, a sign of hope at Manual, is aimed at giving students who have failed elsewhere another chance.

The boy sniffed and said he'd pass along the number. Grismore never heard from the girl, even after calling her home several more times in the coming days. And that was it for the principal's day out. I had expected to spend much of the morning tracking down missing students, or at least sticking it out until we found one. But Grismore had meetings to attend and crises to deal with back at school. And this was mostly for show. So without any success to claim, we got back in his Audi and drove the short distance back to the school.

For the first time, Grismore talked to me without my having asked a question. He was thinking about Abigail, the stoned boy's sister. "We do a good job with the kids who show up," he said. "We do a good job with the kids who stay here for four years. But the problems are huge. The broken homes. The mobility issues. That's what gets in the way of their education. Sure, there are a few knuckleheads who won't do the right things. But for most of these kids, their problems are no fault of their own." And, he said, "We can't teach them, we can't work with them, we can't make anything happen if we can't get them in the classroom."

Back at school Grismore and others spent the following days trying to round up more students. They talked often about the school's ADM (average daily membership), the number of students who would be counted on the roster that determines district funding. After years of declining enrollment within Indianapolis Public Schools and a series of budget cuts, everyone understood the importance of the number. Everyone understood the importance of each seventy-five hundred dollars.

Lyon, the school social worker, was among the many Manual employees given the task of tracking down students. That assignment was a painfully shortsighted decision driven solely by the bottom line. It took Lyon away from the serious problems facing so many students. In her office she told me about a student who had just been kicked out of her house and was in need of help. She talked about students whose family issues threatened their ability to stay in school. But then she pointed to a stack of files containing information on students who hadn't shown up for school. Her task wasn't to help them deal with whatever problem was standing in their way. It was to find them and persuade them to walk through Manual's doors at least once.

As I had discovered during my brief ride-along with Grismore, the task is a killer. Disconnected numbers, lies, apathetic parents, and a poverty problem that leads to a highly transient student population regularly impede success. It was disturbing to see a caring social worker with a master's degree being reduced to acting like a bill collector, calling people who in many cases didn't want to be called in the hope of bringing more much-needed cash into the district's account. "It's politics," Lyon explained. "This is how the game is played. That's how schools get their money. It's sad, but that's how it is."

During her calls, Lyon heard a never-ending stream of excuses from parents whose children were AWOL. Some excuses were serious, such as a sickness in the family. Some were less so, as with the students who didn't like the dress code. In most cases there was no specific answer. "Apathy," Lyon said. "A lot of apathy."

She opened the first file. A teacher had reached the family and written a vague note at the top of the student's record: "Dad says son is not coming to school this year. Having a lot of problems." "Okay, that doesn't tell me much," Lyon said, dialing her office phone.

The student's father answered and after a quick explanation from Lyon talked for a couple of minutes about his son's absence. The boy was on probation for assault, he said, and refused to go to school. Even when he left in the morning for Manual, he never made it there. The dad called police and his son's probation officers. He had asked friends for advice. He had begged his son to give school a chance. He had driven around the neighborhood during school hours looking for his boy. He was out of ideas. "Well," Lyon said. "What are we going to do? Because this isn't going to work." The man had no answers. "I think when you go before the judge, you have an opportunity to share with him what you've shared with me," Lyon said. "Hang in there."

That was seventy-five hundred dollars the school district would not be getting. That was one more student risking his future and wandering the city with little more than trouble on the horizon. Lyon shook her head like a worried grandmother after hanging up the phone. Then she asked me a question she would often ask me throughout the year: "Can you believe this?" I was starting to. The school was filled with seemingly countless stories that explained the empty chairs in most classrooms. And the problem was deeper than funding. There were many students who had met the ridiculous ADM requirement but rarely showed up. There were others who tried to get there but often failed.

Natasha Ellison was one who struggled to make it to school. She walked into Manual after the final bell of the day, having missed all of her classes but eager to collect her homework. As she walked the halls, a school employee scolded her for missing another day. "I didn't have a babysitter," Natasha said in a sharp tone. "Can I bring him here?" She was told that wasn't allowed. "Then what am I supposed to do?" There was no easy answer. As many teachers had already told me, there rarely are easy answers to the problems facing schools like Manual.

Nearly a month later Grismore sat in his cluttered office. Another school day had just ended. Another mountain of problems had passed through his office. But he was smiling. He called me into the office and proudly announced, "We made it." I asked what he meant, not realizing that day represented the end of the period that determines the district's funding. Grismore had surpassed his goal of 946 students. Barely. "Our final number is nine hundred forty-seven," he said.

It was a victory. A much-needed one for a beleaguered administrator. Grismore continued to smile a relaxed smile. A lot of work had gone into that 947. Disappointingly, though, the urgency of getting students to school stopped that day. I never again saw administrators stress in the same way, with the same intensity, over the number of students who walked through their doors. I never again took a ride through the surrounding neighborhoods with Grismore. And by the end of the school year, the enrollment had dropped to about 750 students.

5

★ ★ ★

I HATE THIS SCHOOL.

I parked my car in front of Manual at about noon and walked toward the front door one day early in the school year. In recent days I had filled several notebooks as I wandered the school in search of column material, meeting dozens of teachers and students along the way. My initial column on the school, which I'd written the night before and had spent the morning polishing, would be running in three days. But there's always another deadline, and my next one wasn't far off.

As I approached the school, one of its doors crashed open. A man in a T-shirt and jeans barged out, his teenage son trailing him. The man was furious and mumbling to himself. As they walked, the boy, who I would later learn had been sent home for violating the dress code policy, meekly asked his father if he could drop him off somewhere.

I had already seen many parents leave Manual in anger. Actually, most who came into the school did so because their son or daughter was in trouble, meaning they invariably left irritated. So this wasn't a particularly noteworthy scene. Not yet, anyway. That changed within a second. The man stopped and turned to his son with a face filled with fury. "I ain't dropping you off nowhere, motherfucker," he said sharply.

I turned and stared at the two. The boy was perhaps fifteen. He didn't look scared, just irritated. His father, like most parents I came across at Manual, was probably in his mid-thirties. We all stood there for a second as the father and I made eye contact. I was stunned. Had I just heard a man call his own son a motherfucker?

Apparently I stared too long. The man pointed at me. "Get your nose out of my business, bitch," he said, before turning and walking fast toward the work van he had parked a few more steps away. He yelled at his son to get in and before long sped off.

I remained on the front steps of the school for several seconds, still stunned. When I finally walked inside, I mentioned the incident to a secretary at the front desk. She shook her head and told me she wasn't surprised. Parents can be a problem at Manual. The man was likely upset over being called from work to pick up his son. Parents around here don't have jobs that make accommodations for their parental responsibilities. That's money out of his paycheck.

But I was new to life at the poverty-stricken school, and that moment stuck with me during my entire stay at Manual. I saw it as a symbol of the lives many of the students lived. I wondered why a father couldn't see that his son's own problems with teachers and school rules might stem from the way *he* behaved. I wondered whether a boy spoken to like that by his own parent could ever develop the social skills needed to survive. And, I thought, if a father talked to his son like that on the grounds of a high school, and to a man in a suit who could have been a teacher or vice principal, how does he act at home?

It wasn't the worst thing I would see during the school year. Not by a mile. But it was the biggest lesson I'd learned up to that point about life at the struggling south-side school, a school to which many students go through the front door each morning carrying baggage that is far heavier than their backpacks. Unfortunately, I would encounter many other lessons in the opening weeks of the school year—lessons that seemed to have at their core the common denominator of anger.

That same week, I sat in an English class without knowing that just two floors up school police were responding to a violent hallway disturbance. When they arrived they found a teacher holding back a fifteen-year-old boy who had just attacked his ex-girlfriend. The attack came a day after the girl told school officials the boy had been harassing her. The boy responded by finding her, screaming at, and choking her. When police arrived, the girl's neck was marked with bruises.

"You got me suspended," the boy screamed as he shoved the girl into a row of lockers. He stopped choking the girl only after a teacher heard the ruckus and rushed into the hallway.

The boy was arrested and sent to the county juvenile lockup. It was the second arrest of the year at Manual and just the latest in a long line for the young man. His rap sheet included arrests stretching back to when he had been busted for stealing a golf cart at age eleven. Things had gotten worse in the past year. He had been arrested for exposing himself in public, belligerently interfering with police at a crime scene, and stealing a car. The previous summer he'd been accused of molesting a three-year-old relative. Now his crime spree had spread to Manual.

Days after that incident, I came across a troubled eighteen-year-old student whom school police considered one of Manual's toughest. His name was Stephon, and one police officer told me he was "straight-up street." As in, you don't mess with him. I could understand why. His record was already approaching career-criminal status. At the age of nine he was arrested on charges of sexual battery and intimidation after he and two friends allegedly attacked a young girl. By thirteen he was running away regularly from foster families and group homes. He was arrested at fourteen for theft and, a year later, for driving without a license.

His problems often spilled into school. When he was a fifteen-year-old middle school student, for instance, he got into an argument with a girl over a basketball in gym class. As they argued, Stephon called the girl a bitch and hurled her onto a set of bleachers, pinning her down with his knees and choking her. He hit her in the face and wildly shouted, "I'm tired of all these bitches in this school." When a teacher arrived, the girl had a black eye and bruises on her back and shoulders. Stephon began shouting even louder and more violently. "I'll beat all you bitches," he said, according to a police report. "I don't give a fuck." He was hauled off to jail. A year later Stephon was causing trouble in a class at another high school when a fed-up teacher told him to go to the office. Instead, Stephon cursed and then charged at him. He rammed him hard with his shoulder and was preparing to pummel him when, thankfully, a few students stepped in the way. Again he was hauled off to jail. And now he was Manual's problem.

Stephon had made it through the first two weeks of school without any major problems. And everything seemed calm when he stepped into a history class led by veteran teacher Robert Palmer on a Friday afternoon. The week was so close to being over. As Stephon entered the room, Sergeant Barrow was standing near an exit on the first floor talking to students and telling them to hurry to class. One girl he'd long been trying to get to take school seriously, a girl who had been expelled the previous year, walked up with a big smile and stuck a piece of paper in his face. It was her progress report documenting her work during the first weeks of the year. "Look at these," she said. The paper showed a line of As and Bs. "Now, that's what I'm talking about," Barrow said, holding his fist out for a congratulatory bump.

It hadn't been a bad day. Sure, there'd been a couple fights and a lot of class-skippers whom police spent much of the day clearing from the hallways. But now the halls were unusually quiet. The only noise was the sound of teachers' voices spilling out of classrooms. The quiet was due in part to the fact that many of the students who often trolled the halls during classes had already called it a week and headed out. By the last period of the last day of the week, teachers often told me, many of the school's biggest troublemakers were gone. Things were peaceful, and at times like that Manual could seem like an all-American high school.

Barrow and I stood chatting about the upcoming Indianapolis Colts season. With little going on, I was trying to decide if I needed to spend the rest of the day at the school. Then the call came over Barrow's police radio. That call changed everything. Help was needed in Room 134, the call said. Right now.

That wasn't a problem. We were only a ten-second walk away from the room, and as we came around the corner, the problem stood directly in front of us. Stephon, the student, and Palmer, the teacher, were squared off in the middle of the hallway. They were arguing. As Barrow stepped between them, Stephon complained that Palmer had made a crack about his age; he was nearly nineteen and still far from graduating. Palmer said the student had been goofing off and disrupting the class.

Whatever the cause, Barrow knew this situation wasn't going to be resolved peacefully or quickly in the hallway. He calmly told Stephon to follow him to the office so that they could work the problem out. Stephon agreed, but for some reason Palmer didn't return to his classroom. Instead he ordered his student to give him back a textbook he was holding. Stephon hurled it at his feet. The book landed with a loud thud on the hard floor.

With that, Barrow knew it was time to speed things up. This was going from bad to worse, and his only goal at that moment was to de-escalate the situation before it got uglier. He wanted to keep a student with a lifetime of trouble from adding one more incident to that history. He told Stephon to walk with him.

But again the teacher didn't simply walk away. Instead he turned to me and shook his head as I jotted details about the scene in my notebook, saying, "Do you see what we have to deal with?"

That set Stephon off and turned what had been a quiet afternoon just a few minutes earlier into a scary scene. "Fuck you," the student screamed. "I'll slap those glasses off your face, motherfucker. Fuck you, bitch."

By now Barrow had his chest out and was guiding Stephon forcefully down the hallway, making sure to stay between him and Palmer. He repeatedly urged the young man to calm down; if possible, he didn't want to handcuff him. But Stephon's eyes and rage were zeroed in on his teacher. "That motherfucker's lucky," he shouted. "I don't make threats." I didn't doubt him.

The three of us walked past several classrooms as curious students peered up from their desks. Some teachers walked over to close their doors. Eventually Stephon stopped yelling and began walking to the office. Barrow, meanwhile, was clearly irritated that the situation had turned so ugly. It was bad to begin with, he told me, but it should have ended differently. He shook his head and said Palmer should have walked away. He knew perfectly well that his needling statement to me would set Stephon off. He wasn't excusing the student's behavior but said the goal in that situation should have been a peaceful resolution. Some teachers always have to have the last word.

Barrow and Stephon walked into Dean Hoover's office a couple of minutes later. She looked up from her desk and sighed. It was nearly 2:00 PM, and after a morning full of student problems, she was finally getting around to lunch. But she soon realized her green beans would have to wait. She pushed them aside and reached into one of her ever-present Pringles canisters to grab a quick snack before tackling the school's latest problem. "This school is stupid," Stephon said repeatedly. "This is the worst school I've ever gone to. I ain't coming back."

Hoover gave him a motherly look of disappointment and talked straight. As Stephon sat in a chair on the other side of her cluttered desk, she promised to look into the teacher's comments in the classroom. Teachers shouldn't be mocking students, she agreed. Still, she said, he would have to be suspended for three days for his outburst. That wasn't acceptable behavior. "I don't even care," Stephon said quietly. "I ain't coming back. This school sucks."

As the end of the day approached, Barrow sat down next to the boy and, in his typical fashion, turned into a quasi social worker. He looked him in the eyes and reminded Stephon that they had talked about his anger and what it costs him. "You can't keep responding like this," he said. "Don't let people's words control you."

"What?" Stephon said. "Am I supposed to just walk away?"

"Sometimes you have to," Barrow said as Stephon looked at the wall. "It doesn't mean you're wrong. But look at what happened now. You didn't win anything. You have to think before you go off like that. It only hurts you."

Stephon's face relaxed, and he looked at the floor. His angry glare went away, and I thought he seemed sad. For a moment I thought this story might end like an after-school special from the 1970s, with the young student agreeing he'd made a mistake and promising to do better next time. I wanted that to happen. Despite the violent threats and despite his past, Stephon at times seemed like a nice and intelligent kid, with a great smile when he showed it. But Barrow's message couldn't break through the years of toughness. "I don't even care," Stephon mumbled. "I hate this school. I'm done with it." He did return to school the next week, though. And then he made it another week before he was kicked out after being arrested on drug charges.

Many of Manual's students have painful emotional issues, school social workers and police officers told me time and again. So when incidents escalated, even without the presence of a teacher intent on fueling the situation, calming things down was often impossible. That was the case a few days after Stephon was suspended, when police spent a harrowing few minutes dealing with a sixteen-year-old named Thomas.

Thomas had spent years bouncing in and out of foster care and the juvenile lockup. On this afternoon the school's lone female police officer, Donnita Miller, found Thomas roaming the third-floor halls. One month later he would be arrested for punching two women in the face during a robbery in a CVS drugstore parking lot. This day, however, he was just wandering. Miller asked him to come over to her. He didn't. Instead, he kept walking. He then ignored several more orders to come to Miller, dismissing her and saying he was headed to a class that had begun a half hour earlier. Miller called for backup and received it a few seconds later when Officer Alonzo Bass appeared. After he, too, was ignored, Bass placed his hand on the student's shoulder and tried to guide him to the dean's office. "Don't touch me," Thomas warned, yanking away. "I'll fuck you up." He repeated that warning several times, yelling so loudly that several teachers poured into the hallway. As they did, Thomas clenched his fist and bumped Officer Bass's chest with his shoulder, yelling, "You don't know me. I will fuck you up." Finally Miller was able to cuff him and lead him downstairs. He was sent to the county's juvenile lockup, a place that, sadly, he knew well.

Time and again I would leave the school curious about the lives of the students I had seen getting in trouble or violently losing their tempers. They were in some cases violent and mean, but they were still children. Their faces still had traces of youthful innocence. Repeatedly, after researching the students' backgrounds, I found lives filled with sad tales of abuse or neglect.

I found that while looking into the story of a tough-talking sixteen-year-old girl named Kanesha, whom I first came across while I walked toward the main office one afternoon. As I got to the office Sergeant Barrow was heading the other way, so I turned around and walked with him. I didn't initially realize he was escorting a very angry Kanesha to the in-school-suspension room because she'd been caught skipping class. I would later learn that she had just sat in Barrow's office trying without success to call her mom for a ride home and had unleashed her anger when the phone call went unanswered. "That fucking bitch won't answer the phone," she had said. "I know she ain't out looking for a fucking job."

A few minutes later we were walking down the hall. Oblivious, apparently, I still hadn't picked up on the tension right in front of me.

"I'm sick of you," she said, scowling.

"She's talking about me," Barrow said, shrugging his shoulders.

I smiled. That wasn't a good idea.

"What do you want?" Kanesha said, glaring at me.

"I'm just talking to Sarge," I said.

She continued to glare, and for a second I pondered how embarrassing it would be to get beat up by a sixteen-year-old girl in the middle of the school. Although that would have been humiliating, I could tell by the rage in her eyes that it would have been the likely outcome if she came after me.

"I'll snap on any motherfucker who looks at me," she warned.

"I'm not looking," I promised.

Later I found a dozen pages of police reports involving Kanesha. The story of her life was heartbreaking. When she was only nine, her mom reported that an eighteen-year-old family friend had repeatedly sexually abused her. When she was twelve, her family had been evicted from their home and was left to squat in a trailer without electricity or running water. When she was fifteen, she was arrested for threatening to attack a woman, and her mom was arrested for public intoxication. And a few months after she glared at me, police were called to her home on Christmas Eve as she and her mother argued loudly. The officers who responded said the teenager was out of control, apparently suffering from deep mental illness.

The police report documenting the girl's behavior on Christmas Eve is painful to read. It reported that Kanesha repeatedly said she didn't want to live any longer, "that she hated her life and wanted it to end." As officers tried to calm her, she screamed and said she couldn't control her actions or feelings and that she felt "that she was going to explode." She rocked back and forth and tried to pull her hair out and, police said, "would growl like an animal." The house was a mess. In a fit of anger, Kanesha had ransacked the kitchen, sending food and dishes onto the ground. "She gets like this sometimes," her mom told the cops. Police detained Kanesha and transported her to a local hospital for a psychological evaluation and for her own safety.

I didn't see that event. I'd only seen a girl walking down the hallway, furious at the world around her, or maybe at herself. She had come to school that morning hobbled by a life filled with pain. As I learned more about her, I told myself to be careful about judging students solely on one event or one outburst. There was often much more to the story. Kanesha had provided a sad lesson about the challenges schools like Manual face and about the recklessness of judging every school on the same criteria. But stories like hers are also what make the inefficiencies, apathy, and dysfunction of schools like Manual so infuriating.

Over and over throughout the year, readers asked me whether I thought a school like Manual could succeed. In response I would say that it seemed unlikely without some sort of miraculous change in thinking among district and school leaders. The problems are sweeping and mind-boggling, I would say, so the response must be ambitious and equally sweeping in scope. After the series concluded, I posed a similar question—Can schools like Manual be transformed?—to Joel Klein, the former chancellor of New York City schools. Klein had spent eight years trying both to reverse decades of decline in New York schools and to buck the apathetic mentality that stood in the way of progress. "I don't think it's possible to change an existing school without bringing in new people," he said. "It is one of the delusions of education—that the same people who have contributed to the problem can fix it. If you don't change the adults, you're not going to change the mind-set of a school. You can always have hope, but if they have developed a culture of low expectations and an unwillingness to work differently and harder, I don't think there is much hope."

His proposed strategy was to shut down such schools and start over. At Manual I often found myself believing that might be the best option available. The school starts each year miles behind schools thirty minutes to the north, south, east, and west. Its children face tremendous obstacles. So it should be filled with the strongest administrators, most dedicated teachers, and most nimble district leaders. It isn't, of course. And that just makes the obstacles long-suffering schools face even bigger.

6

★ ★ ★

GO TO CLASS, ZACH.

It feels a bit strange to bump into someone the day after you've put them on the front page of the newspaper. You never know what the reaction is going to be. Are they happy? Are they ticked off? Did you write something they want to complain about? What kind of reaction did they receive from friends, colleagues, neighbors, and even strangers? This is particularly true for columnists. We are expected to make judgments about our subjects, to say things a reporter cannot, and to express our own feelings. The praise or complaints that come after a column can make for an awkward moment. I typically prefer for a few days to pass before coming across the person I've profiled.

Not that I worry too much about the potential for a complaint. I am a columnist, and that means sometimes writing critically about someone, some organization, or some program. My job isn't to make everyone happy. In fact, it's often the opposite. I'm supposed to offer my opinions and my analysis of the issues and people in the news—good, bad, or otherwise. Pick any issue worth writing about, take any side on it, and you're guaranteed to tick someone off. At different times, I've been on the receiving end of complaints from governors, mayors, and a long line of other public officials I've put in the paper. Ultimately, though, the only reaction I fear is the charge that I got something wrong. Not a complaint that I was on the wrong side of an issue, or that my analysis was harebrained, but that I simply and indisputably got a fact wrong. Like misspelling someone's name. Or getting an age wrong. Or writing that a new state program would cost taxpayers $45 billion as opposed to $45 million. Those types of facts—those nitty-gritty details that are so easy to screw up on deadline and that are peppered throughout any newspaper piece—keep me up at night.

But I wasn't concerned about factual errors as I pulled into Manual's parking lot on the morning after my first column ran on the front page—at the top of the fold and in the Sunday newspaper. I had obsessively checked every fact and detail, then double-checked them, and then checked them again. I didn't want a little error to diminish the column. Still, I was unusually nervous about the reaction I would soon receive. The column was different from the hundreds of others I had written over the years. After all, I had noted the lackluster attempts of a burned-out teacher to survive another class and the arrest of the fifteen-year-old pot smoker. I had written about the pregnant girls in the building, the low test scores and attendance rate, and the kids dealing with mental illnesses. And the subjects of this column weren't public officials. They were average people. The teachers and staff were government employees, but they were nonetheless average citizens who hadn't sought the spotlight. The students, meanwhile, were just teenagers trying to get through life. I had dropped into this school for two weeks and put my analysis of it on the front page of the local paper. I had tried to be fair, truly balanced, and accurate. I didn't want to hurt anyone. But a lot of dirty laundry had been aired in that two-thousand-word column.

There was another thing adding to the unusual feeling in my stomach. Typically a newspaper series like this one would have been handled differently. Two years earlier, when I had written a nine-part series on the most crime-ridden apartment complex in the city, I'd spent months reporting on it before I wrote the first word. I had met tenants of the Section 8 complex and spent time in their apartments. I'd gotten to know ex-cons who hung out there, and I'd met residents who were up to both good and not-so-good things. I spent day after day in the summer of 2007 on the grounds of the complex. I rode overnight shifts with police and many times just sat quietly in my car in the early morning hours watching the wild nights that had made the complex infamous. The columns I wrote told of nasty fights between tenants and named violent criminals who made the Phoenix Apartments their base of operation. I blasted the out-of-state owners of the complex and wrote of the rodent-infected apartments and a mountain of code violations. I wrote about parents who put their children in harm's way.

But with the Phoenix series, as with most long-term newspaper projects, I did all of the reporting before the columns began to run. Once they began to appear in the paper, I didn't need to go back to the complex or its tenants to do the reporting for another column. With the Manual story, however, I had decided to write the columns in real time, to make it a serial. Week after week I would tell readers what was happening, what was changing, and how the school year was progressing. I loved the idea of doing it this way, of watching the story unfold and change. I wanted a project that would force me to be flexible and would allow me to change my focus from week to week. With that in mind, I arrived without an end date or overall battle plan in mind. It was exciting. But I also knew this approach meant I would have to walk through the door every week and face critiques about the work that had most recently appeared in the paper. And since I was not going to pull punches in my writing, I would have to accept any hostility the columns generated and the possibility that the school at some point could curtail my access.

Somewhat surprisingly, Principal Grismore offered me a solid hello when I walked into Manual that Monday morning. "Nice article," he said. My nervousness eased. It was 7:35 AM, a few minutes after the start of first period, and Grismore had just rolled a black cart into the school's entryway to give a pass—literally and figuratively—to the long stream of late students. With each student who wandered in tardy, Grismore would stamp, sign, and hand over a pass that allowed them late entry to class. I thought it was strange that the late students were allowed to wander in without repercussions.

I also thought his greeting to me was strange. Many school administrators take deep offense at even the slightest criticism. At many schools my access would have ended immediately if I had written about incidents much less disturbing than those documented in my column. But Grismore didn't complain that I'd mentioned the teens caught engaging in oral sex, the pervasive class-skipping, or the many other problems I'd highlighted. He didn't mind that we had run a chart showing the school's 39 percent graduation rate or its 32 percent passing rate on state standardized tests. Instead he was pleased because I'd noted that in the past year the school had increased the number of categories in which it made "adequate yearly progress," according to government education rules. The categories in which it improved dealt only with the number of students who had taken standardized tests, not the number who passed them. Still, that had pleased him.

It was a reminder that Grismore, a genuinely nice man, was at this point in his career a beleaguered manager. With district bureaucrats constantly hounding him about things like the dress code and paperwork, his overriding goal was simply survival. He was happy the school had found ways to get more students to take the tests. That made his reports to the district look better. As for improving the academic achievement in the building? That would be another story. And as for adding a feeling of urgency to a building filled with low expectations? Well, tragically, that just wasn't going to happen.

A few students walked in and pointed at me, saying they'd seen my column in the paper. I nodded. Interestingly, they didn't give the column a thumbs-up or thumbs-down. They just mentioned it. I had wondered if the students would take notice of my columns. Newspapers aren't exactly overflowing with readers younger than twenty. Or thirty. Or, to be honest, even forty. So there was a part of me that thought the students might not even notice my series. I was wrong, of course.

The fact that a few late-arriving students had already told me they'd seen the column suggested it would be the talk of the day. And even if the students and their parents weren't subscribers to the *Star*, the column was getting around. Helping with that was Lucy Koors, the school's feisty librarian, a woman who was constantly complaining to Grismore about school procedures. As she would week after week, Koors cut my column out of the paper and neatly taped it on the wall directly opposite the main office. It would be among the first things seen by anyone who walked into the building.

A few feet from where the column hung, Grismore continued handing out the final passes of the morning. As he did, an English teacher named Ted Collins appeared before us. I smiled at him, and in return he gave me a dirty look—an extremely dirty look. It would be the first of many he would give me during the school year. He didn't talk to me. But his look made clear I had found my first critic. I would find a few more before the day was over.

"You think we're a bad school?" The question came from a student who walked up to me in the cafeteria late that morning. He was with a friend and proceeded to tell me that my column seemed to suggest the school was filled with losers and troublemakers. As I would time and again during the school year, I told the student I didn't think the students were losers or stupid. But I did think that the school had tremendous challenges, that the test scores and graduation rates pointed to severe problems, and that the students and the city deserved better. I told him there appeared to be many great students, but there were others who were getting in the way of the school's improvement. He nodded and walked away.

In an English class I sat watching as the teacher walked around the room helping students with their work. I had noticed a group of boys staring at me, occasionally pointing. Over the next couple of weeks I would pick up on the obvious tension between some of the white boys in the school and me. The African American students didn't seem to have a problem. Neither did the Hispanic students. And the white girls were constantly full of friendly suggestions of things I should write about. But the white boys, at least some of them, didn't seem to like me. Sergeant Barrow once suggested that could be because they saw me as one of their own but also as someone who thought he was better than them.

"He said we're all poor," one of the boys said, intentionally loud enough for me to hear.

"Do I look poor?" another asked his confused teacher as she walked by. "I can't believe he's in this class."

A few minutes later I took a deep breath and walked over to the students and asked if they were willing to talk. They weren't. I asked if they'd read the column, and one told me he'd read enough of it to know it wasn't any good. I decided to walk away, telling them I'd be around if they ever wanted to talk. I would often find that students weren't mad at me for anything specific I had written. Many had not read the column and relied instead on evaluations of it that were spreading throughout the school. Rather than read it, they would come up to me and ask me to defend it. Or they would just complain as I walked by in the hallway.

Others, though, had taken the time to read it. Zach had. Zach was a sixteen-year-old troublemaker who came to school nearly every day but hardly ever went to class. He was a skinny but tough white kid from what many of the white boys in school called the hillbilly south side. Like many such kids, he tried to dress and talk and walk like a rapper. Often, when teachers would shout at him to get to class, he would walk away and start spitting out rhymes as he headed up or down the nearest stairway. He was a good-looking kid with a big smile, and he constantly flirted with school police officer Donnita Miller, an attractive forty-something single mom.

"When you gonna marry me?" he said on one of the first days of the school year.

"Go to class, Zach," she said, shaking her head.

"Can I at least have a hug?"

"Go to class, Zach."

On this Monday, though, Zach wasn't flirting with Miller, and he wasn't in a good mood. He was furious, and that fury was aimed in my direction. As it turned out, the young pot smoker who had been arrested on the third day of the school year was Zach's little brother, Jacob. And Zach was angry that I had written about the arrest. I hadn't mentioned his brother's name, not even his first name. But I had written about the tear that fell down his cheek when he was being arrested, and plenty of people in the school knew who I was talking about.

Not aware I was the subject of controversy and criticism, I walked up to Miller around lunchtime on the first floor as she talked to Zach. As I approached, he looked at me and shook his head. "You did him wrong," Zach said. "You weren't supposed to write about him."

I had no idea what he was talking about until Miller informed me that Zach was related to Jacob. "You didn't have any right to do that," Zach said.

I told Zach that he didn't know what he was talking about, that without question I had the right, that I'd come to the school to write exactly about that kind of thing, and that it wasn't my fault his brother had gotten himself arrested. I added that I'd done him a favor by not using his first name. He waved his hand dismissively and walked away, taking long, dramatic steps as he did. "You're a punk," he shouted.

I laughed and looked at Miller, telling her I didn't think I'd been called a punk in twenty years. She laughed, grabbed me by the arm, and pulled me aside. Then she turned quite serious, looking in both directions as she said she needed to tell me something. "You'd better watch your back," she said. "Zach's pretty mad at you."

"That would make a heck of a column," I said, "'Columnist Gets Beaten Up by a Manual Student.'" But I said that while I wasn't a fighter, I thought I could handle myself against a skinny kid who was six inches shorter than me.

"Maybe," she said. "But I mean, he's really mad. He came up here furious, saying he was going to get you. I talked to him. But just watch your back."

I wasn't too worried. If Zach was really planning an attack, informing the police would have been a silly strategic move. Nonetheless, I was a bit irritated by the idea that as a nearly forty-year-old man I would have to spend my workdays worrying about some kid jumping me in the hallway. That irritation wasn't eased a few days later when Miller informed me that school officials had screwed up Jacob's expulsion paperwork and, because of district rules, had been forced to allow him back into the school. Now I had two angry brothers roaming the halls.

I briefly longed for the normal part of my job—the one that left only politicians and readers mad at me. But then I thought about the column possibilities of an angry student. And I reminded myself that one goal of the series was to be flexible and take it in whatever direction the school year dictated. I wondered if Zach would be willing to talk, to let me write about his views of my column, and along the way explain why he never went to class. That never happened. I tried to talk to Zach a few times. He wasn't hard to find; he was always in the hallway, always skipping class. But each time I spotted him in the hall and tried to talk to him, he sped up his pace. He would ignore me or call me a punk, or something similar, and walk away.

Before long, the issue went away. Jacob was allowed back in school, but he was kicked out two weeks later after once again being caught with a bag of pot in his pocket. And Zach was soon sent to a district alternative school after Manual officials determined that nothing they could do would persuade him to go to class. With that, the potential for my first school fight since 1981 had been averted.

By the end of the week, I'd had dozens of conversations with students and teachers about that first column. One of the school's IT (information technology) workers walked up to me while I talked to a math teacher and proactively told me not to ever talk to him. "No problem," I said. Other teachers said they had heard from family members and friends worried about their safety after reading about some of Manual's problems. I also heard from dozens of readers. Some were sympathetic toward the school's students and staff while others were outraged. Some wondered if anything could be done to improve the school; others annoyingly offered the kind of simplistic solutions that too often get in the way of serious education reform debates.

The best responses came from adults who had once been the troublemaking, misguided, or simply troubled students I had written about. These readers urged me not to give up on those students and not to judge them too harshly. "I was the sixteen-year-old pregnant sophomore you'll pass in the hall," a woman named Carey wrote. "My son's father contributed to Manual's dropout rate back in 1996. The three of us were lucky and are thriving today. It only took me fourteen years to obtain my bachelor's degree. I obviously want better for my son."

A local lawyer wrote to tell me that twenty years earlier he'd been "that blond kid with the bag of weed getting thrown out and having to attend night school." If not for the work of his parents and a few caring teachers, he wrote, "I would have grown into the dirt bag everyone expected instead of a successful attorney, although some would argue that being an attorney makes me a dirt bag."

Every column attracts phone calls and e-mails from readers. But there was something different about the reaction that first column about Manual generated. It was more thoughtful. It was more personal. E-mails were filled with pleas for more information, and some asked how they could help. I realized how much people cared about the kids in our city's schools. One column in, there was already no doubt in my mind that in this school I had picked a great topic.

But the most memorable reaction to that first column came on the Friday afternoon when two girls, Allison and Kelly, walked up to me on the back steps of the school and bluntly asked if I was "going to write about the kids who are trying to do the right thing at Manual." I met the two girls in the school library three days after our first brief conversation. We met there again two days later. They wanted me to better understand their school, and I wanted to better understand what the kids at Manual experienced. The conversations provided me with a roadmap for the rest of the series, sending me down a better path than I could have planned.

The two seventeen-year-olds had grown up in the area around Manual and, with the exception of a brief period after an argument in elementary school, had been best friends since the age of six. They were constantly together—before school, in school, and after school. They both participated in the school's bare-boned theater program and were part of a small group hoping to find a way to bring back the school yearbook program, which had died a few years earlier because few kids could afford the books. They sometimes finished each other's sentences, and they laughed a lot. Both wanted to be the first in their families to go to college.

We met thirty minutes before the first-period bell rang on a Monday morning. As I drove to school in the dark that morning, I wondered whether a pair of seventeen-year-olds would actually be able to stick to their promise to get to school so early. They did. And they were smiling and ready to talk when I found them.

Allison told me her story first. Her mom worked at Kmart, and her dad worked in a warehouse. Her goal was to go to college to become a social worker, because she wanted to be able to help young people like the friends she'd seen suffer from problems related to drugs, alcohol, and abuse. She told me she just wanted to have a good life and a good job that she could be passionate about, one that motivated her to get out of bed each day. She said she wanted to make her parents proud and talked a lot about her mom, a woman who had failed to graduate from high school twenty years earlier. "She really wishes she had," Allison said. "That's one of the things that really bothers her. She's always told me, 'I want a better life for you.'"

Next, Kelly told me about her part-time job at a local Walmart and the disappointing news that both of her parents had recently been laid off from their jobs. Times were tough, she said, but both of her parents were taking classes to get certified in new trades, and they were getting by. She hadn't yet decided what career she would pursue but, as with Allison, she was contemplating social work. She told me about friends who had lost their way to drug abuse. "I've seen a lot of people around me fall into it," she said. "I just want to be able to help somebody else."

That issue—the kids who had fallen into deep drug problems—came up often as Allison and Kelly spoke. They talked about losing friends in middle school to the problem and of the many people in their neighborhood who had lost their way. So I asked more about it.

"I never wanted to get involved in any of that, and my parents were big on making sure I knew that wasn't the way I should go," Allison said. "My friends and I, we don't need any of that. Anyway, we're completely insane without it." They both laughed.

"In a good way," Kelly said.

"Yeah," Allison said, as the two continued laughing. "In a fun way."

There was something amazing about these two girls. They were serious and laser-focused. They were funny and sincere. They had never had much money, and they hadn't traveled much outside of the tiny geographic area in which they had lived their lives, but they were thinking big about the world around them. They hadn't come from educated families, but they were not going to let that stop them. They talked loud, as if projecting, something they'd learned from Lannae Stuteville, an English teacher who fought to be able to teach one theater class a year. They were friendly. But they were also pushy. As a journalist, I particularly admired that trait.

Allison and Kelly were looking forward to their senior year and hoped to instill some school spirit into a school that had little. They were talking about creating a fan club for the girls basketball team and had gotten the sparse crowd at the previous Friday night's football game to do a wave. Most important to them this year, they said, was getting their grades up and getting into college. The idea of going to college wasn't one they'd always had. The public schools they'd attended throughout their lives hadn't drilled the message of college into them, and their parents knew little about it. Money would be a huge obstacle, they thought. Perhaps too big. And after arriving at Manual as freshmen, they'd both fallen into the common trap of goofing off a bit and earning poor grades.

Allison talked about the poor grades she received during her freshman year, about being distracted in classes and failing her first class ever, Algebra 2, her sophomore year. Kelly said they'd gotten distracted by the freedom of high school as freshmen. Then something happened. "Toward the end of my sophomore year," Allison said, "I just thought, 'What am I doing? Why am I slacking off?'"

She and Kelly agreed over that summer to come to school as juniors being more focused, more zeroed in on the idea of going to college and having more options available to them. They had come to realize that a diploma from Manual, with no education on top of that, would limit them to jobs at retail stores and restaurants. Kelly stopped me as I wrote down her words and said she wasn't looking down on those jobs or the people who fill them. She just wanted something more. "We got back to school, and we just decided we can't mess around another year," she said. "We got together with a few other friends and supported each other."

Allison retook Algebra 2, and although she still struggled to understand the subject, she replaced the previous F with a hard-fought C. The duo grew closer to Jill Haughawout, the English teacher who had walked me to the gym that first morning of the school year, and who also taught a wonderful class called College Summit. It is aimed at improving the college attainment rate of low-income students nationwide. Haughawout convinced the girls they were college material and egged them on when they had doubts. She forced them to think about their strengths and what they wanted out of life. Rarely a day passed without Haughawout talking to them about college—about what it means and what it takes to get there. By the start of their senior year, the two girls had improved their GPAs to about 2.7. In some schools that might not mean much. But at Manual, where academic failure is profound and widespread, their grades were well above average. And they had time to nudge them up further.

The two talked matter-of-factly about their rough neighborhood and noted that the middle school they'd attended was even worse than Manual. They talked about Manual's problems, problems that seemed normal to them. Like the fight in the courtyard that ended with a student firing a gun into the air during their sophomore year.

"There's lots of drama," Kelly said. "There's lots of crazy stuff happening. But that's what I grew up with. And that kind of stuff happens at every school. It's not just here."

I looked up at her. Then I looked at Allison. They seemed innocent. And they seemed unaware of the remarkable nature of Kelly's statement.

"You know that's not right, though," I said. "Things like that do not happen at every school. It's very unusual for a gun to be fired by a student in a school."

"It is?" Kelly said.

"Yes," I said. "It's not normal."

I had quickly picked up on this type of thinking—an acceptance of stunning failure and problems, and a belief that a school such as Manual was normal. As I sat there talking to these two remarkable young women, I wondered how much it had taken to get them to the point where they considered a gunman in their school courtyard, and a bullet flying during school hours, nothing more than a routine problem. But that's not what we had gathered to discuss. As the morning bell approached, Allison and Kelly got to their main concern—that my series would add to Manual's image problems.

"I think the school's biggest problem is the reputation it has," Kelly said. "The students who want to succeed have to deal with the reputation."

I told her I understood.

"I don't think of myself any less because I went to Manual," she said. "If anything, I think it's an accomplishment."

"Yeah, if it's such a bad school and I did well, that's an accomplishment," Allison added.

"You have to push yourself," Kelly told me. "You have to want to learn. I know some people don't want to. But we're not stupid kids, and we weren't raised by stupid parents, and we don't only have bad teachers. We just want you to write about the fact that there are students in public schools in Indianapolis who are doing the right things, just trying to graduate and go to college."

I told them I understood their concern and that I would indeed write about the good kids and teachers. I had been collecting the names of students who had great stories to tell, and I said I would start with the two of them. I liked them immensely and thought readers would too. But I reminded them that I couldn't write only the good stories. Students like Kelly and Allison deserved to have their school's problems exposed and discussed. "Things will only improve if people truly understand the challenges this school faces," I said. They agreed, and I asked about the friends they'd mentioned who had gotten in trouble and the classmates who dropped out in such high numbers.

"It's scary," Kelly said. "It makes me wonder what my generation is going to look like. I just don't see how they're going to get by. When I look at my senior class, I guess I just thought there would be more people."

"I keep thinking, where did everybody go?" Allison said. "You were here a couple days ago, or you were here last year, and now you're gone."

"It's like they're losing hope," Allison said. "I could never allow that to happen."

Then she turned to Kelly, who added to the point, saying, "We could never allow that to happen."

I wrote down the girls' words, and I observed them in several classes over the next week. Every time I saw them in the hallway they were together and laughing or in deep serious conversation. I talked to teacher after teacher who told me how fun-loving and hardworking they were, and how in a school where few students took part in extracurricular activities they always seemed to be participating in one. When I asked Principal Grismore about the two girls, he smiled and said, "They're a kick."

My column on the girls ran in the newspaper a week after that first interview in the library. I noticed immediately that it struck a chord. A flood of readers wrote and called to tell me how inspired they were by "Allison and Kelly." Everyone seemed to use their names, as if they knew them. Many wrote to ask how they could help the two girls, and several readers sent cards to the school with gifts for them. A professor of social work contacted the school and became the girls' mentor, teaching them about the field and arranging several college visits. Vincennes University in southwestern Indiana reached out, eventually providing the duo with full scholarships.

Meanwhile, I was starting to see that this series might go in a fascinating direction. Readers had reacted with deep compassion for students in a school district that typically drew nothing but scorn. If that column, written quickly after knowing the two girls for only a few days, could inspire such an outpouring, what more could be done? People had been motivated to act, and to give, without being asked. I started to contemplate what I could do to take advantage of that.

Manual principal Richard "Rocky" Grismore during a midday fire drill.

Emmerich Manual High School.

ABOVE Allison Tomlinson and Kelly Leatherbury
laugh during lunch early in the school year.

FACING TOP Math teacher Connie Johnston helps a student.

FACING BOTTOM Jammyra Weekly prepares for a scholarship event.

Busy traffic outside the school on the night of the annual holiday concert.

Manual supporters crowd the school on a December
night to attend the annual holiday concert.

Choir director Spencer Lloyd leaves his classroom on the night of
the holiday concert on his way to the school's auditorium.

Choir teacher Spencer Lloyd talks to the overflow
crowd on the night of the holiday concert.

Sgt. John Barrow, head of the school's police unit,
talks to students during a lunch period.

Michael Robinson collects himself during a frustrating afternoon in the dean's office.

FACING TOP Dean Terry Hoover takes a short
break between meetings with students.

FACING BOTTOM Former Manual student Brent Walls, who was sent
to prison after his arrest at the school, talks about his troubled life.

ABOVE Brent Jones hugs his birth mother, Elizabeth Jones-
Gati, after seeing her for the first time in eighteen years. Kim
Roberson, who raised Brent, stands behind them.

Manual graduates celebrate in the school courtyard.

7

* * *

WE'RE NOT GOING TO BE AVERAGE HERE.

The thirty-one-year-old father of a Manual freshman walked into Dean Hoover's office one morning. He moved fast and angrily and wore camouflage pants, a tan workman's jacket, and a black cap. He came into the office without an appointment and spoke before being spoken to. "I want to talk to security," he announced, interrupting a conversation I was having with Hoover and yanking off the cap to show a blond buzzed haircut and an earring in his left ear.

Hoover immediately recognized the man from previous visits and calmly asked him to sit down. He declined, pacing the room instead for a few seconds as he told Hoover that a boy at the school was harassing his daughter and that he was a few inches from handling the situation on his own, even if that meant throttling the boy. He said the boy, his daughter's ex-boyfriend, was stalking her. The bullshit had been going on for a year, he shouted, but lately the situation had gotten worse.

Hoover looked up the girl's class schedule on her computer as the man continued to talk, repeating his threat to take matters into his own hands. At one point Hoover hushed him as she held the phone to her ear and dialed the daughter's third-period classroom, asking the teacher to send her down. Then she called Sergeant Barrow, aware that he might be the only one able to calm the man standing in front of her. As she hung up the phone, the father finally sat down. He began rubbing his face and looked just as flustered as he did when he walked in. "He's been stalking my daughter for a year," he said. "And now he's hanging out with the guy who raped her last year. I don't know what sick thing that's about."

I sat and listened as the man explained that his daughter had been raped by an older boy, a Manual dropout who was now eighteen, after he'd snuck into the family's home the previous year. His daughter was thirteen years old at the time and had been hurting emotionally ever since. Meanwhile, likely because the girl waited several days before telling her parents about the attack, charges had never been filed in the case. The father said he hadn't sought a restraining order. "I don't know law," he said, frustrated. "I know towing."

An hour or so before the man arrived at the school that morning, his daughter had sent her mother a text message. In a scarier version of a typical gossip-fueled high school argument, she'd gotten into a dispute with her ex-boyfriend over something that one of her friends told him she'd said. She insisted she'd been misquoted, that her friend was trying to start a fight. That didn't matter. The boy angrily confronted her, even as he was trying to win her back. He called her names. He yelled at her. The text the girl had sent to her mother sent her dad into a rage, landing him in Hoover's office.

Soon the girl, a freshman with a blond streak in her dark hair, arrived. She looked at her dad, at Hoover, at Barrow, and then at me. Understandably nervous, she carried her books pressed against her right side and answered questions quickly, eager to get out of a room filled with painful questions that embarrassed her. As she sat down, her dad repeated his earlier words about her ex-boyfriend hanging out with the boy who raped her. The girl began to cry, and Hoover handed her a box of tissues, a box that got quite a workout in an office filled with painful conversations. But even for Hoover, who dealt with the worst of the worst problems at the school, this case was particularly touching. "It's going to be okay," she said.

As we all listened, the girl then told Hoover and Barrow that the boy had confronted her that morning as she stood by her locker. She didn't remember his exact words but said she had resorted to texting her mom because of other recent events in the neighborhood she shared with her ex-boyfriend and the boy who had attacked her. On multiple occasions, she said, the two boys had spotted her on the sidewalk and began shouting sexually explicit taunts. Sometimes they would begin humping each other as if to simulate sex, or a rape, laughing and shouting at the girl as they did.

She cried again. But just like the previous time, the tears burst out quickly and then came to an equally quick stop. She sat there, sniffling and composing herself, her hair falling over her left eye before she brushed it away. It was obvious that she desperately wanted to get out of the room. She offered fast "yeps" and "uh-huhs" to the adults' advice. She nodded her head quickly when Barrow told her to stop talking to her girlfriends about the boy. She agreed when Hoover told her to avoid the two boys any way she could. She politely and obediently said, "I know, I know, I know," when Hoover reminded her that this wasn't her fault but that because the boys were such fools she was going to have to take the high road in this case.

"Thank you," the girl said. "Can I go to class?"

"Yes," Hoover said.

The girl raced away. After she left, Barrow made sure she was out of earshot before turning to her father. He had threatened several more times to take care of the situation himself, and Barrow was irritated by the tough talk. He said a stint in jail wasn't going to help his daughter. He told him the bravado wasn't doing a girl in pain any good. And he reminded him that taking on two streetwise teenagers might not end as well as he imagined.

The father agreed. Then he began to cry. "My daughter's been raped by one kid, and now she's being stalked by another and they're hanging out together," he said. "I don't know what I'm going to do."

There was no obvious answer. Hoover encouraged the man to obtain a restraining order against the dropout, who would be arrested on a felony burglary charge a few months later, and said she would have a talk with the boy who still wandered Manual's halls. But that was it. There would be no remedy for the situation. The school couldn't do anything about encounters off of its grounds, particularly with the boy who wasn't even a student. The man left, still in grief but calmer than when he had arrived. He was a reminder of the heavy load so many families carry.

On days like that it was easy to get depressed. As I listened to the young girl talk and watched her sweetly shake her head while answering questions, I almost cried myself as thoughts raced through my mind: Why does a young girl have to go through this kind of thing? What effect will all of this have on her as she gets older? Does she have any real chance of succeeding in a school filled with emotional landmines that would cause someone twice her age to stumble? Jesus Christ, I thought, she was only fourteen years old. She should be studying, hanging out with friends, and planning her future. Not dealing with the pain of being a crime victim and having the cruelest taunts thrown in her face. She should still be a year away from going to the movies with nervous boys whose parents have talked to them about respecting girls, not being harassed by degenerates who see girls as targets. She shouldn't have to roam the same halls as a boy who seemed to be intent on ruining her life.

On days like that, when the sad stories at Manual got to me and when I seriously began to doubt that the school had any chance of being turned around, I often headed away from the main office and walked down the long first-floor south hallway, stopping just before I got to Manual's back door. There I found a classroom that always cheered me up. The class did much more than that, though. It gave me a much-needed dose of optimism and became my oasis from the school's drama and heartbreak, providing me with inspiring lessons about what American schools must to do improve. It was where I went, time and again, in search of hope. Eventually it also led to one of the most inspiring nights of my life. This was Spencer Lloyd's choir class.

I walked into the classroom for the first time on the first day of the school year and was immediately struck by the energy spinning out of the passionate twenty-five-year-old teacher standing at the front of the class. He joked and sang and did impressions as he talked to the ten students in his third-period class about his love of music and his hope that music might become something important for them too. Every minute or so, Lloyd would jump off of the metal stool he sat on to make a point or to demonstrate a song the class might be singing later in the year. He mentioned Cole Porter and was soon belting out a few bars of the show tune "Another Op'nin', Another Show." He talked about learning to control your voice and then belted out a high note. He didn't let many seconds pass without doing something to grab his students' attention. He told them about himself—about his "hot wife" and the weird sounds and cute smiles his infant son made. He found a way to work words like *noogie* and *swirlie* into his stories, breaking the class up in laughter.

One of the first things I jotted in my notebook that morning was that Lloyd reminded me of a slightly—and only slightly—less manic version of comedian Robin Williams. Even as the rest of the school was barely functioning on that first day of the new year, Lloyd insisted on getting to work and making it clear to his students that his class would be different from many of the others they attended. He said he wanted everyone to enjoy his class, a break from the routines of math and science, but he also wanted to make sure nobody saw it as an easy grade or a chance to goof off. He talked about expectations.

He told his class that the cussing you could hear often in other classes and in the hallways would not be accepted in his class. Not even once. He said this would be a class filled with respect. Making the students laugh while also making his point, he strolled up to a freshman named Brittany and began waving his hands in her face, making a menacing face as he did. "Respect your classmates in my class," he said. "If you don't want someone in your face saying 'Yo Mama,' then don't get in their face saying 'Yo Mama.'"

His goal was to set the tone from the beginning. "We're going to sing, and we're going to sing well," he told the students. "We're going to have fun. But we're also going to work hard. We're going to improve day after day. We're going to end the year much stronger than we started it. We have goals, and reaching goals takes work."

"The difference between average and excellence is attention to detail," he said, walking among his students and making eye contact with each of them. "If you want to be an average choir, go to a different high school. We're not going to be average here."

It was a message I rarely heard during my year at Manual. This was a building where mediocrity was sometimes celebrated and mass failure was tolerated. Often, actually, teachers and administrators would tell me with pride or excitement about an accomplishment that made clear the school's low expectations. Once, for instance, after updating the school's data, Principal Grismore happily announced to me that Manual's most recent graduation rate was actually higher than previously believed. It wasn't 39 percent, as had been reported earlier, he said. "It's actually forty." When I stared at him for a few seconds, unsure of how to respond, he informed me that any improvement was welcome.

That was true. And though I understood the challenges the school faced, with students who often arrived lagging academically and with personal lives filled with obstacles, I didn't understand why there was so little belief in setting high standards. I couldn't imagine how a high school principal could be anything short of shattered by a 40 percent graduation rate, or even by the further revised 44 percent rate that would be announced later in the year.

Fortunately, Spencer Lloyd hadn't learned to accept failure or set low expectations. He had high hopes for his program. That's what kept me coming back. On that first day, though, even before he got around to talking about the great music he hoped to hear the students sing, Lloyd talked to his students about how far he was willing to go to help them. He told them he was available to talk about the problems he knew were holding many of them back. "Everyone needs to vent," he said, offering himself up as a sounding board. He wanted them to know they could trust him, and that his class, with its high ceilings and grand piano, could be a special place if they wanted it to be. "I want this to be your island," he told his class. "When you come in here, I want you to be able to leave any baggage you have at the door. I know you might need to pick it back up on your way out. But while you're in here, you can try to forget about it and just sing."

As he talked, two freshmen girls sat next to each other in the front row. Later in the fall, one would spend a few nights at a women's shelter with her mom because of troubles at home. The school would have to call Child Protective Services regarding the other girl, because she was unsure of where she would be staying one weekend. The latter girl would often seek me out in the hallway to tell me about the latest problem she was having at home or the other classes she was struggling in. But in Lloyd's class, she and her friend wore nearly constant smiles.

What I liked about Lloyd from the beginning, in addition to his energy, was that while he had compassion for his students' lives, he was unwilling to use their backgrounds as an easy excuse. He argued that students deserve the chance to achieve great heights and that making excuses for them would only prevent them from doing so. He knew that unlike children in the suburbs, his students hadn't received private voice lessons or had much attention paid to their talents. They hadn't performed routinely at recitals filled with parents, grandparents, aunts, and uncles. His students were still learning basics that their counterparts from better school districts had learned in junior high or even earlier. Despite all of that, and despite a tiny choir budget, he believed Manual could have a great program.

It was going to take a lot of work. But the twenty-five-year-old with the goatee and spiky brown hair insisted he was up for the challenge. "I consider myself—and many people who know me agree with this—almost fatally optimistic," Lloyd told me as we talked in his small office one day. "I just think if there's a possibility something great can happen, it will. That might make me look unrealistic, but you know what? It gives the kids hope."

A group of students in the heart of urban America was getting that hope from a guy who wasn't much older than many of them and who came from a background that could hardly be more different from theirs. Lloyd grew up in a city whose name paints the perfect picture of it: Farmland, Indiana, a tiny rural town two hours north of the city where he now taught. His family life was as peaceful as every child's should be. His dad owned an insurance agency while his mom took care of a household full of kids. They went to church regularly, had enough money, and knew education was important—advantages his students lacked. Few of them received the support at home that he had. They couldn't turn to a parent for advice or money for an extracurricular activity. "It often takes an internal drive for these students to excel," he said, "or even to simply show up every day. The expectations that they do so just don't exist. If they stopped coming to school, as many students at Manual eventually do, that would sadly be acceptable to many people in their lives." That knowledge drives Lloyd to be a memorable part of their lives. It is what motivates him. It makes him glad he took a job in a district where he never intended to work.

By the time Lloyd graduated from Indiana Wesleyan University with a degree in music education, IPS's reputation around central Indiana had long ago been battered, and many young teachers didn't feel safe or prepared to take on the monumental challenges facing the urban core of Indianapolis. Lloyd laughed one day when he told me that when his first assignment as a student teacher put him at another high school in the district, he wasn't sure he could do it. He was scared when he found out about the assignment and when he encountered students who were often bigger, and almost as old, as he was. But it clicked. He enjoyed the chance to work with students who desperately needed a hand. The students who refused to let life prevent them from succeeding inspired him. He loved introducing them to new ideas.

So he pursued and won a job at a local middle school and then arrived at Manual a year before I met him. Manual's choir program was nearly nonexistent when he was hired. Along with many other faltering, dwindling programs, it was in jeopardy. The budget cuts that are haunting schools in low-income parts of the country had claimed many programs in recent years at Manual and soon would be claiming more. The district had frequently threatened to shut down programs with low participation and lackluster results.

When Lloyd got his class rosters that first year, there were only a dozen students signed up to take choir. It was a school, he learned, in which most students stayed away from programs that occasionally required attendance after school hours. Students had jobs and siblings and their own children to care for. For them, spending a few hours after school was not possible. Others simply chose to spend as little time in the building as possible—before, after, or even during school hours. As with everything else in the building, apathy dealt a damaging blow to programs like choir.

Lloyd didn't worry about that. Rather, he began going from class to class on a recruiting mission. He walked into math, history, and science classes, asking for a few minutes to talk to students about what they could achieve by taking choir. He chatted up teenagers in the hallway and urged his small number of students to tell their friends about the program. It was about building memories and traditions and learning how to improve your skills. It was about being part of something, he would say. "Even if you've never sung before," he told students, "come on over and give it a try." He said it would be hard work but promised there would also be fun. Before long he had thirty students. He kept recruiting, and by the end of his first year he had forty-five. By the start of his second year his class rosters totaled nearly sixty students. Even that number grew as his reputation spread throughout the building and as music poured out of his room period after period.

Still, the life of a new teacher in the district is not an easy one. Lloyd's first year at Manual ended with the fear that he would lose his job. His name was on a potential layoff list the district put together because of budget problems. The district's strict union seniority policies resulted in new teachers like Lloyd being included on that list, even though school administrators considered him their most promising teacher. With a baby at home, he stressed about his future for several weeks before the district announced that attrition had spared his job. For now. He worried about being put on such a list the following year and struggled to understand why so many of the district's top teachers, including several Teacher of the Year nominees, had been at risk of unemployment simply because of their junior status. The problem can be found increasingly at many low-income urban schools, schools that have had to make dramatic spending cuts in recent years because of declining enrollment and funding cuts.

"This is the reality for our public schools nationwide," read a 2009 report from the New Teacher Project, a nonprofit research organization that seeks to close the heartbreaking achievement gap among America's students. "Put simply, they fail to distinguish great teaching from good, and fair from poor. A teacher's effectiveness—the most important factor for schools in improving student achievement—is not measured, recorded, or used to inform decision making in any meaningful way." The report, called "The Widget Effect," found that a majority of teachers and 81 percent of administrators reported the presence of a poor-performing teacher in their school. "Troublingly, the percentages are higher in high-poverty schools," it states.

But instead of clearing such teachers out of schools, instead of thinking about what is best for students, districts too often simply cut the most junior teachers when faced with the need to reduce staff. As such, Lloyd arrived at Manual for his second year still slightly bruised and even more skeptical about the union's hard stance on seniority and other issues, but no less energetic. As the first class I watched came to an end, he told his students to get ready for a year filled with wonderful music. "This year can be special," he told them. I had no idea how right he was.

A few days later the class was in full swing. Shortly after the bell rang, nine students sat up straight in their chairs as Lloyd guided them through "Another Op'nin', Another Show," waving his arms and occasionally pointing to his mouth to remind the students to smile when possible. "Fill the room!" he said. "Come on. Let's hear it. This song has a lot of energy, I want to hear it."

He looked at the altos, moving in closer. "Come on, altos," he said. "Rock your part. Yes, that's good. That's what we're looking for."

Lloyd's forehead was starting to sweat when the song came to an end. The students breathed loud sighs of relief and slumped in their seats. They took a short break, and the girls in the class began to talk and laugh. The only boy, a shy junior named Luis, sat quietly. He raised his hand and asked Lloyd if he'd had time to look into something they'd talked about the day before. Lloyd assured him he was looking into his other classes to see where Luis might fit.

"You're leaving?" Brittany asked loudly, her south-side twang filling the room. "Why?"

"No reason."

That wasn't enough for Brittany. She was inquisitive and wanted to know why someone would be leaving her favorite class. She asked again. And again. Finally, Luis, almost in a whisper, told her he didn't like being the only boy in the class.

"We'll work it out," Lloyd said, aware that Luis was getting embarrassed and trying to redirect the conversation.

Brittany, though, still didn't pick up on the social cues. "Why would you want to leave a class where you're surrounded by girls?" she said. "You should enjoy this. A lot of guys would love to be in a class with all girls."

I can't be sure, but it seemed like that little piece of advice got through to Luis. He smiled nervously, and when the singing resumed a minute later, he sang a little louder.

The class, meanwhile, began to work on a piece called "Fascinating Rhythm" by George Gershwin, a song I'd hear dozens of times in Lloyd's class, a song that would remain stuck in my head for months. Lloyd reminded the class it would have its first performance in less than two months. The students had a lot of work to do. They wanted to sound good in front of the audience.

Later he reminded them of what he'd said about excellence. That hadn't been just an opening-day message he would forget. He hadn't said that because there was a journalist in the room or because he was full of energy after a summer off. Excellence was the goal of every class. And excellence on stage in front of a crowd would be achieved only if everyone's full efforts were made in class.

"Do any of you doubt that I'm giving one hundred percent?" Lloyd asked. He was sweating from running around the room. The class agreed he was giving his all. "Then it wouldn't be fair for you to give me less than one hundred percent. I want to feel the tension in your voice."

They sang louder, taking his instructions. "Sit up straight. Focus. Push the sound out from your foreheads," he said. That last one stumped them, and Lloyd could tell they were confused. He elaborated. "If you were superheroes, and your superpower was that you could shoot supersonic sound out of your bodies, where would it come from?" he asked. "Your foreheads. So think about that when you sing. Push forward. Sing it out of your foreheads."

"You have quite an imagination," Brittany said.

When they finished the song, Lloyd told them that when he sang the song, he thought of the tension heard in the voice of Aerosmith's lead singer, Steven Tyler. To demonstrate, he sang a few lines—"more rhythm, more rhythm, more rhythm"—while impersonating the shrieking rock star. The only problem was that most of the students didn't seem to know much about Aerosmith.

"You actually sound like Jack Black," one student said.

Lloyd jumped up, excited, and shouted, "Yes!" He then delivered a line from *School of Rock*, in which Black's character introduces a young classical cello student to the bass guitar. "Instead of playing it like this," Lloyd said, acting as if he were playing a cello, "you tip it on its side and . . . cello, you've got a bass!" The students quoted other lines from the movie, and Lloyd looked at me. "Sometimes," he said, "I feel like my life is *School of Rock*."

Every class was like this, filled with energy and excitement. I noticed that after many classes, students would walk up to Lloyd to talk about a problem they were having at home, or in another class, or even with a song. He always listened. And when I would bump into him in the hallway or the main office, he always had something to tell me about a performance he was planning, a long-term goal he was setting, or a student who was making progress. Meanwhile, I'd come to learn there was a sharp difference in the way many of his students acted in other classes. The same students I would see working hard in his class caused trouble in others. Students who would always attend his class skipped others and were near-constant fixtures in the dean's office.

I walked into Lloyd's class later in the year's first quarter and almost wondered if his students had been replaced by others with more experience. They were already much more polished as they belted out "Another Op'nin', Another Show." Luis, who had been so quiet earlier, was still in the class. But he was more energetic and during breaks would sing loudly, not at all unnerved by the many girls in the class or the sound of his solo voice filling the room. And Lloyd was still pleading for excellence, telling his students they could never get a bad note back. "Once it's out there," he said, "it's gone. And if you don't focus, you've wasted all that energy on a bad note." The class nodded as he talked.

After the class ended, I wondered what Manual's test scores and graduation rate would be if every class were filled with the energy I'd found in this one. The problems that hurt the school wouldn't disappear. Bad parents wouldn't suddenly become engaged in their children's education, and the social ills that affect so many students wouldn't end. But many students could be saved. Many would hear an important message: that they are capable of great things. The achievement gap that has created two classes in cities like Indianapolis would begin to shrink. It wouldn't be easy to instill such a culture in schools like Manual, or to fill so many classrooms with the best teachers. It might actually be the hardest chore this nation has ever undertaken. But it could also result in one of the nation's most important victories.

"The research shows teachers can have a tremendous impact on even the most disadvantaged kids," David Harris, CEO of The Mind Trust, an Indianapolis-based nonprofit organization promoting education reform and innovation, told me one day. Harris pointed to studies, detailed in the Brookings Institution report "Identifying Effective Teachers Using Performance on the Job," that looked at the performance of students of similar backgrounds in classes taught by top-ranked and bottom-ranked teachers. In one year in Los Angeles schools, students with the top teachers "gained five percentile points relative to students with similar baseline scores and demographics," the report states, while those with the worst teachers fell by an equal amount. "Moving up or down ten percentile points in one year is a massive impact," the report insists. "For some perspective, the black-white achievement gap nationally is roughly 34 percentile points. Therefore, if the effects were to accumulate, having a [top] teacher rather than an [ineffective] teacher four years in a row would be enough to close the black-white test score gap." Still, many people fight efforts to make sure that teachers like Lloyd greet students in every classroom, and many continue to question the ability of teachers to have such an impact.

That morning, as Lloyd's students filed out of his classroom, he told me about the October recital he was holding and the annual holiday concert that would be coming in December. That concert typically draws only seventy-five or so people, he had told me, which was barely enough to fill the first few rows of the school's vast auditorium. "We don't get a lot of people," he said. Not even many parents show up. But it's still important for the students to have a tradition. "And who knows," he added, "if we keep getting better, maybe more people will show up. It would be great for the kids." I thought about those words for months.

8

★ ★ ★

WHERE'S THE SCHOOL SPIRIT?

The missing pieces of Manual were everywhere. The school didn't have a student council, I learned one day. Or a newspaper. Or a yearbook. Or so many of the things that scream high school and that are just as routine as math and science at other schools. Day after day, I would notice one more element of high school life that the cash-strapped school didn't have. Once, I stopped as I wandered one of the hallways and jotted a few words into my notebook: "This school doesn't seem to have anything."

I wasn't talking only about the programs and extracurricular activities. The school simply had no spirit. It felt like a sterile factory, and its students were the widgets. The goal was just to keep the dilapidated assembly line moving as much as possible and not to do anything more than that. I walked through the halls another day counting the many empty glass-enclosed cases that at other schools would be filled with memorabilia, photos, and information about student achievements. The only signs I saw on the wall had been taped up by the football coach. "Any student with the desire to play football, this is your last opportunity," they read.

The coach was essentially begging boys to come out for the team—even though the first game of the season had been played three weeks earlier. Meanwhile, the sports trophy cases in the back of the school seemed to have been frozen in time—as if Manual athletes had accomplished nothing since the 1980s. The school was clean. There was no graffiti on the walls, and the building had been recently renovated. But it was soulless. When I walked down the halls, I often felt like I was in a hospital.

For some reason, the lack of a yearbook struck me hardest. It was a little thing, inconsequential in the larger picture and superficial when compared with the school's monumental issues of academic failure, student behavior problems, and high dropout rates. And I understood that times were changing and print products of every kind were suffering. All I had to do was look at my paycheck or the roster of reporters at my paper—both were significantly smaller than a year earlier—to understand that point. But the yearbook program had not been killed a few years earlier because of changing technology, because people preferred to store their high school memories on a disc or a computer file, or because Facebook had overtaken hard-cover books in the hearts of today's students. It had faded from existence after a century of tradition because too few students had been able to afford the books, and the school had been forced to eat several thousand dollars' worth of them. Many unopened 2005 yearbooks remained stacked in a room in the back of the school.

Seniors graduating at the end of the current school year would never have a yearbook to fill with signatures and notes from friends, classmates, and teachers. They wouldn't have a book to dust off twenty years from now when they were feeling nostalgic for high school. Again, I knew it wasn't the biggest issue. But it bothered me. And it bothered some students. One day a group of them met with two twenty-something AmeriCorps workers who had been assigned to the school. The workers' job was to get more students engaged in activities— a task they acknowledged they'd failed at miserably. On this day the women had sprung for pizza and invited students to meet to talk about the yearbook program and whether there was a way to bring it back. Seven students, all girls, showed up at the meeting.

One of the AmeriCorps workers was surprised when the girls said they'd be willing to stay after school on Fridays to work on a yearbook project. For months she and her partner had been hampered by the inability to get students to show up for meetings or participate in activities aimed at tackling the depressing culture in the school. She smiled at the commitment from the girls in front of her.

"You'll really stay after school on Fridays?" she asked.

The girls nodded, smiling as they ate slices of pizza.

"Wow, you really want a yearbook."

"We do," one girl said.

"It's memories," senior Susan Lynn added. "You only go to high school once. For some people these are going to be the best years of their lives. It'd be nice to have a book where all those memories are stored. We want to be able to look back at these years." But, she warned, charging for the book was likely to doom it. Too many kids simply could not afford the forty- or fifty-dollar price tag. And she added that it was hard to get students excited about anything related to school. Susan was on the tennis team, which had struggled to compete at the varsity level because rules required that seven students be on such a team. The team was up to five, and even with promises from others, it hadn't found a way to get to seven. And despite the optimistic yearbook meeting, the idea sputtered. The AmeriCorps workers ended their stints at Manual a few weeks later without having held another meeting, disappointing those students who had offered to help.

The school newspaper had suffered a fate similar to the yearbook, dying off after the district killed a multimedia class whose students had long produced the paper. That was one in a long line of budget cuts that is robbing schools in America's urban core of the extras that can help pull students in to a school, that can sometimes connect students to school in a way traditional classes cannot. That was crucial here; rather than cutting such programs, Manual needed to be expanding them and doing anything it could to give students on the edge a reason to show up in the morning. With a thriving school paper, students could develop an interest in writing, photography or graphic design. Without an official class during normal school hours, however, the newspaper was long gone. Teachers said getting students to stay after school to voluntarily work on a paper had proven impossible. And even if it weren't, it didn't matter. It was clear that nobody was trying to resurrect the paper—the *Manual Booster.*

The student council, meanwhile, had been killed three years earlier, replaced by a barely functioning student group organized by administrators. As such, there was no vote for class president, no banners taped up for different candidates, and no debates among students vying for one office or another.

In an attempted defense, school officials handed me a long list of student groups that were active at the school. But they acknowledged that few of them ever met. And the school's leaders had other things to worry about—things that district headquarters cared much more about than the elusive issue of school spirit. Like the attendance rate. And the dress code. And the behavior in the lunchroom.

One administrator, though, had only recently arrived at Manual. Vice principal Lauren Franklin was in her early thirties, not far removed from her own years at nearby Broad Ripple High School, famous locally for having educated David Letterman. She was one of the district's brightest stars and would soon be a principal at her own school, most of her colleagues predicted. She was tough but connected with students, and she hadn't yet bought into the low expectations that seemed to dominate Manual.

Franklin had arrived at the beginning of the year and noticed the same things I had—the lack of decorations and trophies and programs. She went to football games on Friday nights and wondered where the students were. "Where's the school spirit?" she said. "The things we all wanted to do in high school, there's just not a lot of interest here. Here, everyone says they won't participate. I think we give our kids a bad rap. If we're not offering the right programs, we have to ask ourselves if we're doing enough for them." Clearly, the school wasn't.

I found myself feeling silly as I asked students about school spirit. It's such an indefinable, elusive thing. And I remembered my own high school days and my general opposition to spending any minute at school that I could avoid. But this was a school from which thousands of students in the past generation had dropped out, and the lack of routine programs was yet another sign of the apathy and lack of urgency that dominated the place. The old traditions and programs had faded away and weren't being replaced by new efforts to engage students.

"You'll schedule a meeting after school, and you'll wait in your office until three thirty and nobody will show up," history teacher Cheryl McManama told me as we sat in her classroom one afternoon. "These are things that should be mainstays in high school, and we don't have them. Sometimes I wonder, Will these kids have a reunion in ten years? Or is that a tradition that will go away too?"

Many teachers did little to help with the problems, declining to stay after school or push students to take part in programs. The small cheerleading squad relied on an off-duty police officer to lead it. At most games and performances I attended, the crowds included only a few teachers, typically Manual's most dedicated. McManama, though, was one of the teachers at the school who refused to accept the death of the high school traditions. She had single-handedly kept the annual prom going, insisting that teenage boys and girls need a bit of pomp at the tail end of a long school year. Although few students were involved in planning the prom, it was still well attended every spring. It was a tradition that had survived.

There was also a theater program run by fun-loving theater buff Lannae Stuteville. But she struggled mightily to get students to participate and had to fund it largely out of her own pocket. She smiled and said she considered that contribution her tithing. Turnout from potential actors was so low that the previous year she found herself unable to round up enough students to stage a production of 12 *Angry Men*. So she sat down and rewrote the play, emerging with the newly titled *A Jury of Six*. Early in this school year, Stuteville had held auditions for *The Curious Savage*, a mystery she would be staging in the fall. There were not enough interested students to have the luxury of competitive tryouts, and Stuteville left the first rehearsal knowing she might have to turn to a theater friend to fill out the small cast. The program was hurt by students who were unwilling to stay after school and by new magnet programs throughout the district that were attracting top students from schools like Manual.

Down the hall, Spencer Lloyd, the choir teacher, had been researching the school's musical history. He had discovered that the school had abandoned its tradition of an annual musical play about twenty years earlier. "That's a tradition every school should have," he said, pointing to annual offerings of *Grease* and *Godspell*, which were his favorite high school memories. So he went on the Internet and spent one dollar for a copy of a book, *Let's Put on a Musical*, with the goal of staging one the next school year. "The problem starts outside of the building," he said. "There's a million things that get in the way of these kids participating, and there's this overwhelming sense of apathy. And on the other side of the issue, there aren't a lot of opportunities for the students here at school."

Then there was the problem of sparse attendance at plays and games and concerts. Football games often attracted only a few dozen fans. Plays were even less well attended. Stuteville had addressed the problem the previous school year by having her actors perform with their backs to the sprawling auditorium. She put chairs on stage for the forty or so people who showed up and placed a wall between the actors and the auditorium. It was just too depressing for the kids to have to look at all the empty seats. Lloyd faced a similar problem. His choir concerts drew tiny crowds. He hoped to change that. "It's just about the experience," he said when I asked why he put on the concerts if even parents failed to show. "It gives the kids something to belong to."

All of that was on the mind of Superintendent White when he walked through Manual's doors one morning. He arrived clad in a blue pinstriped suit, and, at six-foot-five, he towered over everyone in the building. White, in his fifth year of leading the district, had come to Manual that morning to talk to the students. He did it every year, at every high school in the district. He met with them in groups and on this morning started with the freshmen and sophomore boys. They filed into the auditorium as White watched from the front of the room. Principal Grismore, Sergeant Barrow, and a few other school staffers stood nervously around him. He studied the students and looked carefully at how they were dressed. Occasionally a student would wave to him, and he would smile back. Above him, on a large screen, were the words "It is time." He started with that message.

"I don't think you realize time is getting away from you," he told the boys, who collectively were the most likely in the school to drop out. "I don't think you understand that." He talked for several minutes, asking them what they believed and what traits defined them, before spotting a boy talking a few rows away. He didn't hesitate. "Get up," he said.

The boy did hesitate, looking around the room.

"Get up," White ordered, louder this time. "Do I have to do sign language?"

As a school police officer escorted the boy out of the room, White used the moment to talk to the students about the need to focus and take advantage of their talents. None of the students talked after that, but quite a few yawned or looked at the floor. Over the next fifteen minutes, White covered everything from the attendance rate to the likelihood that dropping out would doom the students to, at best, low-wage jobs. He made fun of boys walking down the street with their pants sagging and girls who wore shirts that were sizes too small.

And then he offered a warning. Manual's football team had not yet won a game. It hadn't even come close, and White didn't like seeing the district's schools lose to their suburban competition week after week. It was embarrassing. This was the state's largest school district, yet it had some of the worst teams. The basketball team hadn't had enough players the previous year for a freshman team. Other sports saw few people trying out partly because of the 2.0 grade point average requirement. Additionally, the music classes were nowhere near capacity.

"If you're not going to be on the teams, I'm going to cut the teams," White said. "I have to save money anyway. I want a football program. But why should I pay for a football team with only twenty guys on it?" Students should be flocking to the sports programs, he said, rather than wasting their time hanging out on the corners after school. And Manual should have a great band and a top-notch choir. It should be known for its sports and music programs, as it once was. "It's not going to happen if you don't get involved," he said. "Manual will never be all it could if you don't get involved. If you are just getting on the bus, going to class, and getting back on the bus to go home, you're only taking advantage of one-half of your education. Right now we're begging people to go out for the band and to go out for football. I'm tired of it."

Cedric Lloyd, the school's beleaguered football coach, wasn't in the room. But the message carried quickly to his office on the other end of the school. He needed to prove that his program was relevant and worth the district's investment, and that he could turn it into an important part of the school. His team had a game two days later, and he knew he needed a win. Lloyd, who was not related to choir teacher Spencer Lloyd, needed both that elusive win and more players. Without either, his program was in jeopardy.

9

★ ★ ★

I DON'T LIKE BEING CALLED STUPID.

As fall approached, I realized that my initial idea of spending perhaps the first quarter of the school year at Manual was not nearly ambitious enough. There were far too many columns to be written, far too many students with amazing stories to tell, and far too many complex issues to dig into. Plus, the readers were responding. Nine weeks would give me enough time to scratch the surface and to write a few thousand words of copy before returning to the grind of covering the state's political scene. But I wasn't interested in that. Manual was too fascinating, the scope of the subject matter was too complex, and my access was too good. I had been lucky to be a columnist for the previous four years—it's the best job in newspapers—but there was something special going on, and I didn't like the idea of stopping short. I was beginning to notice the story arc of the school year, and after investing so many hours into it at the start, I wanted to see how the story progressed.

The first nine-week period of the school year had been a particularly tough one. Attendance was a huge problem, with teachers reporting a quarter or more of their students routinely missing classes. And the halls continued to be filled hour after hour with class-skippers. That problem had gotten so bad that a group of teachers was complaining to administrators, and to me, almost daily about the lack of attention school leaders were paying to all of the students who wandered the halls and who occasionally stepped in and out of class when they felt like doing so. The teachers' frustrations weren't eased by Principal Grismore's insistence that more students would go to class if the classes were just more engaging. Attendance was just one of many problems that had plagued the school's opening nine weeks, though.

Some problems weren't that serious—at least when compared with other issues—but they still nagged at the school and reminded students of Manual's battered reputation. Nothing underscored that reputation more than the school's undermanned football team. By the first week of October, the team had suffered one humiliating loss after another. The Manual Redskins, who struggled to have even twenty players on their roster, had lost to suburban schools by scores of 54–6, 56–6, and 66–6. Even fellow schools in the IPS district, many of which shared Manual's on-the-field problems, walked away with one-sided victories. The Redskins were winless after their first seven games, with only two remaining. In only one game, the most recent, had Manual lost by fewer than thirty-five points.

Meanwhile, by the time teachers handed out their first-quarter grades in mid-October, police had arrested twenty students—in a school that roughly seven hundred students attended with regularity. The charges ranged from violent attacks on teachers and fellow students to drugs and robbery. City police had come one day to arrest a boy who had skipped a class, walked to a nearby park, and assaulted a woman as she jogged. Another day, police were relieved to have to deal with an old-fashioned prank. A pair of students, who were later sent to the juvenile lockup after being spotted on a security camera, had spent the day pulling the school's fire alarms. It was irritating, disruptive, and even potentially dangerous. But police appreciated that there were no punches or threats involved. Most crimes were more serious, however, and they were so consistent that the staff rarely got worked up by incidents that would have caused major uproars elsewhere.

A sophomore named Sean was one of the school's biggest headaches. With almost daily frequency, the sixteen-year-old was sent to the main office for one infraction or another. It seemed he was perpetually skipping class, yelling at a teacher, or getting into a hallway dustup. The funny thing was, he seemed like a nice kid. His carefully styled blond hair hung low over his face, often covering his left eye. When he wasn't causing trouble he was shy and polite, even nervous. His parents told school administrators he had ADHD (attention deficit hyperactivity disorder) and was suffering from emotional issues. One day police found him banging his head against the wall. Other days he was friendly. His mood could change fast, and dramatically.

One afternoon, Sean was sent to the dean's office after causing trouble in a class. Dean Hoover shook her head as he arrived at her door and in her no-nonsense motherly way told him to sit down. "Why are you getting yourself in trouble all the time?" she asked. "You need to find a way to remain calm in class." She gave him a sweet but disappointed smile as she talked. Sean, however, wasn't ready to listen. He was still upset and for no obvious reason began screaming. He hurled his book bag on the ground and called Hoover a bitch as he left the office, his loud voice carrying through the hall. By the time police found him wandering on the second floor a half hour later, he seemed to have calmed down. So they returned him to the dean's office, where Hoover, who was dealing with a dozen other student problems, had him call his aunt for a ride home. That was the only option at that point. Sending him back to class, she knew, wouldn't do anybody any good. Not Sean. Not his teachers. And not his fellow students.

Hoover returned to her paperwork and Sean sat in a chair waiting for a ride, not saying anything. For a few minutes, that is. Suddenly, as Hoover was talking to a visiting teacher, Sean got up and began to leave the office. With Hoover sitting a few feet away, he mumbled a few sentences and then made a threat. "I'm going to kill you," he said. With that, he became one of the twenty students arrested during that first nine-week period. He was cuffed, processed, and sent to the juvenile lockup. Later that night, his mom drove to the facility to pick him up. But police were waiting for her when she walked in and arrested her on her own outstanding warrant.

These were the complex and sweeping challenges I was trying to explain in my columns, challenges that could not be easily overcome. Readers would often write to me with easy solutions based on the great-sounding concept of more parental responsibility. "That sounds wonderful," I would say, "but what do we do about the kid whose mom is in prison? Or about the dad whose presence causes more troubles than it solves? Or the many students still in high school who are already poorly equipped parents themselves?" These problems are immense, I would insist in response to the readers and policymakers who contacted me, and they can't be fixed with sound bites uttered by people who don't understand what truly goes on in the neighborhoods and homes surrounding many of the nation's worst schools.

A few days later, I was sitting in Hoover's office, talking with her as Heart's "Crazy on You" played on the radio. Sean and his father walked in for a scheduled meeting, both of them looking nervous as they entered. Sean's dad had driven to Indianapolis from a city forty-five minutes away and from the first minute seemed eager to get the meeting over with as quickly as possible. He rarely saw Sean and needed to get back home. Sean was staying with relatives while his mom was locked up.

The meeting had a surreal quality. Here was a boy who just a few days earlier had threatened to kill a school employee, and without much debate he was being welcomed back to school. Hoover didn't hold a grudge, and although she was tough and quick with a suspension form, she had a soft spot for the kids who were the biggest troublemakers, the ones she knew most needed her attention and her advice. With her glasses hanging low on the tip of her nose, she leaned in close and lectured Sean. "You can't threaten to kill someone," she said.

"Yes, ma'am," said Sean, back to his polite and quiet self.

"You need some guidance," Hoover continued. "You need some help. You can't do these things and get away with it. You're not going to threaten another person in this building, and you're not going to curse at another person in this building."

Sean shook his head obediently as his father cut in. "We had a long talk about that, about Columbine and things," he said, referring to a conversation they'd had earlier after Sean had threatened to blow up the building. "We talked. And then he turns around and does this."

Sean apologized. Hoover was used to apologies. She got them every day. She'd gotten many from Sean in the past. She knew not to get too excited about apologies. "He always says he's sorry afterward," she said. "But that doesn't matter."

Then she leaned in even closer, her eyes just a foot or two from Sean's. There was one message she wanted to deliver more than any other. It was a message I would hear her deliver often, and it was an example of why I found her to be such a remarkable character. It was a message she knew was crucial for students to hear.

"Sean," she said. "I need you to understand that even though you said what you said, I'm not afraid. I'm never afraid. Not of you or anyone else. Because if I'm ever afraid of anything or anyone around here, I need to retire. Do you understand?"

"Yes."

"Good, because I'm watching you."

Sean's dad was standing up, hoping to leave. But Hoover wasn't finished. She pulled out Sean's file and scanned it. She noticed he was doing well in art and that he rarely skipped that class. She asked him about it and Sean perked up, saying he loved art and wished he could spend more time on it. With that, Hoover looked over his electives and asked if he'd like her to move him from one of those classes to a second art period. He smiled. So did I. The first quarter of the year had been so tough, so filled with frustration, that a nice ending to a post-suspension meeting with a student who had threatened to kill the dean seemed like a highlight.

Most meetings with angry students didn't end so well. But when they did, I felt like I was watching one of those inspiring movies about a struggling inner-city school. I never felt that more than one day when I wandered blindly into Sergeant Barrow's office.

Barrow was sitting a few feet from a fourteen-year-old student named Patrick when I walked in. Patrick was sitting in a chair with his hands cuffed behind his back. He looked angry or sad. It was hard to tell. Barrow's expression was more obvious. He leaned back in his chair, shaking his head. He was clearly disappointed and not happy to be an inch from officially arresting Patrick and sending the student to the juvenile lockup. They'd spent the past five minutes in deep conversation and were now taking a short break. Barrow waved me in and offered a seat. He brought me up to speed as Patrick looked at the floor.

A half hour earlier Patrick had been wandering the second-floor hall, loudly and angrily shouting obscenities at someone. He was heading toward a math teacher named Bob Lyon, the type of teacher who gave his students his cell phone number on the first day of school in case they ever needed his help and who desperately wanted to see the school improve.

Lyon had heard the shouting and then the cursing and ordered Patrick to stop as he approached. But Patrick didn't stop. He pushed Lyon out of his way, and when Lyon continued after him and put his hand on the boy's shoulder, Patrick aggressively slapped it away. The police were called over and brought Patrick, now even angrier, down to the dean's office. There, he refused to talk, ignoring Hoover when she tried to get him to explain the problem he was having. He put on his angriest face and glared hard at her. In many cases, that would have been the end of the story. Patrick would have been arrested on a charge of battery and shipped to the juvenile facility, another young student with a rap sheet and possibly an expulsion. The story didn't head in that direction, though. Not after Barrow got involved.

Barrow had gotten to know Patrick, just as he'd gotten to know many of Manual's students, during the opening months of the school year. He had talked to him in the hallways and liked him. He knew that Patrick's defiance in Hoover's office had taken an already serious situation to another level. But nobody had been hurt, no threats had been issued, and, he thought, if it was possible he'd like to see this incident end without another kid down at the juvenile jail.

So he let Patrick sit quietly for a few minutes before starting the paperwork needed to officially arrest him. Then he began to talk about the situation. When I arrived, he calmly told the story. He knew Patrick was listening, so he went out of his way to talk about how much he'd like to see the situation resolved and how silly it was for a student to let his anger or pride get in the way of his freedom. Finally he turned to Patrick and asked if he was ready to talk. Patrick said he was. He said he'd had a bad day, was sorry, and didn't want to go to jail.

"Why didn't you just say that to them in the dean's office then?" Barrow asked. "That's all you had to do."

"I know."

"What?" Barrow said loudly.

"I know, sir," he said.

Barrow looked around and took a few deep breaths. He wanted Patrick to feel the magnitude of the moment. He understood the importance of dramatic pauses. After one such pause, he spoke, asking Patrick if he'd be willing to apologize to Lyon. He said that was the only possible way out of this mess; he couldn't unilaterally decide to drop the charges. Only the victim could do that. "So," he asked again, "are you man enough to apologize?"

"Yes, sir."

Barrow grabbed his office phone and looked at the boy, frowning. He was still putting on a show, one he knew Patrick needed to see. He dialed Lyon's classroom. "I'm about to sell my soul for you," he said as the phone rang. Barrow asked Lyon if he'd be willing to receive an apology. He knew that Lyon, unlike a few other teachers in the building, would happily come down. He was a dedicated teacher, and although he was frustrated with the behavior problems at Manual, he didn't enjoy the thought of a fourteen-year-old going to jail. He cared about the students at Manual and said he was on his way.

Barrow used the five minutes it took Lyon to get there to prepare Patrick for his big moment. He told him to stand up and then to stand up straighter, and then he removed the handcuffs. "Okay, I'm going to say this once," he said. "Are you listening?"

"Yes."

"What?" the army veteran said, giving the toughest look he could muster.

"Yes, sir."

Barrow asked Patrick if he had ever given an apology. He said he had not. "Okay, then you need to know a few things. Remember, every pencil has an eraser. So you need to use one now. It's not too late." He told Patrick to look Lyon in the eye and to sound sincere. He asked Patrick if he knew what sincere meant. Patrick nodded and said he did. "You need to mean it," Barrow said. "It has to come from inside. You made a mistake. You need to own it." He paused and leaned in for one more piece of advice as Lyon arrived. "Be a man."

Barrow reintroduced the two as I stood a few feet away, caught up in the moment. At times, I was finding, Manual got to me. And the regret I heard in Patrick's voice, as well as the fatherly concern in Barrow's, had socked me hard. As I held my emotions in, Patrick looked Mr. Lyon in the eyes.

"The way I acted, I acted offensively because I had a bad day," he said. "I didn't mean to take it out on you like that." He stopped for a second, and Barrow nudged him along with a slight nod and a look. "I'm trying to sincerely apologize to you."

Lyon was as calm as could be. He reminded Patrick that he needed to listen to teachers in the hallway and to show respect. He told him to think before he acted and to try to imagine the consequences of his mistakes. "I have no issue with you," Lyon said. "I know you're young. We all make mistakes. There are no problems between us. No grudges. We're cool."

Lyon and Patrick shook hands, ending the Friday drama. A few minutes later, after Lyon left, Barrow gave Patrick one final lesson. "You could be in jail or expelled right now," he said. "You see how quick your life can change? Remember this day for the rest of your life. You got a do-over." He walked him to the door. "Do you understand me?"

"Yes, sir."

A week later I wrote a column about the fifteen minutes I had observed. The headline writer titled the column "Another Angry Kid, but a Different Ending," which I thought perfectly summed it up. The incident underscored everything I liked about Barrow—his compassion, his ability to get through to kids nobody else could reach, and his interest in doing more than what the job required. It was also a reminder that the relationship he'd built with Patrick in the hallway earlier in the year had paid off. It stood as an example of the type of front-end investments—from early childhood learning programs to outreach to at-risk students—that communities and schools must be willing to make.

The first quarter of the year was ending, and that short scene in Barrow's office had been the best moment I had witnessed at Manual. That, unfortunately, was a reminder of how rough the quarter had been. I felt like I'd received a master's degree in urban education. I had written eight columns so far, and readers were writing to me in larger numbers than I was used to, telling me not to stop. They'd become connected to the school, they said.

An early sign of that occurred one afternoon when a retired senior citizen named Kay Sauer showed up at the school's front door. Sauer had read a column I wrote about Jammyra Weekly, an inspiring senior who had overcome neglectful parents to become one of the school's best and most active students, and been struck by one paragraph. In it, Jammyra had spoken of her concern for students who relied on the school for their breakfasts and lunches and, thus, sometimes didn't know what they were going to eat on the weekends. "That just hit me," Sauer said when I met her in the school's parking lot. As we talked, she was smiling and standing next to her car. It was filled with groceries.

Earlier, Sauer had driven to many of the area's big-box discount stores. She went to Meijer and Kmart. She drove to Target and Walmart. At each store she wandered the aisles looking for nonperishable foods on sale. If Kraft Macaroni & Cheese was on sale at one store, she piled boxes of it into her shopping cart. If Rice-A-Roni was on special at another store, she grabbed a handful. During her shopping trips, she had bought bags of canned tuna and peanut butter and anything else she could find. She only stopped when there was no more room in her car. "I just wanted to do something," Sauer said as two students carried the bags into the school. "I was just so moved by what that girl said."

It was a sweet moment, and I enjoyed writing about it. But I was constantly focused on keeping the story of Manual in balance. So while I wrote about motivated students such as Allison, Kelly, and Jammyra, and about school employees like Barrow, I also told the other side of the story—the stories that didn't end well. At times, doing so added to the school's rough first quarter.

That was never clearer than in early October when I wrote a column based on my observation that so many students cursed at school employees. It wasn't just that they cursed while talking to friends or rivals in the hallway or in class. I had worked in newsrooms for nearly eighteen years and certainly wasn't bothered by obscenities. I cursed as much as the students. Or at least as much as some of them. But what struck me was how often students cursed directly at teachers, and how often teachers and other school workers accepted it.

"Go to class, Margaret," a school police officer told a girl one morning after the bell rang.

"Leave me the fuck alone," the girl responded as she walked away.

Another day, the school nurse walked up to me as I was talking to a school worker near her office. "Something's going on today," she said. "I've been called an F-ing B three times."

Sometimes the curses came amid a major student meltdown or were part of a threat as the student was being kicked out of class or arrested. I understood those situations. More surprising, though, was the routine F-bomb hurled at a teacher who was trying to clear the hallways, to get students to work, or to obey the dress code.

Vickie Winslow had become one of my favorite teachers. She was short and friendly and in her thirteenth year at Manual. She taught English and knew how to engage students, often laughing with them as they had conversations about the subject matter of the day. She was also one of a small number of teachers who were active in after-school activities. It seemed like every time I went to a school meeting or after-school event Winslow was among the minority of teachers who showed up. She was optimistic and always had a story to share about a student who was doing something cool. She was also frank about the issues facing Manual, which I appreciated.

So after several weeks of witnessing episodes of cursing aimed at teachers, I walked into Winslow's classroom during an open period and asked if she would be willing to be interviewed on the issue. She told me to have a seat and said, "What do you want to know?"

"Tell me everything."

"It happens a lot," she said. "Since I got here, I've become the Bitch. Or the Fucking Bitch. Or the Stupid this and that. It's the Stupid one that bothers me. I don't mind being called a bitch. But I don't like being called stupid." She smiled slightly and told me that her best estimate was that she got called a bitch thirty to forty times a year, mostly by students in the hallway irritated at being told to get to class or tuck in their shirts. "It gets old," she said, "but you get used to it."

"Teachers shouldn't have to get used to it," I said.

But the school picked its battles, and officials said they couldn't afford to overreact to every occasion of a student blowing off steam. Rules, for instance, mandated that students with special needs could not be suspended for more than ten days a year. That designation included a huge swath of Manual's student population, so administrators were careful about doling out suspensions for minor offenses. They wanted to make sure the penalty was available for bigger problems encountered later in the year.

Police, meanwhile, spent their days dealing with problems far more serious than the hurling of obscenities. Students had attacked at least two teachers by this point in the year. Twenty students had been arrested. Many more had been suspended and several expelled. The problem I was asking about didn't rank that high.

Still, the behavior seemed to be a perfect example of the low expectations that gripped the school. The bar for what was considered a serious problem was extremely high, and the bar for what was labeled success was sadly low. I imagined what a suburban teacher would do if a student told them to fuck off as he walked down the hallway. I felt like a fuddy-duddy but was extremely bothered by all of this. It seemed so easy to tie the apathy in so many classrooms to the low standards the school accepted. Few workers at the school agreed it was a big deal; it was just a part of life, they said. "I learned to curse in this job," Dean Hoover told me one day. "It's what the kids hear when they're at home, so they don't give it a second thought. I've been cursed at or threatened so many times I've lost count. And by students and parents. I've been called everything but my given name."

My column on the issue ran October 11. I included several scenes I had observed of students cursing at Manual teachers and staff. Some were simple brush-offs while others were violent outbursts. The column was filled with carefully placed dashes, as I had lost a fierce argument with my editors over how to represent the obscenities. I would have preferred to use the words I was writing about, or at least allowed to use the first letters of all of them. I was partially overruled. "Fuck you" became "—— you." "Bitch" became "b----."

The reaction to the column left no doubt about whether readers fully grasped my point. They understood the environment teachers and students were being forced to live within. In the column, I called the issue "one of the things about life at Manual that shouldn't be normal, shouldn't be accepted, but often is." I quoted Winslow and wrote that students knew there were few consequences for directing an obscenity at a teacher. Toward the end of the column, I got a little preachy. I wrote about all of the great, hardworking students I'd met and the message they were receiving: they didn't deserve the same standards of behavior as those set at suburban schools. "Until the district demands a better culture within its buildings," I wrote, "the dramatic improvements in achievement and behavior that we'd all like to see won't happen."

The headline blared on the front page: "Violence in Verbal Form? Manual Lets It Pass." Readers flooded my e-mail in-box and voice mail with messages of outrage. They felt for the good students and teachers and wanted to know why IPS tolerated such behavior. They angrily demanded that something be done and told me that the scenes in my column explained why they'd sent their children to suburban or private schools.

I didn't know it at the time, but IPS Superintendent White, sitting in his plush home on the north side of the city, was fuming just as much as other readers as he read the column. He wasn't mad at me, not this time, but rather at the leaders of his south-side school. The following day he railed in a staff meeting about the details included in the column and demanded that Principal Grismore explain himself. He said his schools would not let this type of behavior continue. He said he was horrified at the idea of teachers being treated disrespectfully. It was the right message but a ridiculous response, one that showed White was either putting on a show or oblivious to the reality of what was going on in his district's schools.

As the new week began, I remained unaware of White's reaction and the uproar it had caused until I walked into the school a few minutes after the final afternoon bell on Tuesday. I knew I would have to spend some time repairing bruised feelings. As a columnist, I was used to that. And this column had been the toughest I'd written about Manual; it unquestionably made the school look bad. It told an ugly side of the Manual story. I figured Grismore was getting some kickback. I just didn't know how much.

The halls were quiet when I arrived. Grismore's office was empty, and the only person around was a secretary. She told me the principal was in a staff meeting. She gave me a strange look, as if she was trying to warn me about something. I chose to ignore the warning and headed to the auditorium. When I got there I peered through the small glass window in one of the auditorium doors. Grismore was standing at the front of the room, looking serious as he talked to the teachers sitting before him. Officer Miller, standing on the other side of the door, noticed me. She looked surprised to see me as she shook her head and opened the door. "This is about you," she whispered as I nudged my way into the room.

The meeting, though, was ending. Teachers walked out and passed by me without saying much. Some smiled, and others avoided eye contact. They had just been told that the tolerance for student misbehavior would be lower from this point forward and that Superintendent White was upset and not inclined to take much more bad publicity. "You got us in trouble," Miller said.

Things were tense at the school for the next few days. Police and teachers took a harder line toward students who trolled the halls during class periods. They cracked down on students who caused trouble or cursed during passing periods. Dean Hoover's office was more crowded than ever, as teachers began to send down students who a few days earlier would have received a free pass. Some of the teachers were less inclined to talk to me.

One day, Ted Collins, the English teacher who had glared at me weeks earlier in the year as I stood talking to Grismore, met me as I walked into his room. I'd had full access to the school up to this point and would often wander into a classroom before the bell, ask the teacher if I could observe the class, and then grab a seat at the back of the room. It was a great way to see how the school functioned and to get a sense of the students. All of the teachers I'd approached had opened their rooms to me. Until now. "I'd rather not have you in here," Collins said. A few students laughed, and at first I thought he was kidding. But he wasn't. He didn't like me, and this was one class I wouldn't be observing. A few other teachers grew colder when we passed in the hallways. Vice Principal Franklin, who had been so friendly and blunt about the school's issues earlier, now looked down and sped up when we crossed paths.

Meanwhile, school police and administrators were dealing with the fallout from Superintendent White's anger. Dean Hoover would be forced to reapply for her job, even though her only sin in the column was being threatened with assassination by a student. "You got me in hot water," she said one morning, giving me the same smiling look of disapproval she gave so many of her students. I apologized, but she waved me off, reminding me that she wasn't scared of anyone—not the most out-of-control student, not the angriest parent, and not even Dr. White. "Don't worry," she said.

Grismore wasn't so easily calmed. He was taking the brunt of the complaints from district headquarters and had been forced to compile a detailed report about the episodes I had included in my column. That seemed to be the district's response to every controversy: force school leaders to spend hours on a report defending themselves. Exasperated, Grismore sent me an e-mail one day asking for the name of a girl I had written about who had tossed over a desk and screamed obscenities at the teacher in an after-school class. Among the pile of police reports, he'd missed that one. "The superintendent," he wrote, "is trying to ascertain if we are turning a blind eye to this sort of thing." That was his subtle way of telling me I'd made his life miserable.

Not everyone was mad, though. Some teachers thanked me for putting a spotlight on the ridiculous things that went on in the school. They wanted the public to understand the obstacles they faced. Jammyra, the senior who worked so hard, came up to me one day and said she appreciated my exposing the ridiculous antics of some of her classmates.

I was looking forward to moving on and, thus, cringed one day after noticing that the school librarian had taped the column on the wall outside the main office, near all of the others. Nonetheless, things did get better. Although it took a few days, by the end of the week it seemed that I had smoothed things over with most of the adults in the building. By the end of the day Friday, I no longer felt like a pariah.

Then I picked up the Saturday paper. There on the opinions page was a letter from Dr. White. He'd written a scathing indictment of the Manual teachers and administrators who "accept this inappropriate behavior." He said the tolerance was setting students up for failure. He wrote that "some teachers and administrators are failing to live up to the district value of courage." Employees, he said, "must end this nightmare." He wrote that any teacher who accepts being called a bitch should not be working in the district.

That last line was directed at Vickie Winslow, the friendly English teacher who had been so open with me, and she knew it. The word *courage* hit her particularly hard. A year earlier she had been punched repeatedly by a boy—a boy who would later be sent to prison for another crime—as she tried to break up a fight. The year before that, a girl had punched her in the head as she tried desperately to stop another fight. "I hear I don't have any courage," she said when I stopped in her classroom a few days after White's letter ran. "That stung." I felt horrible. My column had led to a good teacher's being targeted by her boss in the newspaper.

I agreed with White's message that the school needed to set its standards higher and that cursing at teachers shouldn't ever be tolerated. I appreciated his public display of frustration about the apathy within schools that in so many cases leads to low standards being placed on student behavior. But his outrage rang hollow. Teachers from schools throughout the district, including elementary schools, had contacted me to tell me they faced the same problems as those I'd written about. This wasn't something new or unique to Manual. The superintendent's letter came across as a face-saving public relations campaign. He should have taken steps to protect his teachers; instead, he abandoned them.

"I'm sorry," I told Winslow.

"Hey," she said. "Everything you wrote was true."

The first quarter of the school year had come to an end. It had been a tough one at Manual.

10

★ ★ ★

YOU HAVE TO CRAWL FIRST.

Every Sunday my latest column on Manual would run on the front page of the newspaper. That was an unusually high-profile location for columns. For four years most of my work had appeared on pages deeper inside the paper—the traditional home for opinion columns. But Manual was so full of amazing tales, interesting people, and wonderfully mind-boggling issues that the bosses had given these columns more valuable real estate. The depressing state of newspapers had no doubt contributed to their decision, as we simply had fewer reporters than ever to produce the copy needed to fill seven newspapers each week. My column had become a reliable filler of space every Sunday. Either way, I wasn't complaining. The front-page placement had given the series a profile it never would have enjoyed on a less-prominent page. Everywhere I went, people brought up the series, the students, and teachers I was writing about. They asked about Allison and Kelly. They told me to say hi to Sarge. The attention the columns received made the decision to keep going back to Manual an easy one.

The thing that kept me coming back the most, however, was the constant intrigue and the knowledge that with each visit I would meet a compelling person, or hear about a new vexing problem, or watch a dramatic scene play out. I was having more fun than I'd ever had as a journalist. There was humor in the hallway dialogue, drama in the office, and every day I was learning a tremendous amount, even though I would routinely note that I was a trained observer and not an education expert. I hated to skip even a day. So much so that on the many days when I had to report and write columns on completely unrelated issues—such as upcoming elections or political scandals—I would find a way to slip away from the newspaper for an hour or two and head over to Manual. Even on those days I wanted to at least check in, to stop in the dean's office or observe a class. I wanted to get the latest on students I was planning to write about. Fortunately the school was a straight three-mile drive from my office. It was a drive I made hundreds of times during the school year.

One morning I walked in at about 9:00 AM and found the main office largely empty. With nothing going on there, I began to head down to Spencer Lloyd's choir class to see how he and his students were doing. But along the way I noticed a buzz of activity coming from one of the school's auditoriums. Curious, I stepped in and saw more than a hundred students in the auditorium's seats and aisles. Vice Principal Liz Owens was talking on the stage. "This is a point in life where you make a pledge," she told the students, "and a promise to graduate so that you'll have the opportunities you deserve later on."

The idea for the meeting stemmed from research Owens had done into the school's long history. She had discovered a long-forgotten tradition that stretched back more than one hundred years, to a time when Manual Training High School was based out of another building even closer to downtown. In its earliest days, Manual seniors would come to school at the beginning of the year carrying carnations. Then, in an annual ceremony, the senior class would present the carnations to Charles Emmerich, the school's legendary first principal, along with a promise to stick with school and graduate.

A century later Owens knew the school needed to find ways to persuade more students to graduate. So she conceived a plan to bring back the tradition, which had faded away decades earlier. Switching it up for an era in which students were unlikely to come to school bearing flowers, the updated ceremony would have administrators handing the carnations to the seniors. The pledge, the promise to graduate, would remain the same. That, after all, was the more important part of this tradition.

For all of Manual's problems, most of the students who actually made it to their senior year would graduate. (The school's low graduation rate was due largely to the many freshmen and sophomores who dropped out each year.) Still, Owens knew that many of these seniors were vulnerable and in need of a push. For some, the struggle to graduate would continue until the last days and hours of the school year as they raced to make up for failed classes and other mistakes. Not everyone would make it. But on this day they would all pledge to do so.

Students slowly headed up the steps leading to the stage, walked over to Principal Grismore, and shook his hand. They then made their pledge and received a carnation from Owens or one of the other vice principals. The boys walked out of the room with white carnations, and the girls left with red ones. Many laughed at the ceremony and shook their heads at the spectacle, but nobody complained. And none of the students passed up the chance to walk across the stage.

"I promise to graduate," the first student in line said.

"All right," Grismore said approvingly.

Next up was a girl named Deauntee. She was more specific. "I promise to graduate with honors on May nineteenth," she said.

"Then we'll do this again in May," Grismore said.

"I know I'm graduating," one boy said. "I'm getting out of here."

Occasionally Grismore stopped the line to deliver a pointed message. "You need to do everything right," he firmly told one boy. "This is the time to stay focused."

"I know."

"You need to be where you're supposed to be," he told another boy who had been in and out of trouble during his years at Manual. "You need to be in class. And you need to keep what's going on outside, outside. Okay? Can you do that?" The student nodded.

A boy named Eric arrived on stage next. If things had gone right, he would have graduated the previous year. But they hadn't. He'd missed too much school, failed too many courses, suffered too many suspensions, and thus was back for another year. He was what school staffers called a Super Senior. There were many of them in the building—students who were nineteen or twenty years old and still working toward a diploma.

Eric looked sheepish as he approached Grismore. They had a long history. "You know what you need to do," Grismore said, grabbing Eric's hand tightly and refusing to let go. He stared the student in the eye. "You need to do everything you need to do to graduate. You need to keep your shirt tucked in and your pants up. You need to be in class. You need to do the homework."

Eric nodded. But Grismore continued the handshake. "All the homework," he said, pausing for effect, his concern for the young man as clear as the morning's blue sky. "All the classes. You have to follow the rules."

"I will," Eric promised.

I thought about the search for tradition as I sat in the athletics office on another day talking to football coach Cedric Lloyd. He was an intense, often frustrated forty-year-old, a veteran of several high schools, and was now trying to bring back a tradition of winning football to Manual. It was an effort that so far had not produced results. But Lloyd was trying.

Friday after Friday during the season, as we talked about football, Lloyd would lay out for me a scenario explaining how Manual could beat that particular week's opponent—an opponent that was inevitably bigger and better and enjoyed more resources and players. He always had a game plan. "If we can keep it close until halftime," he'd say one Friday, "we might be able to surprise them in the second half." "If we can just do the things we've been working on," he'd say another Friday, "we can squeak out a win." "If our defense can make its tackles," or "If we can stop fumbling," he'd say, "our running game could carry us through." He offered a constant message of optimism as game time approached. Week after week, though, he would give me a Monday morning shrug when we passed in the hall. I rarely had the heart to ask about the latest monumental blowout. Instead, we would talk later in the week, after the wound had healed a bit, and he would once again lay out a scenario in which the Redskins could win. He never disappointed.

But now it was the Friday before his team's eighth game of the year, the second-to-last regular-season game, a game that would be played against nearby Howe Community High School. The good news was that Howe was the second-worst team in the city, coming into this game with only one win. Like Manual, Howe had struggled to attract players and play competitively. The student enrollment at the two schools was about the same. This could be a fair fight. This could be Lloyd's week. This was a team Manual could beat. Making things even more promising, the game was being played on Manual's home field, and because it was homecoming week, there was a chance that a larger than normal home crowd would turn out. "Who knows," Lloyd said, "maybe all of the players on the roster will show up for a change. We have a shot tonight," he said.

Throughout the week, he'd been in his office constantly, working on plays, checking in on players at home, and even tracking the weather. He studied game film and urged his players to focus on that Friday's game. He had asked Sergeant Barrow to talk to some of the boys most likely to miss the game, and he'd put together a booklet for his players filled with tips and motivational phrases. In it, he wrote that the players needed to play without fear and believe in their ability to win. He included a page titled "How to Tell a Winner from a Loser" and another that included "Five Signs of an 'I' Guy." Number one was "A chronic feeling of being under-appreciated." Based on the small crowds Manual's games had attracted, that one was particularly important for the players to see. The booklet included inspirational quotes from professional football coaches and even Lloyd's own sayings. "I will not let my teammates down," he wrote, "and I will not let myself down."

This is what Lloyd loved. His life was football. He often talked about his belief that the sport was the ultimate team game and argued that it mirrored life's challenges. Each down was like an obstacle standing in the way of success in life but also an opportunity. Each new possession provided another chance to improve. Each loss was something to learn from. "Life tells me I'm going to win or lose at different times, just like in football," he said. "But what's important is how you respond to those times when you win and those times when you lose."

Lloyd had graduated from another district high school twenty-two years earlier after spending four years playing football and running track. He left for two years in the army and then spent several years in Florida. He returned to Indianapolis in his mid-twenties and worked his way up the coaching ladder, starting as a volunteer assistant. He eventually became the head coach of his alma mater and had a few decent seasons before leaving for a job in the suburbs. It didn't take, and he decided to come back to the city. "Manual was a program that people said couldn't be successful," he said. "I came in wanting to change the culture and change the lives of young people. We have a ways to go." The team won three games his first year. But this second year was proving to be the school's worst ever.

When I walked into his office that Friday morning, Coach Lloyd wore a crisp red button-down shirt with *Redskins* written in white above a pocket. His desk was covered with papers—plays and rosters and student forms. He looked tired, and I wondered if he'd slept the night before. As always, he welcomed me in with a smile and offered me a seat. I took it and asked how he thought the evening's game would play out. The muted response he gave surprised me. Unlike all of those other weeks, he was now downplaying his team's chances. He said he didn't know if his players had another game in them. They were tired and beaten down. He said he was hoping for the best, but he knew his Redskins would be outmanned once again.

As Lloyd talked, I sensed he was being cautious. He knew a win was possible this night, unlike so many other nights earlier in the season. There was nothing about Howe that scared him, but he didn't want his team to be overconfident. He didn't want to take anything for granted. He was treating this game as if he were facing the state's toughest powerhouse. He knew Manual's biggest opponent would be itself. His players were young and mistake-prone. They hadn't spent summers at football camps learning the basics of the game. "At this point they're better than us," he said of Howe, looking and sounding as serious as an NFL coach standing before dozens of reporters before a play-off game. "They've got a win. Believe it or not, that alone makes a difference. It tells you something about yourself, that winning is possible. It's like being a baby. You have to crawl first. Then you can stand up all wobbly. And then you can walk. We need to learn how to walk. We're barely crawling at this point." He stopped talking for a few seconds. "It would be huge to get a win," he said. "This year's been difficult."

Lloyd wasn't exaggerating. The season had been the type that few high school coaches had ever endured. It wasn't simply the losses—the unending stream of blowout defeats, games that without mercy would have been lost by even wider gaps. Along the way to his 0–7 record, he had also struggled mightily to recruit players. He tried, but nothing had worked. He couldn't get parents interested in the idea of having their sons join a team that might offer a few months of needed structure. He urged boys throughout the school to give football a try. Time and again, though, they declined. Or they'd show up for a few practices and give up. This wasn't a school where the football players or cheerleaders were considered special. This wasn't a school with a cool crowd. There often seemed to be no crowds. Everyone was on his or her own.

Meanwhile, the best upper-class players had either transferred out of Manual or dropped out of school altogether. At most Lloyd had only three juniors and two seniors who showed up for games. He had lost players of all ages to poor grades and discipline problems, and he was in a constant struggle to persuade students to show up for practice. Often only nine or ten showed up, making it impossible to prepare effectively for the next game. He had lost players because they had to get jobs to help out their moms, siblings, or to take care of their own children. The previous week a player had told Coach Lloyd he would not be at practice because he was getting a haircut. That type of indifference particularly irritated him. He'd had to kick several boys off the team for constantly causing trouble on game nights. And while he wanted to be stricter—he loved the idea of being a no-nonsense coach—he was at the mercy of a thin roster. That roster was filled with freshmen and sophomores who were both inexperienced and undersized. At most other schools, the players on his small offensive and defensive lines would be playing on the junior varsity team. But he didn't have enough players for such a team, so everyone played at the varsity level. As such, other teams typically fielded lines that towered over his.

On this Friday Lloyd was hoping twenty-four students would show up for the game. But he knew even that was optimistic. He knew that some players who had promised to play would turn up missing. They always did. The football program was not immune to the apathy that strangled the rest of the school. "Over here there's somewhat of a culture we're trying to beat," he said. "For some it's a lot easier to start something and quit. That's the message they get at home. It's hard to fight it." He wouldn't say it at that point, but Lloyd knew this was his last chance at a win. The next game, the last of the regular season, would be against Arlington Community High School. The school was about ten miles to the north and had a mountain of problems. It was in the middle of one of the city's roughest neighborhoods, one far more dangerous than Manual's. But Arlington also fielded the district's best football team. Manual would be no match.

So this was it. This was a Friday night filled with opportunity. This was Lloyd's best chance of seeing his team win during a miserable season. It would be just one win. But maybe that would be enough to persuade more of the students and teachers in the school to start supporting the team. Maybe it would give the Redskins some momentum for next season.

As we talked in his office, Lloyd pointed to a few boxes in a corner filled with T-shirts. They were a sign of the lack of support the team had received from students. He had spent a chunk of his football budget on the shirts, which were gray and decorated with the school's mascot. He'd ordered dozens in the hope of making a small but much-needed profit for the athletic department. It hadn't worked. So far he'd sold only a few. He tossed one to me, saying they weren't doing any good sitting in a box. "It's taking longer than I expected to turn things around over here," he said. "But we're trying to do things the right way. I want people to look at us and say we're doing things the right way."

I went back to the office to work for a couple of hours and returned to Manual after the end of the school day. The pep rally for that night's homecoming game had recently ended, and the halls were quiet and empty. It was homecoming week, but there were few decorations on the walls.

I noticed Principal Grismore sitting in the library. He was leaning back in a chair in front of a blank computer screen and looked exhausted. Before I could say hello, a teacher stopped by and told me what had caused the principal's latest bout of exhaustion. During the pep rally, he said, two girls and a boy had performed a dance routine for their classmates on the gym floor. It was a fun homecoming-week moment. For a few minutes. The fun took a wrong turn, the teacher said, when the two girls straddled the boy's legs and appeared to wildly hump them. Teachers gasped, and students cheered and laughed uproariously. School administrators cut off the music and Grismore abruptly ended the program.

I walked into the library and sat down next to him. "Tough afternoon, huh?" I said.

He rubbed his face for a few seconds and stared at me. He had just wanted the students to have a little fun. His face seemed to be asking: Can't anything around here be easy? "I don't know why I didn't see that one coming," he said, looking away. "If I'd have known they were going to do that . . ." His voice trailed off, and he didn't finish his sentence. I understood. I figured he needed some quiet time, so I wished him well and headed back to see the football coach.

Earlier in the day I had stopped in the alumni office, a small room tucked in the back of the school, just beyond the band room. The office is filled with old yearbooks and school newspapers. Pictures of students from the 1920s and 1930s sit on the floor. The room is a reminder of Manual's deep history.

I browsed through a book of newspaper clippings and came across a timely story from 1958. "Unbeaten Manual, Howe Clash Tonight," the headline read. The story told of the two best football programs in the city that year and the upcoming game to determine which team would continue to pursue a perfect season. On that night Manual had won on its way to its best season ever—a 10–0 finish. A picture of the storied team sat on a bookcase in the office with the words *mythical state champions* underneath it. At the time, Indiana did not have high school football championship games. But those who followed high school football in the Hoosier state in 1958 considered Manual to be the best. Fifty-one years later the same two teams were playing again. Little else was the same. As the season approached its end, Manual and Howe had combined for one win. That comprised the fewest wins of any two teams playing anywhere in the state that night. This game meant little.

You wouldn't know it by walking into Lloyd's office four hours before kickoff. He had taped a quote on his office door: "We must believe in what we do." He was on the phone checking on the availability of a player. His face was a constant frown. The air in his office was filled with tension. He'd already learned that his goal of a twenty-four-man roster for the night's game was shot. Now he was hoping for at least twenty. He was also hoping to see a few of the students from a middle school that feeds into Manual at the game. He had visited the school often to build relationships with some of the seventh- and eighth-graders, trying to persuade them to do the things they needed to do to play high school football. Win or lose tonight, this season was a lost one. But if he could win in front of a few middle-school stars, that could help in future years. Long-term plans aside, though, Lloyd wanted to win. Desperately.

"You want to know improvements are happening," he said as his quarterback, a freshman named Jaynard Keys, walked in with a tray of brownies his mom had dropped off. "If you can't win a game, it's hard to convince yourself of that."

An hour later Lloyd met with the members of his team in a nearby classroom as they ate their pregame meal. They were relaxed. He was not. "This is your game," Lloyd told them. "It's your opportunity. When you get the chance to be on the field, do your job. I know you're going to be tired, but we need dogs out there. We need guys who finish, guys who stick with it." The players left the room a few minutes later, not saying much. They were beaten down after a season of losing. They were tired. And they knew what Lloyd knew—that because so few had shown up, most of the players would have to play both offense and defense. Adding to that, it was starting to drizzle outside. It was going to be a cold, wet, muddy, and long night.

Henry Crittenden, one of two seniors in the room, wasn't worried. Before heading off to suit up he talked about the season that was concluding. It was his first on the football team; he'd joined as a way to make his senior year special. He wanted to be a teacher and thought football would look good on his college application. He thought of himself as a survivor on a team from which many had fallen. "I'm not a quitter," he said. "I'm sticking with it no matter what happens. Even though we lose, we're still trying. We still want it. We haven't given up."

I asked if it had been frustrating. "All you can do is play your butt off," Henry said, telling me he had played every play—on offense, defense, and special teams—the previous week. "You can't worry about the guys who didn't stick with it. But if more of them would show up, we'd be able to get a break once in a while."

"They think the team isn't good enough," added a freshman named Tre'von Sevion. "And they don't want to put in the effort to make it better. But we do. We go out and try as hard as we can."

I walked out to the field fifteen minutes before kickoff. The school band was playing "Get Ready" and roughly 150 people were in the stands. Across the field, fewer than a dozen Howe fans would be in the stands at kickoff. But Howe did have an advantage. Thirty players were available. Back in the Manual locker room, Lloyd counted his players. It didn't take long, because in the end only seventeen had shown up. The team walked to the door leading from the locker room and gathered around Lloyd for a final pep talk. He wanted to inspire the team. But he ran into a problem. There was always a problem. In this case Lloyd had turned to an injured player—a junior named Donnie—and asked him to help with the yard chains that mark field position. Donnie didn't want to; he wanted to stay on Manual's side of the field, and the chains would be on the other side.

"Just do the chains," Lloyd said, turning back to the rest of the players and starting to give his pep talk.

Donnie interrupted. "I'm not doing the chains," he said.

Lloyd looked at him, frustrated, just as he had been all season by students who wouldn't show up for practice or listen to him when they did. He was supposed to be delivering his final words of inspiration before his team took the field. Instead, he was dealing with another headache. "Donnie, I'm asking you to be a leader and do the chains," he said, leaning in close, begging him with his eyes to stop making him look foolish. The student just shook his head no. The coach let out a loud sigh and looked around the room before settling back on Donnie. "If you're not going to do it, then don't sit on my sideline."

Finally, Donnie begrudgingly agreed to the request. But the moment was gone. Lloyd was so frustrated that he forgot to give his pep talk before telling the team to take the field. "Let's go, it's our game," one of the players said. "Let's go!"

The seventeen players jogged to the field, passing the ROTC color guard and the four cheerleaders who stood on the track between the field and the stands. They gathered on the sidelines, which were already turning muddy from the rain, and listened as Lloyd told them that everyone would be playing most of the game. There would be no benchwarmers. Manual couldn't afford them.

The first drive was Manual's most successful of the season. Jaynard Keys, the quarterback, piled up yards during a series of runs and then scored with a long dash midway through the first quarter. The band played "We Will Rock You" as Keys scored again on a two-point conversion. Manual was up 8–0. It was the team's biggest lead of the season. It was its first lead of the season. Lloyd clapped and shouted instructions as his mud-covered players came to the sidelines. He told them to focus, to keep pounding. A minute later he jumped up and pumped his fist as Howe fumbled the ball.

I stood in the rain, scribbling notes into a wet notebook and imagining the Hollywood ending this game offered my column: the winless team, with barely enough players to participate in a game, finally taking home a victory. That would be a good one, I thought. And not just for the column material. Looking at the players and the small contingent of students in the stands, I agreed with what the coach had said earlier. This would indeed be an important moment for the school.

Sophomore running back Jordan Hughes, who, like Keys, was a star of the team, nearly crawled off the field a few plays later. He had just moved the ball forward ten yards, and Manual needed him on the field as much as possible. But he was in pain. "My balls," he screamed. "God, my balls hurt." The coaching staff traded looks. Lloyd shook his head and told Hughes to keep it down. "Squats," an assistant coach said. "Do squats."

A few minutes later Hughes was back in the game, this time wearing a jock strap, and before long he'd scored on a twenty-nine-yard run. Lloyd didn't have a player who could handle a long snap in the heat of a game, so he went for the two-point conversion again. But this time Howe stopped Hughes as he tried to run it in. No matter. The halftime buzzer went off a few minutes later, and Manual was up 14–0. The players were breathing hard. They jogged slowly off the field. It had been a rough hour. They were smaller than Howe's team, which had more upperclassmen. They were wet and muddy. But they had a lead.

"They're tired," Coach Lloyd said as he walked toward the locker room. "It's gonna hit us. But right now it's good. They're running on adrenaline. We'll see where it goes from here."

In the locker room, Lloyd stood before his team. Some players were gasping for air. Others washed mud off their hands. "This is about us," he said. "This isn't about them. Do you want it?"

"We want it!" they shouted.

"Then finish. Get it done. That's all I want. We can't take one play off. Have the heart and the guts to get it done. They're going to come out and try to take this game from you. You've got to finish this up. Finish it up strong. This is on us. This is about finishing. It ain't about looking good. You with me?"

They nodded.

"You with me?"

The team shouted back. "This is us!" they said.

Back on the field, Manual teachers and administrators were announcing the homecoming king and queen. They were relieved to see that Tricia Tharpe, a hardworking senior who often shared with me stories of her troubled home life, had won as queen. They'd had trouble recruiting candidates, and most of them hadn't shown up that night. "It would have been embarrassing if one of the others had won," a teacher said. Regardless, it was a sweet moment. Tricia was crying as her name was called. She was still teary-eyed when the team jogged back onto the field a few minutes later. "I can't believe this," she said.

Lloyd could hardly believe he was potentially an hour away from his first win of the season. But he was worried. His players seemed not only tired but also unfocused. One player had just shown up, missing kickoff by more than an hour. Another was complaining that he couldn't see. He'd forgotten his contacts, something he hadn't mentioned during the first half. "He's a lineman," an assistant coach shouted. "How good does he have to see? The guy in front of him is two hundred pounds. He can't see that?"

The field was even muddier and wetter now, and Howe's bigger roster began wearing Manual down. The Redskins fumbled shortly after the second half began and gave up a quick touchdown. And then another. They couldn't seem to hold on to the ball. After just a few minutes, the lead was gone. The score was 14–14. Even that didn't last. Howe scored its third touchdown as the quarter came to a close. The fourth and final quarter began with Manual trailing 22–14. Lloyd shook his head as he stood in the rain. His players looked dejected. It had all happened so fast. "I'm so tired," Keys said.

Corey Parchman, a 1996 Manual graduate who went on to play a couple of years in the National Football League, stood on the sidelines. He was one of the team's unofficial assistant coaches. He gathered the players. "We still have time," he said. "But you gotta fight."

They did. Sophomore Shawn Jackson scored a touchdown on a run midway through the quarter, bringing the score to 22–20. It stayed there when Manual failed on a two-point-conversion attempt. After that there were a few more minutes of crashing into the mud on attempted runs and a few desperation passes. But that was it. The game ended. The Redskins had lost once again. This time they'd lost by two points, after a season in which they had routinely lost games by thirty or forty points. They were now 0–8 and would finish the season winless.

The game was over, and few people remained in the stands. Most had left by the end of the third quarter. But Lloyd wasn't finished. He gathered his players under a goalpost on the north end of the field. Few had any spots on their uniforms not covered in mud. "Don't hold your head down," he told one player. "No way, no how. You shot yourselves in the foot a few times. We're still giving up the ball. But now you know you can play four quarters." The players listened intently. This had been their best game of the season. "You can wallow in pity if you want," Lloyd said. "You can hold your head down. You can listen to whatever people tell you about this team. But I wouldn't. It was a good game. You played hard."

Lloyd walked off the field. The team stayed behind and began to chant the Manual football creed, something Lloyd had put together. "Winning begins with us, and I won't let you down," the players said halfheartedly. Lloyd was thirty yards away by now, and he could tell some of his players were indifferently going through the motions. He stopped walking and shouted. "No way," he said. "Either you're going to do it with pride, or you're going to get off my field." The players, all of them, raised their helmets above their heads. The crowd was gone. The rain had finally stopped. They were alone under a goalpost on a muddy field. They returned to the creed. Only louder this time. "Believing is only part of the battle," they said. "I want to win the full battle, and it starts with me."

I wrote a column about the team a few days later, detailing the close call and the heart in the small group of players who continued fighting until the end of a long, hard season. I said the football program was an example of the many programs at Manual that failed to attract many students and suffered because of the chronic academic, attendance, and discipline problems at the school. It was also an example of the gap in resources between schools in poor and wealthier school districts. Manual had less money for equipment, staff, and training than schools not far away. I wrote, though, that this wasn't a gloomy column about a losing football team but rather a tale about a small group who hadn't given up. I warned readers early in the column that there wouldn't be a tidy Hollywood ending.

I later regretted that line. Sure, the team hadn't won. But as the weeks passed, I thought often about that scene under the goalpost, with the exhausted teammates holding their helmets high and vowing to keep fighting. That, I thought, is right out of a movie script.

11

★ ★ ★

WE'RE DROPPING OUT.

Two boys stood in the main office on a Thursday afternoon, talking quietly to each other as their mom sat in a chair a few feet away. They were an example of the dropout epidemic that is devastating many American cities and the mind-boggling lack of urgency that can be found in far too many communities. The boys, brothers named Tyler and Chris, were sixteen and seventeen, respectively. They were Manual students, but only officially. They hadn't been inside the school in a few weeks, and they'd shown up only occasionally before that. And they didn't plan on coming anymore. Their mom, a single thirty-something mother of six, had driven them to Manual that morning so that they could formally drop out. They were intent on becoming part of the huge collection of Manual students who failed to graduate.

The brothers were waiting to find someone to talk to when vice principal Alan Smith raced through the room. He was heading from one mess to another but stopped suddenly when he saw the boys. He'd gotten to know them during the previous school year—largely because they were frequently in the office answering to one infraction or another. Their biggest problems had been an unwillingness to show up for class and an inability to live by the school's strict dress code. Despite the problems, and despite their unwillingness to give school much effort, Smith liked them. He gave a puzzled smile. "Long time no see," he said.

The brothers nodded back and then looked away, embarrassed.

Smith walked over. "Are you signing in or signing out?" he said.

"Out," Chris said. "We're dropping out. Gonna get a GED."

At that point Smith committed to the conversation. He'd been in a hurry to deal with the latest headache on his schedule, but this one had jumped to the front of the line. He put a pile of papers he was holding on the front office counter and pounced on Chris's declaration. "You can't drop out," he said, definitively. "You're not eighteen. You can't just drop out. It's actually against the law." He told them they didn't have a choice in the matter, because the state legislature had recently passed a law requiring all students to attend school until their eighteenth birthday unless they've graduated. He didn't tell them the other part of the story—that the law was well-intentioned but rarely enforced. On any given day the city could fill every police squad car it had with minors who had stopped going to school. But with all the crime problems that plague bigger cities, truancy didn't occupy much time in the minds of the local police chief or prosecutor. Law enforcement tends to treat the symptoms rather than the diseases. That means spending lots of time on the latest burglary or drug bust but little time on the problem of kids who weren't getting an education, the very kids who in some cases would later commit the burglaries or drug crimes police spent so much time on.

That is the depressing and shortsighted reality in cities across the country. Despite the push for dramatic education reforms and the increased attention being paid to the national dropout problem, it continues largely unimpeded. Estimating the economic impact of America's dropout epidemic is not an exact science. But the problem undeniably costs the nation heavily. In a report issued just weeks before Chris and Tyler showed up at Manual that morning, the Alliance for Excellent Education estimated that if all the students who dropped out of the class of 2009 had instead graduated, "the nation's economy would have benefited from nearly $335 billion in additional income over the course of their lifetimes."

Two examples of that loss stood quietly in the Manual office as Smith waited for a response that morning. They'd hoped to get in and out of the school without much notice or hassle. Smith, a veteran school administrator with an eerie resemblance to Stephen King, was in the mood to get in their way. He was used to students who didn't have much to say. He moved in closer. "You've got some good scores," he told the boys. "You were doing okay in some ways. You just need to come to school."

For the first time, their mom, who was still sitting in the chair, spoke up. "I tell them that all the time," she said. She didn't sound the least bit sincere.

Still, Smith took advantage of the opening. He saw before him a pair of students who should be in school. Plenty of kids drop out, and he would have tried to persuade any of them to come back, but this case was a no-brainer. These two were bright. They got good grades when they put in even the slightest effort. It wasn't a hard school; even students who missed far more classes than they should could do well. These two could easily succeed. "Do you guys need to see your scores?" Smith asked. "Do you need something that shows you can do it?"

He got a shrug on that one. The boys had come to drop out, and at this moment their mission remained the same. They were tired of school and hadn't gotten very far yet. So why give it another shot? It seemed like a waste of time.

Smith mentioned night school, and Tyler said he couldn't afford to come to school after normal hours, because he had to work at a nearby White Castle. The family needed the money, he said. Smith then went through a series of other options. He talked about half-day programs for students who had trouble committing to a full day. He talked about online classes that could be taken from home and about a program called the Opportunity Center, which is targeted toward students who have had trouble in normal classroom settings and like to work at their own pace. The boys were listening. But they were skeptical.

"What will happen since they missed a lot of days already?" their mom asked. It was a common problem, Smith said. The school was filled with students who had skipped weeks or even semesters of school but eventually came back. It provided a challenge, but there was another program for such students, he said. It was called Vestibule, an intense program intended to get students caught up by assigning them to work closely with one teacher for three weeks.

"There is a light at the end of the tunnel if you stick with it, especially for you guys," Smith said. "You guys have so much ability." He looked at them, hoping for a response. He still didn't get one, so he turned back to their mom.

"I don't want them to drop out," she said. "I told them it's hard to get a job without a high school diploma. I already gave them that talk." Smith asked her if she thought the boys could commit to school. "If they're willing to work with you, I'm all for that, because I really don't want them dropping out," she said.

I stood to the side taking notes, puzzled by how lightly the mother, Henrietta, was taking the idea of her two oldest children dropping out of school. I didn't want to judge her, though. She was a single mother of six who worked at KFC and had dropped out of Manual herself twenty years earlier. She had a lot on her plate. "They need an education," she said. "Life is hard without one."

The boys had barely spoken. Smith let a long pause pass to see if they would finally bite at his offer. When they didn't, he asked them to be honest and promised that the answer to his next question would be off the record. "Do you guys have a problem with drugs that will make it hard for you to stay in school?" he asked. "I'm just asking. Just be straight with me." They shook their heads no. He asked if they wanted to at least learn more about the reentry program, aware that it was far too early to ask for a commitment beyond that. The brothers didn't speak but shook their heads. "So you're interested?" Smith asked. He told them he needed to hear it.

"Yeah, we can learn more about it," Tyler said.

Smith looked relieved. His ten-minute detour from a day filled with nonstop activity had at least resulted in something. Nothing was certain yet. The boys would still have to meet with Principal Grismore the following Monday to get his blessing to join a program that didn't have a lot of extra room. And after that they would have to show up fifteen days in a row, an almost unthinkable task for a pair of students who later told me they didn't think they'd been to school that many days in a row since the sixth grade. If even then.

"You'll have to come here fifteen days in a row and not get caught up with the old crowds and the old problems," Smith reiterated as they said good-bye. The brothers looked like they were being scolded, but they weren't. "This isn't punishment," Smith continued. "What it's meant to do is change the behavior while you're in school. You do it for a day, and then you do it another day, and then maybe you'll get used to it." He kept talking, kept selling the program. Then he stopped. "I'm talking and talking, guys," he said. "I want you to stay here. But it's up to you."

They nodded and a few seconds later headed out of the school, promising to return a few days later. I walked out of the building with them that morning and asked why they rarely came to school. Their answers weren't unique. Chris said school was boring and the teachers didn't seem to care. He said Manual didn't have enough interesting electives, which was true. Tyler talked about his job, and both said they had a hard time getting up in the morning. Meanwhile, they had a cousin who'd gotten a good job at a warehouse and that's what they wanted. A GED would be sufficient, they said.

I asked about their dad, and they said they hadn't seen him in a year. That problem was so common at the school I sometimes thought it was universal.

I looked at their mom, and she told me her biggest dream was for her sons to graduate from high school and go to college. That sounded great. But she'd loaded them in her car that morning and driven them to school so that they could drop out. I asked why, and she told me they were adults and she didn't have the authority to tell them what to do. "But," she said, "I want something better for them. I want them to be good men and have good jobs and be there for their kids. Not like their father. I want more for them."

They seemed like a close trio as they said good-bye and walked into the chilly Thursday morning air. The two brothers had only agreed to another conversation about their education. They hadn't agreed to anything beyond that. But they'd taken a nice step forward. The question now was whether they would show up the following Monday to have that conversation they'd promised to have.

Monday morning arrived, but Tyler and Chris did not. One of them had called the school and asked if they could postpone the appointment until Tuesday. No reason was given. But they did show up the following day.

I walked toward the main office just before 11:00 AM on Tuesday so that I could sit in on the meeting and noticed the boys and their mother standing just outside the room. They were looking at my most recent column, which the school librarian had again helpfully taped on a wall at the front of the school. The column had asked readers to demand more from the school district, and the brothers were pointing at a paragraph I had included about "parents who just don't care." Without including any names, I had followed up that sentence with another that described the family's visit to the school the week before. I wrote about a mother who had come to the main office to casually help her sons drop out of school. I said it was an all-too-common scene in a school "where teachers and administrators struggled to get parents involved, or even to answer the phone." The boys and their mom were laughing lightly as they read the paragraph, making me wonder if they would allow me to sit in on the meeting they were about to have. But when I said hello, they didn't seem to hold what I'd written against me. It was strange.

Meanwhile, Grismore was overwhelmed as usual with district directives, student issues, and teacher requests. He had jammed this meeting in between several others, and as Chris and Tyler walked into his office with their mom, he was distracted. He shuffled through a stack of papers and messages before finally coming across the brothers' files. After reviewing them, he announced that his secretary had called their former high school and learned they had a handful of credits they didn't know about. It wasn't much, but it meant they were further into their high school careers than they'd realized.

Now the bad news. They were still far short of the credits they should have by now, and Chris, who would be turning eighteen in a few months, was still at least two full years of credits short of meeting graduation requirements. Clearly, Grismore said, one of the school's credit recovery programs was in order.

As the family sat on the other side of Grismore's desk, Chris paid close attention. He seemed interested and nodded his head as Grismore talked. Tyler, the younger of the two, slumped in his chair and responded only when Grismore looked directly at him and asked a question. This wasn't a surprise. When the two did show up for school, Chris had always been more likely to go to class and turn in his work. But administrators worried about him because Tyler, though younger, was the more dominant brother, and Chris seemed to follow his lead.

Henrietta sat next to her sons in jeans and a hoodie as Grismore continued to study the files. "Well, Chris has got some decent grades," he uttered. He looked up, his eyes peering over his glasses. "Guys," he said, "what's the problem? Why aren't you coming to school?"

He laid the files down on his cluttered desk and leaned back. He wanted an answer. His school was filled with students who struggled academically and arrived as freshmen already years behind in math and English. Why were two smart kids giving up?

The boys and their mother looked at each other, wondering who would speak. Finally, Chris did. "I couldn't get enough credits to graduate no matter what," he said.

Grismore swiveled in his chair and got in front of his computer so that he could look up more records. Chris's point was valid. He had received only one credit the previous school year. To graduate, a student needed to average at minimum more than ten credits each year. "But you can't get credits when you rarely walk through the front door," Grismore said. "That's why you're so far behind." The room fell silent for a minute as Grismore looked at the records and considered Vice Principal Smith's recommendation. The family waited without speaking. "Guys," Grismore finally said, "I can bring you back to school, and you could start catching yourself up."

He was talking about the reentry program that Smith had suggested. It was a wonderful program aimed at addressing the problems facing students like Chris and Tyler. It was based on the understanding that many Indianapolis students lose their way early in their high school years and that giving them another chance was good not only for them but also for the school district and the city. Administrators knew the freshman year was brutal for many students; it was the year when students dropped out in the largest numbers. Many of the students were never seen again within the school's walls. But some realized—late but eventually—that the decisions they made at fourteen were bad.

It wasn't clear that Chris and Tyler had learned that yet. But again, at least they were listening as Grismore offered another chance. It wouldn't be a free one, though. "You'd have to prove yourself with perfect attendance early on," he said, "and you'd have to be doing the course work and living by all the rules here. That means no sagging pants. You need to be in uniform. You need to listen to the teachers. You'd have to obey the rules just like anyone else."

Grismore's life was about paperwork, and Tyler in particular had been a tornado of frustrating paperwork over the years because he so hated the dress code and the structure of class schedules. Grismore looked directly at him as he talked about the rules. "I'm being serious here," he said. But the rules weren't the biggest obstacle in the brothers' way. To break the rules in the first place, a student had to at least show up. And they simply had not done that. "It seems like there's a bigger problem than the course work, because these grades show you can turn it on when you want to," Grismore said.

He turned to Henrietta and asked if she had anything to say. But any hope that she would help him came crashing down when she complained that the school had repeatedly suspended her sons for violating the rules. "What's that supposed to teach them?" she said. "That's giving them exactly what they want, a reason not to be here."

"The rules are the rules," Grismore said. "It used to be in the old days we could just give them a whack with a board and send them back to class. Not anymore."

And then he asked the brothers a question. Did they want to give school another chance? He had more meetings and more problems to address. He needed an answer. After a short pause, Chris leaned forward. "I'll do the program," he said.

"That means every day," Grismore warned. "You have to be here every day and follow all the rules every day."

Chris nodded, agreeing to the conditions. As he did, Tyler mumbled. Everyone else in the room turned to him, unsure of what he had said. He repeated his words. "I'll do it," he said. "Yeah, I'll do it."

They went over the rules again and agreed to start the reentry program later that week. Graduation was still a long shot. A lot of damage had been done already, and even with dedication this would be difficult. Unfortunately, there was nothing in the boys' records to suggest they were willing to suddenly turn it on. "This is a last-ditch thing, fellas," Grismore said as he walked them out of the office, reminding them to be there by 7:30 AM on Thursday—and not a minute later. "If you can't follow the rules, I'm just going to have to send you out," he said. "You need to apply yourself and get busy with the work. You can't do this from home. You need to be here. It's time to man up."

"I've been telling them that for years," Henrietta said.

Two days later Grismore stood by the school's front door wearing a blue suit. It was an uncharacteristically formal look for a guy who usually wore a polo shirt or a cotton button-down shirt with a loosened tie. But this was a big day. A group hired by the state was coming in to monitor Manual in advance of a report it would send to the Indiana Department of Education. It was the latest step in a six-year process—a process now in its fifth year—that could result in the state's taking over Manual and several other of the state's worst-performing schools.

Grismore stood waiting to offer the group a friendly welcome. He looked nervous as he told me about the takeover threat. He didn't want to be the principal who lost his school to state officials. Hence, the suit and the work he and others were doing to craft a school turnaround plan. The state had made clear that Manual had just one more chance. Just like Tyler and Chris.

As Grismore waited, the first bell of the morning rang, notifying students that they had four minutes to get to class. Students shuffled along; some rushed and some didn't. There were hundreds of them in the halls. But there was still no sign of Tyler and Chris. About thirty seconds before the next bell rang, the one that officially started the school day, the brothers finally walked in. Grismore was distracted and not worried that they'd almost missed their first bell. He had other things on his mind, and even after the bell rang, dozens of students remained in the halls and walking through the front doors. Bells, I'd learned, were more of a suggestion than a rule here.

"Welcome back," the principal told Chris and Tyler.

"Thanks."

"Are you excited?" I asked the boys.

They shrugged at what they clearly thought was a stupid question.

Grismore handed them off to Dawn Walker-Seyerle, the energetic forty-three-year-old teacher who led the reentry program. The class was a small one; there were just three students enrolled, allowing her substantial one-on-one time with each student. Her goal was to get them used to being back in school and to studying, and to help them catch up on subjects in which they'd fallen behind. Hopefully, the three weeks would also get them thinking about their futures and the importance of getting that high school diploma. With one teacher so focused on them, there was no chance an absence would go unaddressed. Or that unfinished work would be ignored. Or that empty excuses would be tolerated. And since they would be in one class all day, they couldn't skip the occasional period. If they did, Walker-Seyerle would find them. Her mission was first and foremost to keep them in class.

Chris and Tyler followed her to a second-floor classroom, offering short answers to her questions along the way. They waved and smiled at the occasional friend as they passed by other classes. Walker-Seyerle let them settle in their new classroom for a few minutes before launching into the start of their new life. It was a dramatic change from the lives they'd been living. First up was an assignment in which they were told to identify jobs they'd like to have one day. "It can be anything," their teacher insisted. "Don't limit yourself. This is about having something to look forward to," she said. "I'm sure you guys have goals. Right? There's got to be something you want to do with your life." The brothers said they wanted delivery jobs, or landscaping jobs, something that would give them variety from day to day. Even getting those jobs, their teacher tried to convince them, would be easier with a diploma. "This is the twenty-first century," she said. "It's vital. But we don't give diplomas for just having your butts in those chairs. You can't just show up. You have to do the work."

It was a message she delivered daily. One she hoped was sinking in. It was hard to say whether it was. Each time I stopped in the class, I noticed that Chris was working and Tyler often was not. He continued to talk about getting his GED; he hadn't been convinced of the need for anything more. Once I watched as Walker-Seyerle stood at the board and worked through a history lesson. Chris listened while his brother picked at his fingernails. But three weeks passed, and the boys showed up every day. Sometimes they were late—quite late—and they'd been distracted at times, especially when their mom won twenty-five thousand dollars on a lottery scratch-off ticket and the family went on a shopping spree. Still, they showed up day after day. For them, that was a feat, an educational marathon. One that allowed them to move on to a more traditional class schedule.

"I'm proud of myself," Chris said on the fifteenth day.

"We did it," Tyler said, barely audible.

On their last day in the class, Walker-Seyerle wished them well and reminded them that they'd only made it to the starting line. They had a long way to go and a lot of credits to recover. But they'd accomplished the very important first step. "So," she said, "don't let all that work go to waste. It's important to think about what you need to do to get what you want out of the future. Don't give up."

I wrote a column about Chris and Tyler a few days after their first day back in school, under the headline "Two Brothers, 15 Days: Can They Change Their Lives?" In it I said that finding ways to save students like these two was crucial and would be necessary if Manual was going to improve on its low graduation rate. I said the surrender of students like Chris and Tyler should be seen as a crisis, and massive resources should be directed at the problem just as they would be at a raging fire or a wild crime spree. This was the most important issue facing the future of the city. Manual was filled with many more students at risk of falling by the wayside, and each one should have a teacher or administrator assigned to them, I thought, someone to track his or her progress every week. It would take a uniquely ambitious effort, and likely an investment of more spending, but it could pay off tremendously even if just a few kids were saved each year.

The story I had watched unfold over the past few weeks was moving. The sight of Vice Principal Smith taking an interest in the students and luring them back into school was inspiring. Despite my growing frustration with the apathy in the school, it was a reminder that most of the adults there cared deeply about children. But I kept wondering about what would have happened if the brothers simply hadn't come to Manual that day to officially drop out. The school was doing little to reach out to the many other students who had also stopped coming to school. Principal Grismore had made a nice show of visiting a few homes early in the school year, but that effort had faded. It should have been a daily occurrence. If Chris and Tyler had continued to stay away, no school official would have shown up at their front door. They would have been forgotten. In my column I wrote about the long road and many challenges ahead for the two brothers. Graduation was still a long shot. But, I said, "For now, at least they're where they should be. In school."

They stayed in school for a while longer. But not long enough. Tyler soon began to routinely miss days and eventually stopped coming altogether. Chris was more committed. Even though he occasionally missed a day, and even more occasionally showed up late, he came to Manual through the fall and winter. I sometimes saw him in the hallways. We didn't talk much, but he always returned my hellos. A number of readers had sent cards, and even money, to the two brothers, encouraging them to stick with school. One day Chris told me he was trying. I promised to write an encouraging follow-up column about him if he made it to the end of the year. It never happened.

On a crisp morning in late March, I got an e-mail from Walker-Seyerle, the teacher from the reentry program. She had continued to track Chris's progress even after he'd moved on from her class. "I wanted to let you know Chris is signing himself out of school today," I read as I worked at my desk back at the newspaper. "He is eighteen now, and his mom needs him to get a job to help her support the family. I told him I was disappointed, but not disappointed in him." She continued, telling me she wished he'd landed in her program earlier, before he'd fallen so far behind. He was an example of the need for schools across the nation to tackle at-risk students as early as possible, to identify them young and direct effective resources their way in order to help them avoid the life that too often comes with dropping out.

It's a tough life. A 2009 Northeastern University report found that nearly half of America's dropouts were unemployed the previous year and, when compared to college graduates, were sixty-three times more likely to be imprisoned or institutionalized at some point in their lives. More than a third of dropouts lived in or near poverty, the report found, and over the course of a lifetime a dropout cost the nation more than he or she contributed in tax payments. "There is an overwhelming national economic and social justice need to prevent existing high school students from dropping out and to encourage the re-enrollment of those dropouts who have already left the school system," the report read. Otherwise, it continued, "Their immediate and long-term labor market prospects are likely to be quite bleak."

That seemed to be the likely prognosis for Chris as he gave up on his education that morning. "I just feel like we were too late," Walker-Seyerle wrote in her e-mail. She said that Chris was going to a few of his classes that day to say good-bye to friends and teachers. But she didn't know how long he would stick around.

I wanted to talk to him. So I ran from my desk, rushed to my car, and drove the three miles to Manual. I walked in the front door just after 9:30 AM clutching a copy of Chris's schedule, which Walker-Seyerle had e-mailed me. I headed to the second floor and peeked into Chris's chemistry class. But he wasn't there. A half hour later I stood on the third floor to see if he would walk into his world history class. He didn't. And an hour later he wasn't at lunch. I was too late. He was gone. And another student's name had been added to the nation's dropout epidemic.

12

★ ★ ★

I GET HIT ALL THE TIME.

Dean Hoover was having one of those days. A day when her office was a nonstop burst of activity, filled with troublemaking students, perplexed parents, and enough drama to fill a few soap opera scripts. Shortly after nine o'clock, after Hoover dealt with a handful of other brush fires, a fifteen-year-old boy named Darnell walked into the room with his father, Bryan. Darnell, who had a smooth demeanor and a mild learning disability, was a frequent visitor to the office, and as soon as they entered he fell into a seat and leaned his head against the wall behind him. "Sit up straight," his dad ordered.

The meeting had been scheduled so that Hoover and Jackie Sababu, the head of the school's special education department, could talk about the trouble Darnell was causing. He received help from teachers assigned to students with learning disabilities but attended regular classes. And he was disrupting them constantly of late. Sababu said Darnell's was a tricky case. He had a sweet and innocent way about him that masked much of the trouble he caused. He was friendly and apologetic, she said, a trait that had bought him a lot of leeway earlier in the year. Not anymore. He'd pushed things too far. His teachers were fed up. Darnell stared at the ceiling as she talked. "Look at her," his dad said.

"We're going to have a long talk when you get home. He's already on punishment until December."

For the next few minutes, Hoover and Sababu came within inches of begging the boy's dad to truly crack down on his behavior, to follow through on the threats he made in the office, and to make sure he was studying and coming to school. They persuaded him to agree to take the TV and DVD player out of Darnell's bedroom. "The law says he has to provide you with a roof and four walls," Hoover said, looking at Darnell. "It doesn't say he has to give you a four-star hotel." She then handed his father a sheet showing Darnell's grades and attendance record.

The father looked surprised by what he saw. "He ain't brought homework home except for one day," he said.

"Two days," the boy corrected, earning a cold, hard look from his dad.

"Say something else," he warned. "Roll your eyes again, and they'll be on the floor."

Hoover jumped in, facetiously asking Darnell if he was so smart that he was able to finish all of his homework in class. If so, she told him, then he should have a report card filled with As.

"I don't see any As here," the dad said, staring at his son. "All I see is Ds and Fs. An F in math. An F in science."

"I don't like science," Darnell said.

"That's too bad, so sad," Sababu said, jumping in.

I had come to Hoover's office to do what I did there several days each week: observe. The problems crippling Manual were on clear display in her 150-square-foot domain. The challenges students were going through and the frustrations the school dealt with every minute were all easily found here. I had begun telling groups I spoke to about my Manual series that the ongoing national debate over education policy should start right there in Terry Hoover's office. "There's a lot to be learned in there," I would tell them.

Before Darnell's dad left, Hoover asked for his current phone number, saying she'd had trouble reaching him over the past few weeks. It was then that Hoover and Sababu discovered Darnell had given the school his grandmother's name and number, hoping to keep his dad from being called. His grandmother, Bryan said, was a sucker for Darnell's charm and kept quiet about his misdeeds. Hoover promised to call the dad from now on. "Darnell, you're slick," she said. "But you're not slick enough. We caught you this time, and we'll catch you next time."

After the boy and his dad left, Hoover said that Darnell was a perfect example of the school's freshmen problem. Manual's youngest students dropped out in staggering numbers and were the source of many of its discipline problems.

They struggled to adjust to high school, and those struggles often led to them just giving up. The school's enrollment statistics told the story. In the fall of 2006, roughly 450 freshmen had enrolled at Manual. But the number of students in that class dwindled every year, and by the time those students were seniors, only a third remained.

Darnell's father, meanwhile, was a perfect example of the challenges the school had with parents. He said the right things but clearly didn't spend much time parenting his son. Darnell rarely brought homework home, but until now his dad had not questioned that. Darnell had long struggled in school, but until he was called his dad hadn't taken the time to check on his son's progress.

"A lot of them have a big bark when they're in my office," Hoover said. "The question is whether they'll follow through once they get home."

As Hoover talked, a junior named Tasha stormed into the room, looking angry. She dropped into a chair without saying anything and folded her arms across her chest. She was one of the school's toughest girls and had spent much of her life fighting one rival or another, usually winning. "Come in, grumpy lady," Sababu said after Tasha entered. For the next few minutes, Hoover and Sababu got the story out of Tasha, a girl they both liked and knew extremely well and whom they hoped was learning to control her emotions. They had spent countless hours talking with her about her life and anger and problems, essentially being the nurturing mother figures she didn't have elsewhere. She seemed to appreciate the effort. Even when Hoover had suspended her for previous fights, Tasha didn't get mad.

In this case, as with so many other incidents at Manual, someone had said something to one of Tasha's friends about her, leading to a near fight. She had come into Hoover's office rather than pummeling the other girl. That was a promising step. But she was still mad and thinking about settling the dispute. She said the girl's words made her furious.

"Are you a puppet?" Hoover asked.

"No."

"Then don't let other people pull your strings."

They talked for a few more minutes about the situation and Tasha's life. Hoover asked about the daughter Tasha had given birth to four months earlier and told her to think about her baby before she got into another fight. "Don't you teach your child manners?" Hoover said. "Or aren't you going to? You have to be an example for her. You have to be a mother she can look up to. Don't you want a relationship with your child?"

That one stung, because Tasha rarely saw her own mother. "I was thinking about giving her up for adoption, actually," she said.

With that, she began to cry. I was sitting about five feet away, surprised and touched by the sight of her crying. This was a girl who walked the halls with the toughest possible look painted constantly on her face, who tried at all times to make clear that nothing and nobody scared her.

"It's hard, isn't it?" Hoover said. "Is your baby's daddy in your life?"

"Not anymore."

"That's going to be a hard decision you have to make, whether to give her up for adoption," Hoover said. "That's one where you need to decide what's best for the baby."

For the next hour, Hoover dealt with a laundry list of student problems and disciplinary meetings. One student came into the office with a monitoring bracelet around his ankle. So many students had been in trouble with the law that the county probation department staffed an office a few doors down from Hoover's. At one point Hoover talked to two boys whom she had heard were on the verge of a fight. After twenty minutes of detective work, she learned that the dispute boiled down to an eighth-grade girl who had spent the past few days turning the boys against each other. "That's sad," Hoover said. "Letting a little girl play you boys like fiddles." The boys sat in front of a table, looking embarrassed as Hoover shook her head at them. She smiled as she walked them out of the room and told them to grow up.

There were no smiles a few minutes later, though, when Larissa, a fifteen-year-old girl with blonde hair walked into Hoover's office. She was another tough-looking student with a history of fighting. She'd also spent a lot of time talking to Hoover and occasionally accepting her advice. She had done so on this day, stopping in the office to announce that she had been inches from starting a fight with another girl. She could have just gone and fought. Instead she came to talk first. "Larissa," Hoover said. "What's your dad going to say if I have to call him again to say you got suspended because you got in a fight?"

The girl's answer provided one of the many moments when I realized how deep the problems at Manual were. Larissa said her father was fine with her fighting and had even offered to drop her off at the home of the other girl the previous weekend so that they could do battle. That's how her family solved its problems.

Hoover sighed and realized this was going to be a long conversation. She told Larissa to sit down and pulled up her records on the office computer. They were a mess. Scores of missed classes in the first months of the year. A stream of Fs, and nothing but Fs, on her transcript. Few credits. Numerous disciplinary referrals from teachers. "You were in three schools last year," Hoover said. "You moved a lot."

"We move a lot every year," Larissa said, highlighting a problematic trend in a school district filled with poverty and transient families.

Hoover continued to scan the records. She asked Larissa how she expected to learn if she rarely made it to class. There was no answer. Larissa shrugged as she pulled loose eyelashes out and sprinkled them on the floor. Hoover tried another strategy, saying that surely Larissa didn't want to get hit in the face during another fight. "I get hit all the time," the girl said quietly. "Doesn't matter." The room grew silent for a few seconds. Hoover sensed that Larissa had something to say. Without looking up, Larissa began talking about her problems, many of which Hoover already knew about. Her father had spent time in prison several years ago. Her step-grandfather had molested her when she was thirteen. She had spent time in foster care and under the supervision of the state's Child Protective Services. She lived with her dad, who was now out of prison, and rarely saw her mother. That last one seemed to bother her the most.

"You have a lot of things going on in your life, and it's affecting your school work," Hoover said, handing her forms that would allow her to receive in-school counseling from the county health department. "You're not alone. There are people going through the same thing as you. Right now you're angry, and I think it's because you don't get to see your mom. It would be good to talk to someone."

The same girl who looked so angry a few minutes earlier was now relaxed. "When I was little I had a good childhood, because my mom and dad was married," she said quietly. "But then they got divorced, and that was it."

The next day Larissa was back in the office. Hoover had set up a meeting with her mother in the hope of persuading her to spend more time with her daughter. It was a hard sell. Larissa's mom said she worked nights at a warehouse, slept during the day, and didn't have time to raise a daughter. As she talked, Larissa's face turned painfully sad.

"My daughter is the slickest of the slick," her mom said. "She even outfoxes me a lot of the time. You gotta watch her."

"She's just very angry," Hoover said, again suggesting that Larissa, along with her mother, speak with the counselor assigned to the school.

"Talking ain't gonna help nothing," Larissa said. "I've talked to a ton of counselors."

"I know my daughter's going through a depressed stage right now," her mom added. "But I don't want her on a bunch of medicine."

Finally, though, the mom softened. She looked at her daughter, who was leaning against the wall. "It's not just her fault," she said, turning to Hoover. "She's been through trauma versus trauma versus trauma in the past year."

"That's why she needs you," Hoover insisted. "I know she loves her dad," she said. "But girls her age want to be with their mother."

Larissa didn't say anything. Her mother didn't either, for a few seconds. Then she repeated the point about her job schedule and apologized as she said there just wasn't any way she could have custody of her daughter.

A minute later Hoover asked the girl for her current address, as her file hadn't been updated since a recent move. Larissa turned to her mom, asking if she knew the address of the new apartment she shared with her father. She didn't. "It's by the dollar store and the liquor store and the Pizza Hut," Larissa said, hoping to jog her mom's memory. Her mom shook her head. She hadn't been there yet.

As the meeting wrapped up, Larissa's mom stood and thanked Hoover. She apologized as she again said she couldn't raise a daughter at that point in her life but promised to come back to the school anytime she was needed. She gave her daughter a kiss and a hug. Larissa was on the verge of tears. "I love you," her mom said. "Call me tonight." She turned to Hoover. "It breaks my heart to see her like this," she said. And then she left.

Larissa walked out a few seconds later, passing Jill Haughawout, who was now standing in Hoover's doorway. The popular Ms. H. was carrying a black plastic bag and wearing a slightly nervous expression. She walked to Hoover's desk, handed over the bag, and said a senior named Aaron had crafted the ceramic art inside. Hoover, weary from her previous meeting, opened the bag and immediately shut it, appearing startled. "Oh, my!" she said.

Haughawout nodded her head knowingly.

"If only he could focus this much on his homework," Hoover said.

She waved me over and told me to take a look inside the bag. A giant ceramic penis greeted me. I looked at Haughawout and noticed that in a display of perfect symmetry, "Welcome to the Jungle" was playing on the classic rock station that was constantly on in Hoover's office.

"It gets worse," Haughawout said. "He actually put it in his pants during class and paraded around. And when I took it away, he shouted, 'She took my penis! She took my penis!'"

Hoover sighed and said she would take care of the situation. She called Sergeant Barrow and asked him to come down and then called to have Aaron sent down from his class. When Barrow walked in the room a few minutes later, Hoover handed him the bag without a warning of what it contained. "What's this?" he said. He looked inside, removed the artwork, and then looked at Hoover. It had been a long day for both. They shook their heads, looked at me with serious expressions, and then, after a few seconds, burst out laughing.

Barrow pointed to all of the chips and cracks on the sculpture. "What's with all the open sores?" he said. "Is that herpes?"

They laughed again. Hoover laid her head on her desk in a moment of surrender, and Barrow took a seat. Eventually, between laughs, they walked through the details of the incident. Barrow picked up the office phone and called Haughawout, who had returned to her class before he arrived. "Ms. H.," Barrow said, "I'm going to have to put you on the sex offender list. You took a young man's penis. That's a serious crime."

"No, he gave it to me!" she said.

Again Barrow and Hoover laughed. And for a couple of minutes two stressed-out school employees, two of the hardest workers in one of the state's worst schools, enjoyed a much-needed laugh about their latest headache. Then they collected themselves, opened the office door, and ordered Aaron in.

He wore a crisp ROTC uniform and did not know why he'd been called down. He quickly got his answer, though, as Hoover had strategically placed the ceramic model in the middle of her desk. "Oh, that," he said. "I did it on a dare. It was stupid."

Barrow had been close to tears a minute earlier, but he didn't want Aaron to think this was a laughing matter. He scowled at the student and said the district took sexual harassment seriously. He said this hinted of more serious problems and that he could be charged with a crime. That, he said, would damage Aaron's plan of going into the military. Barrow got angry when Aaron briefly claimed the art was actually a model of a bell. "Don't insult our intelligence," Barrow said. "You're a smart kid. But we've dealt with this kind of stuff for three years. Think about it: thirteen years of school, and you get kicked out during the last year. Is that what you want? What a waste."

Aaron apologized and tried to offer an excuse.

Hoover stopped him. "You've engaged in conduct that is vulgar and profane," she said, handing him a disciplinary form. "You're suspended for five days, and you can't come back without your parents coming to my office. Bye."

Aaron walked out and Barrow followed him to the door, watching as the student left the office complex. Then he closed the door, and he and Hoover burst into laughter once again.

13

★ ★ ★

WE JUST COULDN'T GET
ANYTHING STARTED.

The leaves were falling, and the Indiana weather was turning colder as early November arrived. Manual had settled into its routines, both good and bad, and teachers and students were already looking forward to the winter break that was seven weeks away. The school had spent the year under a microscope. The district was watching it closely. Superintendent White spent many Monday mornings questioning Manual leaders about something he'd read in the paper, something that bothered him or, occasionally, even something that pleased him. But the close examination of the school was not due solely to the weekly front-page columns I was writing. White had long had deep concerns about the indifference that plagued the school and was pondering big shake-ups. Over at the statehouse, meanwhile, the state's new superintendent of education had ordered the deepest look the state had ever taken at the school. It all resulted in November being a month of big changes at Manual with warnings of even bigger changes to come.

Early one Wednesday, Principal Grismore sat in his sprawling suburban home. He was eating a bowl of Cheerios and reading that morning's edition of the *Indianapolis Star*. He had breezed through the front page and metro section on his way to the sports section. The city was in full swoon over the Indianapolis Colts, who had won their eighth consecutive game the previous Sunday and were headed toward an epic showdown against the New England Patriots the following week. The city's rabid football fans were starting to talk about the possibility of an undefeated season and another trip to the Super Bowl.

But Grismore's calm morning slammed to a halt when he turned from the front page of the sports section and came across a short story about White's decision to eliminate football programs at three Indianapolis high schools. The headline didn't specify which schools were losing their teams, and Grismore hadn't received a courtesy call from the district boss, but he had no doubt he would see his school on the list. The team hadn't won a game all season, hadn't been able to field a full roster, and White had come into the job five years earlier with a promise to do whatever it took to restore his district's once-strong tradition of stellar athletic programs. He was tired of programs that always lost. Grismore dug into the story, and there it was. Manual was one of the teams on the list. A football program with nearly a century-long tradition was history and had already played its final game. He knew White well enough to know that this decision would be final, regardless of complaints, protests, or rallies in favor of the Redskins.

Grismore was melancholy in his office later that morning, stung by the idea that a sports reporter had gotten the news out of White before he had. Even now, as teachers and students began asking about the news, he didn't have much to tell them. All he knew was that a school that was already missing many of the basic elements of American high school life was now losing another. "We're trying to build extracurricular programs," he said. "We really are. But here we are now, losing a major piece of that." He wasn't in much of a mood to talk. "I'm surprised," he said. "I'm disappointed. But I knew [White] was looking into this." The hardheaded superintendent had made that clear many times, including two months earlier when he'd spoken to Manual's students in the auditorium. Still, the reality of the loss stung, and it sent another message to the school that it was second-rate. How could a public high school not have a football team? This wasn't math, or English, or science, or any of the classes that were unquestionably more important to the future of Manual's students than football. But this was nonetheless a big loss. In a building filled with apathy and few activities that pulled students in, this would only add to the problem.

White's argument was solid in some ways. He said it wasn't safe to have students forced to play every minute of every game because the rosters were so thin. He said having teams that lost all or most of their games, and that were routinely destroyed by schools from more affluent districts, sent an awful message to the student population. He said the losing programs added to the low self-esteem that afflicted many students. He knew it would be easier to have successful football programs if the district had fewer of them, as many of the players at Manual and the other defunct programs would transfer to schools that still fielded teams. "If we're going to do something, we have to do it well," he said. "It doesn't help their mentality to get slaughtered on the football field every week."

When White talked about sports, he emphasized the high graduation rate among athletes. Football was at the top of the list, with 87 percent of players graduating—in a district where only about 50 percent of boys overall graduated. And although his arguments for killing Manual's program made bottom-line sense, it struck me as another surrender by a district that too often gave up rather than fight for better results. There was little evidence to suggest that the district had done much under White's tenure to address the problem of low participation in football.

Ultimately, few Manual students or parents complained, at least not loudly. One of the other schools affected by White's decision flooded school board meetings with parents and teachers, demanding its program be reinstated. At Manual indifference reigned. But there was still disappointment. "We just couldn't get anything started," said Coach Lloyd, who had also learned about his program's fate by reading the morning paper and would soon leave the school.

At the end of the school day, a student named DeJuan Parker stood by the school's front door waiting for a ride. He had played wide receiver the previous season and told me it helped him keep his grades up. It had been a disappointing season, but he said that hadn't bothered him. "It really helped some kids," he said. "The kids who play graduate. Now you have that big field out there. What are you going to do with it?" Not much, I wrote in my next column. The district, it seemed, was giving up on Manual.

A week later Grismore would learn the lack of a football team wouldn't be his problem. He was called to the district offices one day and told by his bosses that they wanted him to take a job at headquarters. The move would end more than thirty-five consecutive years of working inside schools, work that Grismore deeply loved despite all the problems he encountered. The move wouldn't take full effect until the end of the school year, but he would begin transitioning into the new role almost immediately. For the final several months of the school year, he would spend only about half of his time at Manual, leaving it without a full-time leader. A new principal would be selected soon, he was told, and would spend the school year's second semester preparing for the promotion under his tutelage.

Grismore broke the news to his teachers at a hastily called after-school meeting in mid-November and then told me when I walked into his office the next day. He billed it as a simple transfer, saying White had asked him to help out downtown. But a district official later told me the move had come about because Manual needed new, fresher leadership. The school was not only failing but had also stagnated. There were few signs of progress. Many teachers assumed the columns I had written contributed to the district's move. They had exposed a school filled with problems that were not being adequately addressed. Grismore, however, was popular with the bosses and had been a loyal employee. Since the district rarely got rid of anyone in leadership, he was simply transferred to a new position.

I didn't write much about the move, other than a short blog posting titled "Rocky's Last Year." The problem was that I didn't know what to write. I had such mixed feelings about Grismore. He was extremely hardworking, and there was no doubt he cared deeply about the students in his building. He arrived before sunrise and stayed later than everyone else. He was competent and passionate. He once told me about his dream of winning the lottery and starting a school free of local and state regulations. But dreams aren't enough. And although I routinely acknowledged that I was not within twenty miles of being an education expert, it didn't take an expert to see that Grismore and his school were in a deep funk. He had been swallowed by the district's legendary bureaucracy and was not the outspoken, dynamic leader a school with Manual's problems needed.

The lack of strong and independent leaders at schools like Manual is particularly infuriating. Though some critics of education reform dismiss it as Hollywood fantasy, schools filled with social challenges and disengaged parents desperately need the type of high-profile, energetic, and demanding leader they make movies about. I found myself thinking daily that Manual was home to many students who were living dangerously on the edge. A school filled with urgency and excitement, led by someone who insisted on excellence and was willing to challenge district rules that impeded success, could keep many of them from falling off that edge. Such a leader could also demand more from lackluster teachers and give a boost to those who already gave their all but were hampered by the apathy throughout the building.

As a 2011 report for the National Governors Association stated, "A principal's effectiveness impacts both teachers and students. Although all schools can benefit from an effective school principal, there is an emergent need for schools that are chronically low-performing." Principal effectiveness, the report added, "is second only to teacher effectiveness in terms of the school-based factors that influence student learning." Ultimately, "Students in our nation's low-performing schools are particularly vulnerable to ineffective leadership and turning these institutions around hinges on highly effective leadership and teachers."

The reason for new leadership at Manual was clear, and it was highlighted by November's other big development. The month had begun on the heels of a two-day visit by Cambridge Education, a private education-quality firm hired by the state to compile reports on Manual and nearly two dozen other Indiana schools that faced the threat of a state takeover. For two days a small team wandered the Manual building, observing classrooms and meeting with teachers and students. Team members took notes about the school's problems and programs as well as its successes and plans. The team walked away disappointed after a meeting with parents. Exemplifying one of the school's biggest problems, administrators had been able to round up only two parents who were willing to attend the meeting. In classrooms, meanwhile, they saw what I had seen during dozens of hours spent watching teachers at work: a lack of rigor and engagement. Even some teachers I liked, teachers who clearly cared, often failed to offer the type of dynamic classroom experiences their at-risk students needed. The report's main author visited the school again that month to talk with Grismore and his administrative team about their ideas for a turnaround. All of the meetings and visits would be used to form the basis of a report that would be presented to state and district officials several weeks later.

The report was devastating. It deemed Manual a disaster in nearly every possible way, giving it a rating of poor or unacceptable in all but one of forty-seven categories. "A trend of low achievement in core subjects has been evident for a number of years," the report said, adding that the administration "has not translated the imperative to improve with sufficient rigor or robustness." In a brutally frank review of school leadership, the authors said Grismore had not established a clear vision for his school, that his "resourcefulness and ingenuity is poor," and that in most cases the school was engaged in "crisis management rather than being proactive in addressing the social and personal needs of students." "There is a lack of a clear leadership strategy to promote improvements at the school," it read. Additionally, the report said the school's "culture, environment and student engagement are poor" and that little was done to help students set goals or get involved in school activities. It noted classroom disruptions and the sense that the actions of some teachers "reflected only a token acknowledgment of the need to focus on student achievement." Few areas survived unscathed. Class lessons were deemed unchallenging, parental involvement was called nearly nonexistent, and the professional culture within the school was ruled poor. The school was mired in deep failure, but, the report concluded, there was still no sense of urgency. This was the utter definition of an underperforming school—one of many across the city, state, and nation that was threatening the nation's future.

"It's bullshit," Grismore told me later when I asked about the damning report. He was irritated as he sat at his desk and insisted that the report skirted around the many positive steps Manual had taken, such as magnet programs and more advanced-placement classes. He said the report read as if the group had settled on what to write before stepping into the school. He felt like he was under fire. His school was already under the microscope of the local newspaper, and now it had the state zeroing in. "There are a lot of good things going on at Manual," he said. And he was right. I had found many inspiring stories in my time there.

Nonetheless, the report was accurate. It was filled with exactly the types of fundamental problems and missteps I had seen daily during my months there. The authors had quickly picked up on the apathy that hung heavy in the building even though they'd visited at a time when the school had been on its best behavior. In the end, no temporary push could hide the deep problems that had long kept the school down. Special short-term attention to class-skipping students and hallway troubles couldn't hide the school's below-average test scores, low graduation rate, and poor attendance problems. The lack of life in the school, from the empty walls to the trophy cases devoid of modern-day student athletes, was impossible to miss. The lackluster classes were on daily display.

As much as I had been drawn into Manual's story, and as much as I liked the people inside it, I left nearly every day wondering why more wasn't being done to radically improve the school. A team of outsiders who had spent just two days at the school had exactly the same question.

14
★ ★ ★

WHAT'S GONNA HAPPEN, MR. GRISMORE?

I walked out of Spencer Lloyd's class on the Friday before Thanksgiving after watching his choir prepare for its upcoming holiday concert—the Christmas Extravaganza, he called it—which was less than four weeks away. I was amazed at how far Lloyd had brought the choir in such a short time. The students were more focused and sounded stronger than they had just a few weeks earlier. That seemed to be a pattern. Each time I returned to the class, the improvement was noticeable, even to me, a guy who loved music but couldn't carry a note and didn't know the first thing about singing. Many of the students were just starting to learn the basics of voice control and pitch, but they were improving.

The class had spent the period working on the classic "We Wish You a Merry Christmas." The students' voices filled the room as Lloyd conducted furiously and moved around to hear the different singers, to make sure all of the students were doing their part. "Come on, sing it, sopranos," he said. "Altos, come on, guys!"

I was planning to write about Lloyd's class and hoped that doing so would result in a few more people than normal attending the mid-December concert. He and the students deserved it. Every student in the building who took part in such an activity deserved that. The sports teams and the drama clubs deserved the chance to perform in front of full crowds. But they didn't get them.

The previous weekend, I had gone to see the two girls I wrote about earlier in the year, Kelly and Allison, in the school's production of *The Curious Savage*, a mystery about an elderly woman's fight to keep her greedy heirs from grabbing her money. The girls had claimed the lead roles and worked hard for weeks leading up to the performances. But fewer than forty people attended the shows, and as I walked out into the November evening after one of the performances, I found myself regretting that I hadn't written about the play in the paper.

The school seemed calm that Friday morning as I walked from the choir room and toward the main office. The next class period had already begun, and the halls had mostly cleared. I hummed "We Wish You a Merry Christmas" to myself. But the calm came crashing to an end when one of the doors to the main office flung open hard and a boy sprinted out, yelling as he did. His arms were cuffed behind his back, but he was moving fast. Not fast enough, though, because a pair of police officers caught and tackled him as he reached a door leading to the school's courtyard. He was screaming, squirming, and crying as they dragged him back into the office. His brown hair was a mess. His face was red.

It turned out that while I had been sitting in Lloyd's class, the boy, seventeen-year-old Brent Walls, had been arrested with two friends after police received word that they were arranging drug deals in the locker room near the school gymnasium. The police found the three boys in there and brought them down to the main office for questioning. More than the others, Brent was acting suspicious and fidgeting as police escorted him from the locker room. Once they were all in the office, police had searched the boys. They found marijuana on all of them. Brent carried the biggest bag, but that was just the start of his problems. In one of his back pockets, police found something worse: a loaded semiautomatic handgun. After finding the gun, they had cuffed him and placed him in a chair—a chair that was too close to a door and gave him that last, unsuccessful chance at breaking free.

When I walked into the office, Brent was back in the room with two police officers. I peeked in and saw his red eyes as one of the officers worked through the paperwork needed to have him sent to the juvenile jail facility. The mood was serious. This wasn't a routine arrest. A gun—a loaded gun—had turned it into something bigger.

I walked over to the dean's office, which Principal Grismore was running that day because Dean Hoover was out. As usual, Grismore had more problems than he had time. But now he had the biggest one of all. He would have to deal with the district headquarters, which would issue a press release later in the day because of the loaded weapon. He also had to arrange an automated call to each of his students' homes to let their parents know what had happened. He was hoping to keep the story from spreading until after school. For all of Manual's problems, this was the first time all year Grismore had been forced to deal with a gun issue. It doesn't get much worse for a high school principal.

As things finally began to settle, a loud wail pierced the office complex. The voice wasn't Brent's, though. It was clearly coming from a much older man. Grismore turned to the noise as Charles Walls, Brent's father, burst into the office, a room he had been in many times. He was sobbing uncontrollably and began pacing the small room. He ripped his stocking hat off of his head. "Oh, my God!" he shouted. "I'm sorry. Oh, my God! Oh, my boy's in trouble." He fell into one of the office chairs, buried his face in his hands, and cried some more. He was crying so hard that his body heaved in the chair. The scene continued this way for several more seconds before he began to calm himself, taking deep breaths and wiping his face. "What's gonna happen, Mr. Grismore?" he finally said. "What's gonna happen to my boy?"

"He's in some deep stuff this time, Dad," the principal said, setting off the father's sobs once again.

"Oh, Mr. Grismore, I'm so sorry," Charles said. "I'm so sorry."

"He's just made some pretty stupid choices," Grismore said. "And this is the worst one."

Grismore told the father the details of what had happened. As he got to the worst part of the story, the part about the gun, Charles shook his head and insisted there were no guns in his house. He said he didn't even like guns. "I think it might be the other kid's," he said.

"No, it was his," Grismore said without hesitating. "And it doesn't matter anyway. Possession is nine-tenths of the law, and he was carrying it, so he'll get the charge."

Charles started crying again. "I'm so sorry for you, sir," he told Grismore.

"Don't worry about that, Dad."

Charles sat in the chair staring ahead. He wore jeans and a brown jacket, and a white mustache sat prominently on his weathered fifty-five-year-old face. His graying hair was buzz cut. He said he didn't know why his son liked to mess with guns. He couldn't understand how things had gone so badly so quickly. His son had recently gotten off probation after being on it for five years because of a laundry list of crimes and troubles over the years. He seemed to be improving. Now this.

"Out of one frying pan and into another," Grismore said.

"I brought him to school today," Charles said. "I didn't know. I didn't know. I swear to you, I didn't know."

"You can't be responsible for everything he does," Grismore said.

Composing himself, Charles asked to see his son before he was shipped off to jail but was told that wasn't possible. He would have to deal with the juvenile court system, a system he knew well. And he was told a suspension from school was automatic, with the very real possibility of an expulsion. "Oh, my God," he said.

Charles had gotten the call that Brent had been arrested as he stood in line at a nearby government office applying for Medicaid. He had just talked to his son the day before about keeping clean now that he was freed from probation. He had told him about the ability to have a clean slate since all of his past mistakes had occurred while he was a juvenile in the eyes of the law. He didn't want Brent to make the same mistakes he had made in his own life, mistakes that three decades earlier had landed him in prison. He cried again. "I've got a good heart, Mr. Grismore."

"Brent's old enough now to make his own decisions," the principal said.

"Yes, he is," Charles said, standing up to shake Grismore's hand.

Grismore called a quick staff meeting at the end of the school day. Teachers walked into one of the school's auditoriums just after the afternoon buses rolled out without any idea of why a meeting had been scheduled. Nearly five hours had passed since three boys had been arrested on drug charges and since police had found the loaded handgun. It amazed me that word of the incident had not spread around the school. "I have a bit of information, and I want you to hear it from me," Grismore told the teachers as they took their seats. He walked them through the story, announcing that a tip from a student had led to the arrest of three students on drug charges. He said the police had quickly apprehended the suspects. And then he told them the big news: that one of the students had been carrying a loaded gun. A few of the teachers gasped. "But our crack team of IPS police did a great job," Grismore said quickly. "The gun was never brandished, and nobody was in jeopardy. Our officers were good about getting on this with no disruption to the flow of the day."

He was right. The arrests had not disrupted the flow of the day. But I wondered what that said about the school. Regardless, the meeting came to an end, and the teachers applauded police officers who were standing around the room. "We do take tips," Sergeant Barrow joked as the teachers stood up and left the room.

Brent was sent to the juvenile jail facility, but it was a short stay. The county prosecutor's office quickly charged him with a handful of adult crimes, including a dreaded felony gun charge that effectively guaranteed his actions would result in prison time. Along with four misdemeanors, from resisting arrest to drug possession, Brent faced the prospect of a prison sentence ranging from two to twelve years. Because of the adult charges, he was sent to the county's adult jail, a tough place for a short and thin, though tough and troubled, seventeen-year-old. Several years of mistakes had led him to the jail. His arrest record was long and included three previous arrests at Manual alone—for slugging a female teacher, attacking a fellow student, and attacking his own father during a meeting in the dean's office one day. He'd had nine stays in juvenile placement facilities over the years and had been diagnosed as being bipolar and having ADHD.

I got to know his dad in the days after Brent's arrest. We talked outside a courtroom after Brent's brief hearing one morning, over coffee at a downtown Starbucks one afternoon, and at his home one night. Charles Walls was friendly and brutally honest about the problems plaguing his son and his family and about his own troubled past. He told me he had divorced Brent's mom when his son was six months old and rarely saw him until Brent decided he wanted to live with his father in Indianapolis when he was ten. At the time, Charles was abusing alcohol and crack and could barely keep his own life in order. He was a trucker and often on the road. But he had agreed to let Brent move in with him. The boy left his mom's home in rural Indiana, where he had often fought with her boyfriend, and joined his dad and three brothers at the first of several homes he would inhabit in a downtrodden neighborhood on the south side of Indianapolis.

As we sat on a bench outside the courtroom one day, Charles told me Brent was a good boy but was also following the family pattern of making bad decisions. He said moving to Indianapolis, to a neighborhood full of drugs and petty criminals, had been too much for him, particularly since he had little adult supervision. He couldn't think of a long stretch of time that had passed without Brent's falling into serious trouble. He said his son loved football and eating and dreamed of joining the army one day. But he also loved guns. He was obsessed with them and was always on the lookout for a way to get his hands on one, even stealing one from his grandfather once.

Each time I talked to Charles, I noticed he went out of his way to accept a big chunk of the blame for his son's problems, both past and present. The family was a mess, but when I visited their crowded home I noticed they all stood together. "Probably the most significant thing in Brent's life was that for the first ten years of it, I wasn't a part of it," Charles said. "I didn't spend quality time with him. I know there were always questions: 'Where's Dad?'" Even when Charles had stopped doing drugs three years earlier, Brent's problems continued.

A case report on Brent that school officials completed that fall told the story of a student adrift and at risk of major problems. It said he had trouble "controlling verbal and physical aggression" and was frequently missing from school. He had missed ten days of school during the first six weeks of the year, and it got worse after that. He flunked all but one class during the first quarter. He would turn eighteen in seven months and was old enough to be a senior. But he had earned only a few high school credits. He had been prescribed medication intended to treat his bipolar disorder but had not been taking it at the time of his most recent arrest, because his father's insurance had lapsed. The report said Brent had declined a request that he take part in behavioral counseling. On the other hand, it said that when Brent wasn't getting in trouble or losing his temper, he was at times "polite and goal-oriented." Charles wasn't surprised to read that statement. "Of my four boys, he's my best helper," he said. "He jumps every time I ask for help."

But now Brent was in jail and writing letters to his dad almost daily, reaching out and making promises like so many people in his situation do. As we talked over coffee another day, just a week or so after the arrest, Charles showed me Brent's letters, which were sprinkled with misspellings but neatly written and thoughtful. "I'm not going to lose faith like the devil wants me to," Brent wrote. "Thank you dad for not giving up on me. I thought you'd give up on me like everybody else. Thank you for not. Just to let you know I'm not giving up on my dreams either." He complained about his cellmate, a three-hundred-pound man he said terrified him. But he also wrote of graduating and joining the army—as if his current stay at the county jail was just a blip in the way. "I miss y'all so much," he wrote. "Can't wait till I come home. I want a welcome home party. I'm talking about a big ass cookout. Love you dad. Can't wait till I come home."

Charles's eyes welled up as he read that part. He feared his son did not realize the magnitude of the charges against him and wondered if he understood that this was different from all of those past charges in juvenile court. He railed about his son being put in a cell with an adult twice as big as him but said that as a guy who worked odd jobs for a living, he just didn't have money to either bail him out or get him a decent lawyer. Brent had already missed Thanksgiving at home. He would probably miss Christmas as well, and more. "Brent's in a lot of trouble," Charles told me as we sat in a cheerful Starbucks two miles from Manual High School. "I hate it. But I understand."

15

★ ★ ★

COULD YOU IMAGINE
IF WE FILLED THE HOUSE?

By the time late fall arrived, I had fallen quite hard for Manual. I barely tolerated the idea of spending time on any column that wasn't related to the school. Often I would breeze into my office at the newspaper, fulfill my obligation by cranking out a quick political column for the Wednesday or Friday papers, and then head back to the school. I wrote dozens of columns unrelated to Manual during the school year, but most of them came and went without meaning much to me.

My Manual columns, though, meant something. The students and faculty had pulled me in. They had grabbed me with their stories and personalities and problems and dreams. I loved listening to students talk about their goals of graduating or going to college or just being happy. I enjoyed being pulled aside constantly by students and teachers who wanted to tell me the latest development in their life or class. I truly felt honored to be telling their stories, and I hoped they were helping. I even got a kick out of the occasional student or teacher who made clear they just didn't like my hanging around. Being a witness to scenes like the one that played out after the arrest of Brent Walls, and getting to know his family, gave me an ever-deeper understanding of the issues standing in the way of improvement at the schools in America's hard-hit cities and neighborhoods. It was all part of this amazing world I had tapped into.

The most surprising development, though, had been the reaction from readers. They weren't only reading the columns and sending me e-mails, as readers always did. They were also pulled into the story line in a unique way. They were moved, just as I was, by the people inside the school. With every column I received calls and messages from people who didn't only want to talk but also wanted to help. They were eager to mentor students or help out financially. They wanted to contribute to school programs and send messages of hope to the teenagers and adults in my columns. Throughout the year, several readers sent me money or checks and asked me to pass them along. Some offered to contribute to student college funds. Each time I wrote about a student, readers would send cards and gifts to the school.

One Sunday I profiled the school's sole calculus class. Eight students were enrolled in the class, but on most days a core group of six students actually showed up. There were three boys and three girls. I called them the Calculus Six. They were among the roughly 1.5 percent of their starting freshman class who had made it to the school's highest-level math class. Unlike the overcrowded class that followed it—the one for students who had failed algebra at least twice—most of the seats in the calculus period remained empty. But the Calculus Six were a dedicated bunch of kids who refused to let the vast array of problems within the school hold them down. The students were focused on college, the future, and avoiding any landmines that might get in the way. Their lives had not been easy. They came from the same poverty-filled neighborhoods as everyone else at the school, and they faced many of the same family issues. But they pushed on.

There was Jeff, who wore his crisp green ROTC uniform to class on Wednesdays and, between smart-alecky jokes, talked of his dream of going to West Point. He had stopped me in the hall one day to ask about the application process. I didn't know anything about it but pulled a few forms and tip sheets off of Indiana senator Richard Lugar's website one day and passed them along. I urged Jeff to go to a seminar being held downtown a couple of weeks later, but he said he didn't think he could get the day off work. Ultimately he decided that his grades, while good, probably weren't good enough.

There was Clark. He had watched his parents struggle financially for years and didn't want to spend his life that way. His dad had dropped out of high school, and Clark had been taken away from his mom by social services at one point. "I just want a better life for me and my kids," he told me.

There was Matt. He always had a book in front of him, a long science fiction or historical tome. He dealt with health problems and missed school quite often because of them. But he excelled nonetheless and planned to major in physics.

There was Tricia, the cheerleader and prom queen. Her family life was filled with drama, and she couldn't wait for the peace and quiet of her own college dorm room. Math had never come easy to her, but she, too, was driven to excel. She stressed about her grades, her mother, and her inability to get more girls to go out for cheerleading. But she was motivated by a deep desire to get out of the trouble-filled neighborhood that had been her home.

There was Susan. She didn't know her father, and her family faced constant financial difficulties. But she smiled and laughed frequently, loved math, and was battling for the title of class valedictorian.

And there was Andrea. She was Susan's best friend and main rival for vale-dictorian. Born in Serbia, she had landed in Indianapolis at the age of eight and was sent to a local elementary school without knowing basic English. She picked up the language quickly and soon took on the role of her parents' trans-lator. She had become an American citizen a few years earlier, along with her parents and siblings.

After I wrote about the students of the Calculus Six, a reader sent each of them gift cards to McDonald's. It was a small token. Just a few bucks each. But what a wonderful gesture, I thought. And it was unique to this series. I had been a journalist for more than seventeen years at that point, and I'd rarely seen readers reach out so directly to the people I wrote about. It became routine. Time and again, readers asked me what they could do to help the school, and I would pass along the numbers and addresses of worthy programs. What they wanted to do most, I realized, was to make sure the students knew there were people out there rooting for them.

I had started this project with the idea that it might be the last big thing I did as a newspaperman, because it came at a time when everyone around me seemed to believe newspapers were dying. My own paper, like so many others, had gone through a series of painful layoffs, pay cuts, and furloughs. I had helped good friends carry boxes out to their cars after their journalism careers were cut short by budget slashing. I had started to consider the idea that I would eventually have to find a new line of work. So the reaction to the series not only inspired me but also served as a reminder of the unique power of newspapers. The industry was suffering, but there still was no better way to connect with a community than the local paper. I had quickly realized that walking through the front doors of Manual was the smartest career move I'd ever made, if only because it had given me a jolt of career energy.

After I wrote about the lack of a yearbook program, a group of elderly Manual alumni got together and began a fund-raising campaign. Before long it had raised enough money to bring back the yearbook and provide a free copy to every graduate. The owner of a local print shop, meanwhile, called the school after reading that it no longer had a newspaper. He offered to print the paper for free. "I just thought it was sad," businessman Dave Wise said when I called. "They had no vehicle for students to tell the student population about what's going on in their school. How else do you build school spirit?" It took several months—and was the result of the work of just one student and one teacher—but by the end of the year the *Manual Booster* was back.

There was more. People contributed thousands of dollars to a holiday gift program for low-income families. A company donated materials to the arts department, and a mentoring organization affiliated with Manual was flooded with volunteers. One day a woman dropped off a new bicycle and asked administrators to give it to a student. One night theater teacher Lannae Stuteville went to another print shop to pick up posters for her play. "No charge," the owner told her. "We're Manual fans."

This was cool. Every week I heard another story about outreach from someone in the community. Or Grismore would show me a stack of letters sent to a student I had profiled. It was all just the latest sign that I'd struck gold. My columns were fine, I knew that. But something bigger had grabbed people—the emotion in the words of students, the details of their lives, the stories behind the teachers in every classroom, and the belief in the importance of turning around schools so that children could have the opportunities they deserve. The reaction came after columns about inspiring students and teachers and also after columns documenting the school's tragic problems. It was all a clear signal that the community cared deeply about the students and teachers who spent their days in schools like Manual—schools that are so often the subject of political and social debates but that many people doing the debating rarely spend time in.

It was uplifting. In an era filled with angry bloggers, divisive political rhetoric, and nasty anonymous comments at the end of nearly every online newspaper story, it's easy to think the average person is an unfeeling jerk. But I had come to believe that the response from readers to this series, and the actions they were taking, was much more characteristic of the typical person in any community.

I was enjoying the reaction. For years I had braced myself before checking my voice mail or e-mail messages, because I knew whatever political column I had written would bring out angry partisans. I didn't mind that. I actually enjoyed the give-and-take. But hearing from readers about Manual was a treat. As the weather turned cold, though, I found myself increasingly worried that I wasn't taking full advantage of the emotional connection that readers had to the school. Essentially the outpouring toward Manual happened organically. That was beautiful, I thought. It just wasn't enough.

As a journalist, I had been taught to stay on the sidelines, to write about issues and not get involved in them. That had changed somewhat during my years as a columnist, as my job was now to share my opinion and advocate for one position or another. Still, I remained an outsider, someone looking in and commenting on the news. This time, however, I decided to push things further than I ever had before. I wanted to find a way to answer all of the requests from readers who had called or written to ask how they could help. I started small, simply including a list next to my columns of places and programs to which readers could contribute. It worked. The checks and offers to help arrived in even bigger numbers. But I still wanted something more, something bigger, and something lasting.

One day a reader wrote to talk about the help Manual needed. "I would really like to see your columns spark a community project," she said. That got me thinking. What could I propose? What would send a message that the community deeply cared about the students at Manual and the other schools like it? What could I do to harness the energy to help that so obviously existed?

One chilly afternoon shortly before Thanksgiving, I walked out of my office at the *Indianapolis Star*, got in my car, and began the six-mile drive north to my house. As usual, I was thinking about Manual. Then it hit me. The idea struck so strong that I pulled over to the side of the road and let the afternoon rush-hour traffic zoom past. I pulled out a pen and scrap piece of paper from a cubby under my car stereo and jotted down the idea. I smiled as I scribbled. "I've heard a lot from people who want to help Manual High School," I wrote. "Well, here's an idea. Just come to the school on Dec. 15. Just sit in the auditorium for an hour and listen as a wonderful teacher leads a hard-working group of students through the annual holiday concert."

I had spent many hours in Spencer Lloyd's choir class, and I'd been preparing to write a column about him and his students. The class had remained my oasis from the madness that so often overtook the school, the place where I routinely found hope, and I wanted readers to know about it. I had long ago decided to mention the annual holiday concert—the one that generally attracted tiny crowds—in the hope that a few more people might turn out. But now I had a different idea. Why not turn the concert into a challenge? Why not encourage the readers of my series to pack the house on the night of the concert, sending a direct message to the school and its students that people care about them and that they care deeply? Why not invite people to step inside a school that for years most of us had forgotten?

I continued to think about the idea as I completed my drive home. I'm vulnerable to bad ideas, so I wondered if this was one of them. I thought about the absurdity of it. I wondered how hard it would be to persuade people—even those who do care deeply—to take a midweek evening out of their lives to go to a school many would need MapQuest directions to find. I considered the possibility that the idea would flop, embarrassing me and my paper and, more importantly, disappointing a bunch of kids who didn't need any more disappointments.

Then I mentioned it to my wife. She gave it a thumbs-up. A few days later my boss did the same. And by the time I mentioned the idea to Spencer Lloyd just after Thanksgiving break, I had officially decided to give it a try. He bought in immediately. "Could you imagine if we filled the house?" he said with his characteristic optimism.

"That would be something," I said.

16

★ ★ ★

IT FEELS LIKE I'M A SOMEBODY.

The choir was roaring by early December. From the start of each class until the end, it was a wall of music. The students were filled with more confidence than ever before, and they spent each class eager to impress Spencer Lloyd, who had spent so many classes working with them and so much time after class talking them through their problems. They noticed things about him that were different, such as when he frantically labored through classes one week while suffering from a nasty cold, or when he let a student who wasn't in his class paint a huge mural on the back wall of the class, or when he told them he loved them.

The holiday concert was approaching, and Lloyd had built an ambitious set list with the help of Michael Weber, the young band teacher with whom he'd spent many hours talking about the big things they wanted to accomplish. They had a dream of turning Manual into a school known for its top-notch music program. They thought a decent turnout at the holiday concert could help lead them in that direction. They had seen the demise of the football program and wanted to show the school district that their programs were on the way up. They believed that students desperately needed to feel pride in their school and that such a feeling would make them more likely and eager to come to school and succeed. The Manual music program could provide that inspiration, they insisted.

The students were getting excited about the possibility of a large crowd. They had grown accustomed to having more singers on stage than listeners in their audience. But now they were peppering Lloyd with questions. "Do you think strangers will really come out to see us?" "Do you think the auditorium will be filled?" Lloyd was excited, too, and said such a turnout was indeed possible. But he tried to hold down their expectations. "Even if we get a few hundred people," he told his students one day, "that'll be a lot of people listening to us, more than ever before." Still, the students were hoping for more.

I spent many of my days in early December in Lloyd's class working on the upcoming column. They were some of my favorite times of the school year, as I often just sat back and watched a whirlwind of teaching and singing and camaraderie. The singers still struggled at times—lacking years of training and, in some cases, confidence. But this was special. When I wrote the column, I told readers that Lloyd was an example of exactly the type of teacher we all say we want in our struggling schools. He was optimistic, energetic, and focused on excellence. He wanted to change the culture of a school and a neighborhood where students were rarely pushed to excel. He wanted to bring back some of what Manual once was known for. So why not support his program?

I wrote about students like a fourteen-year-old girl with a golden voice and sad home life, one that involved visits by Child Protective Services. She told me she would have dropped out of school by then, like so many other freshmen, if not for her choir class. "It's where I feel comfortable," she said. I wrote about Luis, the junior who had turned from shy to outgoing in just a few months of working with Lloyd. "This class really does help build self-confidence," he said. "It gives a whole new meaning to school."

I didn't want to exaggerate. After all, Lloyd continued to struggle with the same problems that were found elsewhere in the building. In a school where families were often forced to move from one neighborhood to another when the rent came due, students sometimes disappeared from his class. And some of his students got in trouble in other classes, leading to suspensions that cost them valuable in-class practice time. Others got in trouble outside of school. Some didn't show up for practices. Many of the students were new to organized music. But he fought through every challenge placed in his path.

One day Lloyd sat on a stool in front of his class and talked to the students about the upcoming concert. To groans, he told them that any visible piercings that weren't in their ears would not be allowed when they were on stage. He told them that they'd better be in class the day of the concert if they wanted to perform. He told them to practice at home in the days leading up to the show. He told them to respect the choir department and take this concert seriously. He told them he wanted them to fulfill their potential. "I don't apologize for sounding like your mom and dad," he said. "Remember, nothing in life worth doing is easy."

"My mom says that," one student said.

"Well, your mom is right."

My column ran on December 13, just two days before the concert. I didn't sell it too hard, because I didn't feel I had to. The choir department sold itself, so most of the column was about the classes I had observed, the teacher in charge of the program, and the students who were participating. It was perhaps the easiest column I've ever written, because Lloyd and his students had provided me with such wonderful material. Only the fifth paragraph of the column, and then the final one, even mentioned the concert. "Here's a challenge, and a request," I wrote. "Let's send a message of support to a dedicated teacher and a group of hard-working students. Let's do it by spending an hour listening to them sing 'Silent Night' and 'Jingle Bells' and other holiday songs." The concert was free, I said, though donations would be welcome, and I insisted it would be worth the investment of the readers' time. I ended the column by noting that in a school too often known for failure, Lloyd's program was a success. In a district that was cutting programs, this one was growing. In a place where hope was often hard to find, it was on display daily in this class.

The season and my fondness for the class were probably getting to me by the time I wrote my final paragraph. "With Lloyd's drive and enthusiasm it's easy to imagine Manual in future years earning a reputation for its choir program," I wrote. "You can help by turning out Tuesday night to listen to a group of students and a teacher who deserve your cheers." The column ran on the front page that Sunday, under the headline: "Do You Hear What I Hear? Manual Hits a High Note." And for the next two days I waited, wondering whether anyone would show up.

A secretary sitting at the front desk gave me a disinterested shrug on the morning of the concert when I asked if anybody had called to ask about it.

Principal Grismore said he had no idea what to expect that night. Neither did I. A few readers had e-mailed to say they were planning to attend, but I had also heard from others who had said that as much as they wanted to come, they just couldn't. They had family obligations, a holiday party, or a work commitment. I was worried there would be many more people just like them, people with good intentions but busy lives. I understood. I had made an unusual request in the Sunday paper, asking people to come to a school with which many had no affiliation. Even many of the teachers who worked at Manual said they wouldn't be able to attend.

In the choir classroom, Spencer Lloyd was preparing to take a handful of his best performers to a restaurant twenty miles away so that they could perform in front of a reunion of Manual alums from the 1950s. He said he'd woken up with a feeling that the turnout would be strong. His kids deserved it, he said. There was no doubt about that.

Melissa, a freshman with many family problems, stood in the middle of the classroom and told me she had practiced her "Santa Baby" solo dozens of times. But she was still nervous. She was Lloyd's most talented singer. It wasn't even close. He had told her repeatedly that she would have no trouble getting a music scholarship to college if only she could get her other grades up. But that message was a difficult one to sell. He knew her life was filled with problems and that her family moved so often she might not even be at Manual for much longer. Regardless, this would be a good night for her and the other students, he predicted.

I hung around the school for a while wondering what would happen that night. As I walked the halls a bit later, it struck me that I had asked readers to come to the school just a week after writing a column about Brent Walls, the drug-dealing student who had been arrested for having a loaded handgun on the premises. Would some readers be scared away? Perhaps. But at least I hadn't written about the four students arrested for other crimes in the past week.

The first semester would officially conclude at the end of the week, and as I walked the halls I thought about the many hours I had spent at the school and the inspiring people I'd met. I had still not fulfilled my goal, perhaps the unattainable goal, of telling the full story of the school. There were so many more people and classes I wanted to write about. There were a lot of stories inside this building. Hopefully, I thought, this night would provide another.

Back at my office an hour later, my colleague Beth Murphy, a copyeditor whose office was next to mine, could tell I was nervous about the idea of a flop and the prospect of having to look at the faces of a group of disappointed high school students. "People are going to be there," she assured me, promising to attend with her family. "Don't worry about it."

But I wasn't sure. And I could only laugh when another colleague walked up to me and pointed to the fifteen front-page columns I had written about the school in the previous four months. "If nobody turns out tonight," she said, "that will be a sign that newspapers really are dead." Thanks for the pressure, I thought. But I understood her point. Months of front-page copy in the local newspaper had generated a flood of interest and an outpouring of calls and letters from people eager to help. The voices of the teenagers at Manual High School had told touching stories. It was impossible to not care about them. Their pictures had run in the paper week after week. If all of that couldn't motivate people to come out and listen to an hour of music—in the middle of the holiday season, no less—that probably would indeed be another sign of my industry's waning influence.

Then I told myself to stop being such a drama queen. This was a holiday concert, not a civil rights march in 1963. The show would go on, the students would survive, and the newspaper would continue publishing—whether there were a meager one hundred people in the audience that evening or a standing-room-only crowd ten times that large.

About an hour before the concert, I decided I had spent enough time sitting around. I got up, grabbed my keys, and headed over to Manual. It was thirty degrees, and the sky was already dark as I drove from downtown to the near south side, passing the same graffiti-covered buildings and old struggling neighborhoods that I'd driven by on that first morning of the school year four months earlier. I played my well-worn Elvis Presley Christmas CD for good luck as I drove. The trip to Manual required me to drive past the school before doing a U-turn about three-tenths of a mile down Madison Avenue and returning to the school from the south. It was a little after 5:30 PM when I first drove past the three-story brick building. I slowed and looked beyond the grassy median separating Madison's north and south lanes for any signs of life on the school grounds. There wasn't much—just a few cars in the parking lot, cars that probably belonged to the teachers, administrators, and students who had official roles in the concert. There was no sign advertising the show.

Instead of making my usual U-turn, I drove a few blocks more and pulled into a gas station, filling my Honda's tank even though it was nowhere near empty. The concert wasn't until 6:30 PM, and I just wanted to kill a few more minutes. But then it was time to go. I nervously headed over and pulled into a space directly in front of the school at a quarter till six. I noticed a few cars pulling into the back parking lot as I walked toward one of the school's side entrances. Once inside I was relieved to see that a few dozen people had already arrived. That was a good sign. At least the evening wouldn't be a total flop.

Inside the school the last of Lloyd's choir students were trickling into the choir room, where they would stay until it was time to go on stage. The choir director had enough trouble getting students to his shows on time. He wasn't going to lose any of them once they arrived. "Okay, this is going to be awesome," he told the fifty students who would be performing. "We need to do our best no matter what happens. If we go out there and it's full, don't be nervous. Just sing like there are five people in the audience. No matter how big or small," he said, "enjoy the moment."

I had been in the school for only a few minutes before everything changed. The trickle of visitors turned into a flood in an instant. By six o'clock Manual High School was a madhouse. The ROTC students who had been assigned to politely open the back door for visitors didn't get a chance to shut it for nearly an hour. Each time a group of people walked through the doors, more would arrive. The long hallway leading to the auditorium was packed like a New York City subway car. People were smiling and laughing and shaking their heads in disbelief at the size of the crowd. Some cried. Manual alumni from decades past were shouting "Go Redskins" and other encouragements to their school. "I'm coming home," one middle-aged woman said as she stood with hundreds of others in the hallway. "Redskins grad, nineteen eighty-five!" a man said, pumping his fist in the air.

A group of welding students sat at a table selling metal Christmas tree ornaments made for the occasion. The fifty ornaments the students had thought would be more than enough sold out in minutes, mementos of the night. Visitors also rushed to buy the holiday cards a group of students with learning disabilities had made.

Shortly after six, every seat in the nine-hundred-seat auditorium was filled. But people continued to file in, grabbing any patch of floor they could find. They stood in the aisles and in the back. Younger people who had gotten seats eagerly gave them up to senior citizens. The room was a roar of conversation. And the crowd kept coming.

Spencer Lloyd remained huddled with his students in his classroom, which was separated from the auditorium by the hallway. The noise from the hundreds of people standing in the hall spilled into the room. His students raced around the room, filled with adrenaline. "The kids," he told me later, "were freaking out." Some of the students had joined the choir only recently, so this would be their first concert. Others had sung before small crowds at previous shows. But none had seen anything like this.

Lloyd was too curious to sit in his office, so he cracked open the door and slipped out for a few seconds, telling his students to stay inside. He immediately met a wall of people. The crowd pointed, asking if the man before them was Spencer Lloyd, the great teacher they had read about. He felt like a celebrity. Lloyd waved and ducked back into the classroom to settle his students.

Nearby, Principal Grismore was fighting through the crowd to get to the classroom. He had just cried as he talked to his wife on the phone about the massive audience that had come out to support his school. Finally arriving at Lloyd's room, Grismore snuck in, and he and Lloyd shook their heads in amazement at the turnout. "Where are we going to put all these people?" Lloyd asked.

Grismore laughed and announced that the choir and band would have to put on two shows that night, one at 6:30 and another ninety minutes later. "There are too many people," he said, "and we can't just send them home. The people have spoken."

"It's full out there," Lloyd told his students, who stared at him, stunned. "Like really, really full."

I stood near the main doors of the auditorium, stunned myself, as I watched people enjoying the moment. Many spotted me and told my editor and me that this night was a sign that newspapers still mattered. Many of them wouldn't be able to get inside the auditorium, but they stood ten people deep outside its doors, enjoying the chance to hear echoes of the concert and, more importantly, to be a part of a great moment.

A group of students from another district school had come to the concert holding a large handwritten sign reading "Good Luck Manual." A choir director from nearby Carmel High School, in the state's wealthiest county, fought through the crowd to give her card to a school administrator, nearly begging the administrator to let her school help Manual's choir with anything it needed. It was the start of a partnership that would grow throughout the rest of the school year.

There was no charge to the concert, but a pair of donation boxes had been placed on a table by the doors leading into the auditorium. As two vice principals watched, visitors frantically stuffed money into the boxes. Some put in singles, some put in tens. "Some people are putting in hundred-dollar bills," an amazed vice principal Lauren Franklin said. The boxes filled up so quickly that on four different occasions within less than an hour the administrators had to run to a nearby school office to dump the money on the floor. Then they returned to the auditorium so that more money could be stuffed in. At the end of the night, the choir program had collected ten thousand dollars, roughly ten times its annual budget. The contributions continued in the coming days as people who didn't attend the concert sent cash and checks. By the end of the month, the concert had grossed about twenty thousand dollars.

But this night wasn't about the money. It was about the electric mood inside a school that on so many days felt like a factory. On this night it felt like nothing of the sort. "This is like a Christmas movie," said Cindy Shaw, a special education coordinator. "I'm trying to hold back tears here," said Patrick Viles, a parent liaison at the school.

I walked down the halls as the hour of the concert approached, wading through the crowd and noticing that people were still arriving. I began talking to the visitors and realized that many had come from far outside the school district. They came from the edges of the county and the surrounding suburbs and, I would later learn, even from cities and towns more than a hundred miles away. "How could you not want to help these kids?" said Joanne Gallagher, a woman who had driven thirty miles from a local suburb to attend the concert. "I hope this is sending out a message that we need to reach out to other communities and not just our own. This school has touched my heart."

And then I got a text message. It was from Danese Kenon, the photographer I often worked with on projects. We'd spent many hours wandering the halls of Manual over the months, and I'd been wondering why she had not yet arrived. Her excuse for being late hit me hard. "I'm stuck in traffic!" she wrote. I stared at the text message for a few seconds and then slowly walked from the auditorium to a set of side school doors. I opened them and felt a blast of cold air, and then I saw lights—headlights for as far as I could see. They lit up the night sky from the north and the south on Madison Avenue. Cars were stuck in a sea of holiday gridlock on what would have normally been a quiet Tuesday evening on the city street.

I watched the traffic for a minute, but it wasn't going anywhere. The school's parking lot had long ago filled up. Now people were scouring the surrounding blocks, looking for an empty patch of curb where they could park. Concertgoers later told me they'd never seen such a polite traffic jam. Drivers calmly waved in other cars as they approached congested neighborhood intersections. Many people walked several blocks in the cold and dark evening after finally finding a parking spot. Others told me they sat in traffic for so long that they missed the concert and went home, unaware that a second show had been added. I told them that they were still a part of a beautiful night and that the traffic jam was a symbol of how much people cared about these kids.

I walked back inside. The first concert would be starting soon, and nearly every square foot of space in the auditorium was taken. Many people, including the chief justice of the state supreme court, sat on the aisle floor, happily talking with one another but also making me wonder if the fire marshal might stop by. He didn't. But police had received numerous calls about the strange madness in front of Manual, and at one point a confused police officer came into the building to investigate. He scolded school officials and ordered them to let police know the next time they were expecting so many people. They hadn't expected this, they insisted.

Back in the classroom, I talked with a few nervous students about the upcoming show. "It feels like I'm a somebody," a freshman named Meagan said as she looked at the crowd through the classroom door. "People always tell us we're nobody. Well, no, I'm not."

"People really want to see us and hear us," said Kristen, another freshman. "This is so much more exciting, because we've been working hard. We want people to see how far we've come."

The choir students left their classroom just before 6:30, led by their teacher. As they made the short walk from their room to the auditorium, the hallway crowd parted and began applauding and cheering. A few seconds later the stars of the show were staring at roughly twelve hundred people in an overcrowded auditorium. It was, Grismore estimated, probably the first full house for any Manual performance in at least twenty years. "I think this community was looking for a way to support these kids," he said. He was right.

On stage Lloyd walked to the microphone and announced that there would be a second show for those who couldn't get into the first. The crowd laughed, not realizing at first that there were hundreds of people outside the room, smiling and hugging and patiently waiting for the second show. Some of those waiting relaxed in the school's smaller auditorium. Some left for dinner, promising to return. Others walked over to the gymnasium to watch a girls basketball game.

I stood with my wife on the side of the stage as the students sang. As they did, I noticed for the first time that they didn't have matching outfits. Some wore polo shirts. Some wore their school uniforms. One boy wore his dad's old union T-shirt. On a budget of about one thousand dollars, matching outfits were something the program just couldn't afford, and the school knew it couldn't ask the students' families to spend money they didn't have on choir outfits. On that holiday season evening, the mismatched students made for a beautiful sight and sent a message to those sitting in the crowd.

This night wasn't about the way the students dressed. In a school with a music program that was near death two years earlier, it wasn't even about pitch-perfect performances. It was about effort. And community. And high expectations. And finding a way to make schools like Manual seem special. Still, thanks to the money being collected in the hallway, the choir department's budget problem was being addressed. The students would have matching outfits before their next concert.

That night I watched and listened as a group of students fought through their nerves and received a series of standing ovations. As the crowd listened in rapt attention, the choir sang a haunting version of "Still, Still, Still" and, with the band, a rollicking "Santa Claus Is Coming to Town." Melissa shook as she beautifully and nervously sang "Santa Baby." As fake snow fell on the stage, the choir concluded the show an hour after it began with a jazzy "We Wish You a Merry Christmas." At the end, Lloyd and band director Michael Weber bowed, along with their students, and the crowd stood and applauded for several minutes. Many in the audience left the show wiping their eyes, promising to return for the next year's holiday show. "There hasn't been this much spirit at Manual in a long time," Weber said.

An hour later I was back in my office trying to capture the mood of the evening for a column that would run in the next morning's paper. My e-mail in-box was already being flooded with the first of hundreds of messages I would receive in the following days. Some told me of the beauty of being stuck in traffic for such a good cause. Others said they couldn't remember such an emotional night. Some said they had brought their children from the suburbs and happily watched them appreciate being a part of the experience. They asked me to tell Lloyd and his students how wonderful they had sounded. "I will remember this evening for a long time," a reader named Mary said. "Christmas came a little early this year," wrote another named Kevin. "The spirit and energy in the auditorium," wrote yet another reader, "felt like the movie 'Miracle on 34th Street.' And as I drove home, it dawned on me that we had experienced the 'Miracle on Madison Avenue.'"

I felt like I had too. I had arrived at Manual four months earlier without a plan, or, really, even a clue. I had come to the school because I wanted to do something different from what I'd been doing. I wanted to learn and perhaps write some columns with impact. Along the way I had met amazing people and witnessed unforgettable incidents and events. I had learned a lot about the challenges facing struggling urban schools, and I'd been given a much-needed reminder of just why I loved working for a newspaper. And now I'd had an evening unlike any other I had ever experienced.

But that evening was about much more than a wonderful feel-good holiday moment. It showed just how deeply so many people cared about students at schools like Manual. It was a reminder that students at schools like this one don't often get the experiences that students in other schools not far away consider routine. It provided indisputable evidence that Manual High School and so many schools like it don't need to be forgotten. It was a message to school districts everywhere: there is tremendous energy in communities surrounding struggling schools, and that energy must be harnessed.

The evening had proven Lloyd right. In a building where standards are often far too low, the young teacher had told his students on the first day of school that they would strive for something great. He told them it was possible to excel and that he would demand they do so. On this night they had. And so had their community.

17

★ ★ ★

I USED TO BE BAD.

Students and teachers returned from the two-week holiday break and quickly got to work on the second half of the year. Police resumed patrolling the halls, and administrators continued to prepare for the upcoming transfer of power at the top of the school's leadership chain. In every way, Manual was back to being Manual. Still, the student population was diminished significantly from the first semester, as more than 10 percent of the school's original roster of students had stopped coming or been kicked out. Many classes were now smaller, a clear sign of the city's dropout epidemic. The only silver lining was that this had rid the school of some of its biggest troublemakers. That's not much of a silver lining. Many of those kids were now out of school without a diploma, approaching adulthood with few options and setting examples for their younger siblings and their own children. At Manual the missing kids were like ghosts.

I walked into the building early on the first day of the new semester looking for new column ideas. I wanted to meet new students and teachers, to learn about other education issues and find columns that were different from the ones

I had already written. Nonetheless, it was nice to see the old faces. Sergeant Barrow and the dean. Ms. H. and Ms. Winslow. And students such as Jammyra and Tricia, who were now only a few months away from graduating and heading off to college. Jammyra smiled and gave a loud customary huff, to underscore how busy she was, when I asked her how things were going one morning. She talked about the need to refocus on school. Her grades were still near the top at Manual, but she'd slipped a bit in the fall because of the many extracurricular activities she was involved in. She said she was now fighting a nasty case of senioritis. "I'll fight through it," she promised, and she did.

After a two-week break, it was good to be back. But a part of me had spent the holiday break questioning whether I should return. Although I had initially come to the school without a plan, by December I had decided to spend the entire year at the school. But after the choir concert, I had begun to question whether I'd unwittingly stumbled onto the perfect ending to the series. It seemed hard to imagine anything in the second half of the year that could top that spectacular evening.

Despite my concerns, I knew I couldn't walk away from Manual this early. The story wasn't over. And although the concert might have provided a wonderful fairy-tale ending to my series, the issues facing schools like Manual are far too complex to be solved by one spectacular evening. Leaving early, I decided, would be negligent. Plus, I enjoyed hanging out in the school too much. I had grown used to the drama of the building and the daily surprises. I wanted to see how the year ended. Who knows, I thought, perhaps the ending of the second half of the year would be just as amazing as the first. As hard as it was to believe at the time, that thought would ultimately and amazingly prove true.

The biggest development in the new year had to do with Manual's biggest problem: the profound academic failure that for years had devastated the school. The problem was on display in many ways. There was the low enrollment in advanced courses and the overflowing student population in remedial classes. There were the fundamental reading problems that gripped many students, the standardized test scores that were less than half the state average, and, of course, the devastatingly low graduation rate. During the holiday break, administrators had spent much of their time responding to a new one-size-fits-all district directive that mandated the addition of study hall periods to the school's curriculum. The classes would be required for any student who failed two or more of four core subjects: math, science, English, and social studies.

Of the roughly 840 students who remained at Manual, more than a third had failed at least two core classes during the first semester. Dozens more failed one, and many had also failed electives. But the district couldn't afford to be too ambitious and had drawn the line at those who had failed at least half of their core classes. That much failure in a semester was enough, administrators said, to knock a student wildly off course from graduation. It demanded a response.

The idea that a third of the students had performed so poorly wasn't surprising and seemed to suggest the need for a more radical and fundamental restructuring of how Manual—and schools like it nationwide—did business. After four months at the school, I had become a strong believer in the need for sweeping changes to the way failing schools are run. In a more perfect world, Manual would have implemented intensive tutoring for a majority of students, or it would have filled most of its classes with extra academic assistants charged with both keeping the rooms under control and helping struggling students. The school's leaders could have demanded that parents come in to discuss their children's problems. They could have tried to harness the wide public support the school had won and transform it into a community-wide effort to help its students, aware that many of them were deeply at risk and in need of constant, intensive attention—attention that very well might increase the cost of running the school. The bloated central office could have cut spending and pushed more money into Manual's classrooms. The burned-out or otherwise underperforming members of the teaching staff could have been dismissed and replaced with energetic teachers filled with passion for their profession.

Instead of any of that, the district bosses settled for study hall periods for its most at-risk students. Hundreds of students would now have forty-five minutes a day to work on their homework.

"The numbers could have been worse," Principal Grismore said as we sat in his office one day early in the semester. He was right. But that wasn't saying much. Although the numbers could have been worse, they were downright depressing. One in three Manual students were doing so poorly that they were in jeopardy of not graduating. The problem was worst among sophomores. A whopping 44 percent had failed at least half of their core classes, raising scary questions about how many would even stick around for their junior year. And this didn't include the many students who had started the year on Manual's roster but had since stopped coming.

As Grismore continued to talk about the new study hall program that January morning, it became clear to me that the decision to move him out of the school was a good one. He was a wonderful guy and had dedicated his life to struggling schools. He cared about the students in his building and understood the challenges facing them. But he seemed overwhelmed by the scope of the problems and had succumbed to the vast and suffocating district bureaucracy. He was focused on putting a good face on the problems at his school. He needed to be able to file reports to the district that showed meager improvements or that excused the school's failures. He appeared to be out of big ideas or big ambitions. The system wasn't going to save Manual High School. And after thirty-six years, Grismore was a product of the system.

As he talked about the problem of student failure, for instance, Grismore criticized the teachers in his school for demanding too much of their students—that, in a school where the expectations and the demands were already low. "One of the main complaints teachers have is that so many students just don't do the homework," he said. "Well, many of these kids don't have a place at home where they can do homework, or they don't have time to do it. We have to have more conversations about kids being graded for their mastery of the subject matter and not so much for busywork. If a kid can master the skills without having to do the minutiae, they should get the grade."

By "minutiae" Grismore meant homework. He was calling on his teachers to diminish the importance placed on homework simply because so few students actually completed their assignments. Instead of striving for excellence, Grismore was pushing for something even less than mediocrity. Instead of teaching students about deadlines and the need to follow instructions, Grismore was arguing against that, in the hope it would lead to fewer Fs. Instead of preparing them for the demands of the work world or college, he was looking for a way to boost his numbers. But his argument was flawed for many reasons. First, it sent an awful message to students, telling them they shouldn't be expected to follow instructions and do the work required of them. Second, it sent the wrong message to those teachers who wanted to instill in students a belief that they were capable of succeeding. Third, it ignored the fact that the vast majority of Manual students failed the standardized tests that gauge their mastery of the material.

Even if teachers forgave every missed homework assignment, the epidemic of student failure would remain. Many students faced heartbreakingly difficult home lives, but the school's problems weren't limited to the inability of some to do their homework. The most basic problem the school faced was the apathy that got in its way at every turn and the unwillingness of many to demand higher standards.

Math teacher Connie Johnston outlined the problem perfectly as we sat in her classroom one day, saying she and other teachers felt tremendous pressure to pass students they knew didn't deserve a passing grade. As she ate her lunch, Johnston grabbed a stack of papers and showed me the raw data from her first-quarter grades. In class after class, students had received scores of 30 and 40 and 50 percent—far short of the mark needed to earn a D minus. If those grades were left un-curved, she told me, the vast majority of her students would receive Fs. Her students arrived at high school far behind in their math skills, and most never caught up. Even her small group of calculus students—the ones who tried so hard, the ones who were so inspiring to watch—struggled because of years of apathetic teachers and disruptive classrooms. The best calculus student, she said, would receive only a C if the grades were not dramatically adjusted. The results would be far worse in her other classes. "We really curve our grades, because if we don't pass enough kids, we're written up for it," she said. "We're not allowed to hold students accountable for not doing the work." A student with a raw score of 50 percent could receive a passing grade, she complained. "It's just not right." It wasn't. And it soon became clear that none of these problems would be solved by the addition of a few study hall classes.

The morning bell rang on a Tuesday three weeks into the semester. History teacher Sean Marcum stood outside of a first-floor classroom welcoming students to their study hall period. "Make sure you're getting out books or something to work on," he said. "If you need help, we're here." Two other teachers assigned to the class sat at tables in the back of the room, looking down at papers and not saying anything. They barely moved all during class. A girl wandered in a few minutes after the class began. A boy followed two minutes later. A few students studied; the rest tried to sleep or talk, something Marcum wouldn't allow. "Angel, you need to get to work on something," he told one student. "I don't have anything," she said. "Then you need to go to the back of the room and pick out a book." She followed the instructions, walking to the back of the room, grabbing a book at random, and then returning to her desk. The book was never opened. Manual's problem of student attendance was magnified in the study hall classes. During the first weeks of school, it was routine for a class to have only a fraction of its students in attendance. A few days day after Marcum talked to Angel, only four of twenty-seven students showed up.

Something had to be done to address the sweeping scope of student failure. But it was a Band-Aid approach to a deeper problem. Sitting the worst students in a quiet room for forty-five minutes wouldn't solve serious problems. It was a baby step in a district that needed bold moves but seemed incapable of thinking big. Months later, when I interviewed U.S. Secretary of Education Arne Duncan, he explained the problem well. Improving chronically underperforming schools, he said, "takes a radical measure. There is not one way to do it. This isn't one size fits all. But what doesn't work is incremental change around the margins. Think of it in medical terms. You either have a small cold or a serious illness, and the remedy you choose to deal with it has to fit the problem. Our cures have been woefully insufficient to fight the real issue."

These students at Manual needed something more radical than a quiet room and a free period. They needed something more than old-school thinking and the district's tired and halfhearted approaches to huge problems. Many of the teachers understood that. Marcum was among the large group of teachers who often complained to me about the school leadership's lack of urgency. "But don't get me wrong," he said. "You have to try something. Somewhere along the way, they've lost that value of education, that understanding of what an education can do for them. I don't know how we can tap into that problem. But we have to. We're losing too many of them."

Earlier that month Marcum had learned he was losing one of his favorite students, a girl who had been doing pretty well in his history class. She had turned eighteen, and her parents announced it was time for her to move out. They were tired of supporting her. She dropped out to get a job. The school district's problems ran deep. Its solutions only scratched the surface.

Fortunately there were many students who didn't drop out. The halls were filled in January with seniors who had made it to their final semester and had no intention of quitting. There were younger students who were just as motivated. One of the school's most likable students was a junior named Johnny Willis. Early in his time at Manual, he was what Grismore called "hell on wheels," a constant source of trouble and headaches for teachers. But somehow he had begun to turn things around during his sophomore year, and by the time he was a junior he was making the dean's list. Johnny constantly flashed his huge smile, even after taking a long city bus ride to and from school each day because he'd had to move in with his grandmother on another side of town. "I'm getting out of the ghetto," he told me one day, shaking my hand and flashing that huge smile. "I'm going to make something of myself." His vow was easy to believe. He was now one of Manual's most determined students.

By January some of the school's other most determined students could be found on the second floor in room 229. The room was filled with students who hoped to graduate at the end of the school year but knew that was not guaranteed. They had fallen behind earlier in their high school careers and in many cases had gotten in trouble repeatedly. But now they were in the Opportunity Center, which was aimed at giving students another chance. The program, in its third year, was led by two veteran teachers and based on the concept that one size indeed does not fit all students. Students worked mostly on computers, progressing through classes at their own pace.

Rachel Tucker spent her senior year in the Opportunity Center, one of about thirty students there. I had met Rachel on the first day of the school year, five months earlier, as she sat with two friends on the gymnasium bleachers. She was among the many Manual students who were eager to do what their parents and older siblings had not: graduate from high school. It was a big challenge for Rachel. She had fallen behind in middle school and skipped many days of school during her first two years of high school. By the time she decided to get serious, she was what administrators called "over-age and under-credit" and in serious jeopardy of not graduating. She thrived in the Opportunity Center, though, because of the freedom it offered. The program allowed students to work without the distractions that come with traditional classrooms. That traditional route through high school, the one Rachel took during her first years at Manual, had not worked for her. "When I first got here, I thought school was a joke," she said. "I didn't take it seriously. That was my problem. I've always been able to get good grades if I wanted. But I just wasn't able to shut my mouth, and I skipped the classes I didn't like." Then there was the fighting. "I used to be bad," she said, before smiling. "But not anymore." One day early in the second semester, I asked Rachel if she thought she would graduate in May, as she hoped to. It was a hard question to answer, she said. But she was going to try. She wasn't alone.

As the new semester began, a boy named Tommy was struggling but refused to give up on school. I had met the nineteen-year-old early in the school year when I sat in on Connie Johnston's class for students who had repeatedly flunked algebra. He had spotted me in the back of the classroom and waved me over, shaking my hand. "I'm a father," he said in a whisper. I congratulated him and asked how old his child was. "Well, I'm a father-to-be," he said, adding that his child was due in March. He smiled, as he almost always did. With his hefty frame, goatee, and tattoos, Tommy looked much older than nineteen. He actually looked like the guy you'd expect to knock on your door after calling the plumbing company for help with a leaky faucet. But as old as he was, his focus at the start of the second semester was not graduation. He had accumulated few credits in his years at Manual and had a learning disability. He didn't read well, and a diploma at the time seemed out of reach. But he kept coming to school because of a welding class taught by Jason Wiley, a forty-year-old union welder who'd moved into teaching a few years earlier. His was the type of class that Manual—originally titled Emmerich Manual Training High School—was once known for. These days welding was the sole remaining part of that blue-collar vocational tradition. It was a perfect fit for some students. "Without this program I would have probably dropped out by now," Tommy said as we talked in the welding room one day. "I have trouble paying attention in most classes. But in here I can. I don't understand books that well. But when it's hands-on stuff, I can learn."

For some like Tommy, students with learning disabilities for whom school had always been a struggle, classes like welding offered a way up. His goal was to leave school with a certificate that would earn him an entry-level welding job, something he could do to support his family. He said he liked welding because when you make mistakes, it allows you the opportunity to go back and fix them. It seemed as if he was talking about his own life when he said that. He had failed repeatedly in school. Perhaps welding offered a chance to make up for that. "Ever since I got into welding, it made me love school," he said. "That's what they need more of here. Some people ain't no good at books. This is giving us hope to think we're going to be able to do something."

He was only nineteen but said he knew that without a welding certificate his most likely job would be in a fast-food restaurant. That was a depressing thought for a father-to-be who didn't want to follow in the path of the many friends he had known who had been unable or unwilling to take care of their children. He promised not to follow that path. "I was raised right," he said. "My parents raised me to know if you make a situation for yourself, you stand by it and take care of it. I was raised old-school." He told me about his girlfriend, who was a junior at another Indianapolis high school. He went to every one of her doctor's appointments and was committed to fatherhood. Still, behind his smiles, there was fear. He was nineteen and hadn't yet been able to hold down a job. He couldn't understand many of his classes. His neighborhood was filled with guys who had stumbled out of school and into young fatherhood. Few got very far. "I want to be a good dad, someone a kid can come to and talk to," he said. "I really want to be a good dad. I'm just nervous not knowing what the future holds."

The new semester at Manual was under way. Some students had graduation in their sights. Some were planning for successes beyond that. And others were already staring at the realities of life.

18

★ ★ ★

I KNEW I DIDN'T WANT THAT.

Thirty-five years before I walked into Manual High School I began my own inglorious education career at Kuny Elementary. The one-story brick building sat in the middle of Gary, Indiana, a once-mighty steel town thirty minutes from Chicago that by 1974 was well into its steep and unyielding decline. The local steel industry, which had given healthy middle-class paychecks to generations of Gary residents, was crumbling. A city that was once the heart of northwest Indiana was now full of blight. In a region stung hard by a deep racial divide, whites had fled the city in huge numbers for the area's surrounding cities and towns, leaving behind Gary's increasingly overwhelming poverty and crime problems. The onetime home of the Jackson Five and scenic World War II–era neighborhoods was now home to a growing number of abandoned buildings and social problems. Those problems were only getting worse. The city was in the midst of a staggering population decline that would drop its number of residents by a third, or nearly sixty thousand people, from 1970 to 1990.

When my kindergarten year began at the tail end of the summer of 1974, I was sharing a bedroom with my young single mom and my seven-year-old brother in a small home in the Glen Park section of Gary. In the four previous years, the years that followed my parents' divorce, the three of us had lived in four different apartments or homes in Gary. Ultimately, roughly a year before I started school, we moved into my mom's childhood home, sharing it with my grandparents and an uncle who had recently returned from military service during the Vietnam War.

It was a cramped house but I loved it, and I loved Gary. At the age of five I was oblivious to most of the problems that had plagued the city. And as the mid-seventies settled in there were still remnants of Gary's glory days to be found. The long stretch of Broadway, the once-bustling street that cuts down the middle of the city, continued to be home to a few family restaurants and dime stores—businesses that wouldn't last much longer but were hanging on in 1974. Lake Michigan offered recreation on the north edge of town. And even some of the city's problems—such as all the empty buildings—provided my brother and me with endless summer playgrounds. One of the many neighborhood corner stores that for years had peppered the city sat at the end of our block. It gave us a friendly place to buy candy and sodas and kill time—until the longtime owner was shot in the last of several robberies, that is.

Kuny Elementary was a short walk from our back door. The school was built after my mom's time in Gary schools in the 1950s, and it seemed new and bright. I went there for just one year, before my mom married a man after a brief courtship and we moved to another part of town. My brother, Jeff, and I attended two other schools in Gary over the next four years, taking a city bus to one of them, before moving to a nearby city in 1979. In Gary we left behind a city that over the next decade-plus would compete repeatedly for the title of Murder Capital of the Country and serve as an example of what can happen to industrial towns that rely too heavily on the jobs of yesteryear. The schools we left behind eventually emerged as some of the worst in the state. My only hint of that decline was that the stellar grades I had received in Gary schools instantly turned into a string of Ds and Fs when we moved to a better district.

I thought about my education and childhood often as I talked to Manual students. By the time I met them, my wife and I were living in a nice house and enjoying comfortable salaries. We were college graduates and frequent travelers, and my final days in Gary schools were thirty-year-old memories. Our Indianapolis home was only nine miles from Manual's front door, but like most professionals in the city, we were living in a different world than the one occupied by the kids I'd spent the year profiling.

Still, when I looked at Manual's students and heard their stories, I felt I understood them. I remembered living my first ten years in the same type of rough neighborhoods that many of them lived in—neighborhoods where drugs, home break-ins, and car thefts were common. Like many of the students I met, I'd spent time with my father on only a handful of occasions during my childhood, and after my mom remarried I'd spent the rest of my school years living with an alcoholic stepfather. Despite that, I knew my childhood didn't compare to that of many of the students I was meeting.

I grew up with a loving mother who kept a close eye on my grades as I moved through elementary and junior high school. I had learned to read early, and our homes were always filled with books and newspapers. My father lived six hundred miles away and was largely out of touch, but he sent birthday cards and Christmas presents. His monthly child support payments arrived on time and without fail, and he later helped me with college expenses. My stepfather was often drunk and occasionally an embarrassment to the family, but with the exception of a stint spent in rehab, he held a stable union job. Money was tight, but we never felt poor after he and my mom married. By the time my family moved to a safe blue-collar city to the east of Gary when I was ten, my youth was free of any obvious outside dangers. I got a paper route, played baseball, and lived the life of a typical American kid. Meanwhile, my uncle Rob, the Vietnam vet, served for many years as a reliable and loving father figure. He was a towering and positive presence in my life, a lover of books and travel, the type of role model every child should have but that many Manual students do not.

Decades after my days in Gary, I was spending day after day listening to the painful stories of Manual students. And although nothing in my life had approached their experiences, I had at least a peripheral understanding of what life in their neighborhoods had been like. And like many of them, I had danced on the edge of trouble and struggled mightily in high school.

One day during my year at Manual, I wrote a column about the huge problem of student absenteeism. I quoted teachers who said many of their students had no chance of learning or passing because they missed so many classes. I talked to students who casually told me they just got bored with school and skipped a class or a day whenever they felt like doing so. I wrote of the belief among many that school wasn't important and that the problem was killing any chance Manual had of improving. It was a glaring symbol of the depressing lack of value many students and parents placed on education: too many empty seats.

The funny thing was, if another columnist in another city had written the column in the mid-1980s, I could have been one of the prime examples of the problem of student absenteeism. Day after day during my junior and senior years at Portage High School, I came to school late or not at all. One semester I violated a school rule that limited unexcused absences to nine in a semester and was given automatic failing grades in every class. My grade point average never recovered. School wasn't important to me—or at least not important enough. For most of my high school years, I rarely considered the idea of college; that was something that never came up at home and rarely came up in a neighborhood where most of our parents worked at a mill or retail store. I was more interested in my part-time job than school and spent far too many evenings smoking pot or drinking with my friends, nights that often kept me in bed the next morning. At home a strained relationship with my stepfather was deepening as he approached the worst days of his alcoholism. My mom was overwhelmed by her marriage and a full-time job working nights at a local nursing home. Getting out of the house, rather than getting to college or getting good grades, was my main concern.

Still, unlike many Manual students, I had never thought graduation was optional. Crucially, and despite my apathy toward school, I loved to learn and read. I knew the world was much bigger than the city I lived in. On many of the days I skipped school, I would take the South Shore train to Chicago and spend my time walking up and down Michigan Avenue and dreaming of making it to the big city. I wanted to be a writer of some sort. I wanted to do something big with my life. I wanted to make a good living. I just didn't know how to get there. Or, to be more accurate, I never spent time pondering the path that would take me there. And at school my grades and attendance gave teachers and counselors little reason to believe I had much potential.

I graduated in the spring of 1987 with a C average on my transcript and little idea of what to do next. So I stumbled around for several months, traveling the country on the money I had saved at my part-time job before landing back, humbled and broke, in northwest Indiana. Still without a plan, I settled into my mom's basement and took a series of menial jobs, working at a hardware store and a clothing chain in a local mall. But the most important job I held was as an overnight cashier in an old drugstore just outside of Gary. The job paid minimum wage and required sleeping all day so that I could stay awake through the graveyard shift. It was in that little store, in the early morning hours one winter day, that I realized I could be stuck working in jobs just like that one for the rest of my life. I knew I didn't want that.

Almost immediately I signed up for classes at a local extension of Indiana University. Before long I transferred down to the main campus in Bloomington and settled into the university's wonderful journalism school. I had taken a strange path to college, but I had gotten there. Fortunately, I had an older brother to follow. He had taken his own circuitous path to college but had shown me that the path was possible. Once I arrived, I still wasn't a great student. But I'd luckily escaped a world in which my opportunities would have been severely limited. Despite my lackluster academic career, I had found my way into a good college. Despite the mistakes I'd made, I had survived without making one that would jeopardize my future. I still sometimes sit in my office at the newspaper and wonder how I avoided being stuck in a dead-end job somewhere in northwest Indiana.

Too many of the students I met at Manual lacked the role models I'd had and the understanding that a high school diploma was not optional. They had not been convinced of the idea that there was indeed a path that could take them out of their current circumstances. They had not been exposed to a world beyond their little section of it. Their home lives were filled with heartbreaking details that few of us can fathom. They made mistakes, just like many of us did. Too often, though, those mistakes cost them their high school education and any real chance of recovering from them.

During my months at Manual, I was invited to speak before dozens of audiences, from education reform organizations and colleges to an array of community and civic groups. They wanted to hear about the students I was writing about, the challenges facing struggling schools, and the solutions that were needed to improve them. They wanted to hear my opinions on issues such as union contracts, charter schools, and parental involvement. I was always happy to go out and speak to anyone who wanted to listen to me. When I did, though, I often thought about how absurd it would have seemed twenty-five years earlier to raise the prospect of my having a voice in the debate over public education. My teachers at Portage High School surely would have laughed at the idea. They would have remembered a kid so unfocused he was kicked off the school newspaper. Or they wouldn't have remembered me at all, because I was so frequently absent.

Many of the people in the crowds I spoke to didn't seem to believe me when I said that I could have been one of the kids I was writing about and that I wasn't one of those students for whom college and a career was an early goal. I repeatedly told them that I was just a journalist and not an education expert, and I often joked that I'd been in high school more often during my year at Manual than during my own senior year of high school. It was only partly a joke.

But the path I took through school, however dubious, somehow ended with a college degree and a wonderful career. That degree wasn't from an Ivy League school, and it had come with modest grades. But it did exactly what an education can do. It offered entry into a world of opportunities.

19

★ ★ ★

THERE'S NOBODY THAT CAN'T DO SOMETHING.

Linda Thatcher's classroom was tucked away near the back of the first floor of the school, along a lesser-used hallway, and noise rarely spilled past the closed door. So it was easy to miss the magic inside. Thatcher's students, all with severe mental disabilities, spent most of their school time inside the classroom. They didn't move from teacher to teacher like other Manual students, but rather stayed with Thatcher and her assistants. They were participants in an inspiring and compassionate program aimed at preparing them for life after high school. Their class was an example of something the school did well and was part of a proud tradition within a district that had long taken seriously its treatment of students with special needs. It was filled with the type of creative problem-solving strategies, and heavy attention to each student and each student's challenges, that should be the norm for at-risk schools like Manual.

The goal of this program was to help the students one day live as independently as they possibly could. So while other classes in the building focused on math or language arts, Thatcher's class focused on the true basics, such as how to shop at the grocery store, wash clothes, or make telephone calls. She taught the students about proper behavior, such as the need to show up to school clean and groomed and on time. They were lessons that sometimes took years to sink in. But the fifty-nine-year-old teacher was patient.

Her students faced huge hurdles, and full independence was a stretch. Most would require some form of assistance as adults—a relative or social services worker to check in on them from time to time, perhaps. And some would likely never be able to live on their own. But unlike the students with more profound disabilities in another classroom on the other side of the building, many of Thatcher's were capable of learning skills that would allow them to live semi-independent lives at some point and to contribute to their city.

It was a beautiful class to watch, led by a teacher who was completely absorbed in her mission and who built extremely deep relationships with her students. Her mission was to guide them toward the best life they could live, whatever that was, and to help them find their place in the world. "There's nobody that can't do something," Thatcher said one morning. "I really believe that." There was no doubt she did.

Thatcher's classroom was always filled with conversation and lessons, and often laughter. She worked on concepts and skills that many might consider minor but for her students were crucial elements of their future. She helped them learn how to organize kitchen cabinets so they would know where to find their food. She taught them how to order clothes or other things online and over the phone. She wanted them to be able to work, and getting to work on time was key to that. So she helped them learn how to set their alarm clocks, focusing heavily on the difference between AM and PM. She taught them how to go to the nurse's office and, after getting permission and while being carefully supervised, pull their prescription bottles out of a medicine cabinet. They needed to know how to identify their medications and to be able to determine both the proper amounts to take and when to take them. She and the other teachers took city buses with the students. Since they would not be able to drive, they needed to know how to negotiate the city's mass transit system. The students went to the grocery store after carefully preparing shopping lists, and they learned how to count out the money needed to pay the cashier. Once back at school, they learned how to cook, preparing the same meal week after week. Some learned how to write checks and pay bills. The room was equipped with laundry and kitchen facilities so that they could learn to do basic chores.

Some lessons were based on problems that few people outside of the classroom could have imagined. Thatcher, for instance, realized one day that her students sometimes had trouble determining which bathroom to enter at restaurants, because the doors weren't always labeled "men" and "women." Restaurants sometimes put clever pictures or names on the doors—"Mars" and "Venus," "Thorns" and "Roses," or "Dukes" and "Duchesses"—and that stymied her very literal students. So day after day during one stretch of the school year, she sat with her students and a stack of pictures of bathroom doors. She had collected every example she could find and spent hours helping the students determine which door they should enter. Part of the lesson was memorization as they learned to differentiate between the names on doors of local restaurants. She also tried to help students work through clues that would provide an answer. If necessary, she reminded them, they could ask a restaurant employee. But she wanted them to do be able to do things like this on their own. That's what freedom is all about. "Our goal is to help them learn functional life skills," Thatcher said. "We want our kids to be included in the community and to be able to function as independently as possible. Everything you and I do, all the basic things we do from the time our alarm goes off until we go to bed, that's what we're teaching."

Since the core of the program was about preparing students for the real world, many of them spent up to two days each week working at local stores or restaurants. They stocked shelves, washed dishes, and swept floors. They learned how to be good employees, to show up as scheduled, and to take breaks at the right time. If they needed a particular day off, they were taught to call the employer and ask for it. If they couldn't make it to work, they called in and explained the problem. And when they left Thatcher's program, sometimes not until their early twenties, they had a proven ability to work and a résumé filled with work experience.

I met Thatcher after Spencer Lloyd insisted I check out her class. He ate lunch with her and her students nearly every day and was amazed at the wonderful work she was doing. While his students were becoming better singers with each passing week, hers were becoming more independent. One girl from a troubled home who showed up early in the school year dirty and smelly had learned to bring clothes with her that she could wash and wear the next day. Others learned of the need to shower and be polite. Thatcher taught them to pick up after themselves. Some of her students came from dysfunctional homes with parents who were just as hobbled by disabilities as they were. Because of that, the life lessons they received were learned in this classroom.

Thatcher happily welcomed into her room anybody who showed an interest in her students. She wanted to show them off. She was proud of them, and every one of them was special to her. She talked glowingly about their strengths and offered hope about the chances of improving their weaknesses. When asked about a student, she often started talking about the student by saying "Isn't he cool?" or "Isn't she the neatest?" She seemed to enjoy nothing more than sitting with one of her students and talking or reading. She was another reason to have hope that schools like Manual could be turned around.

Thatcher's class provides a roadmap of sorts for struggling schools. It is aimed at helping students with profound learning disabilities, but the lessons it offers are much wider in scope. Many students at Manual, after all, face tremendous challenges related to poverty and troubled families. Their home lives and emotional baggage stand in the way of academic success. But most do not receive the type of one-on-one assistance or carefully managed strategic plans that the students in Thatcher's program receive. Each school day, students at dire risk of dropping out walk through the doors of America's schools. Too often, little is done to help them with the problems and challenges standing in their way. The infrastructure is not in place to help them. Changing that in a significant way would take a massive infusion of resources and energy. But it is hard to imagine the payoff would not be worth it.

In late January, Thatcher prepared to take a group of her students to a lunch outing on the north side of Indianapolis. The field trip was part of her recurring effort to help the students navigate the real world and to have experiences they otherwise might not have. Six of her nine students had qualified for the lunch. They had done so by doing their work and meeting various goals Thatcher had set, such as showing up to school with their hair combed and teeth brushed, walking quietly through the halls, and bringing their student identification cards with them. These were among the basics, the functional life skills, they would need to master in order to hold down a job later in life.

That's how Thatcher thought. Every school day and every experience within it centered on the idea of preparing the students to be successful on their own, of making sure they would have a chance to be accepted by the people they would spend their adult lives encountering. She avoided the lessons that sounded good but didn't help with her overall mission. "My philosophy is, if you do not do it at home, if it's not part of your life, then don't teach it to my kids," she said. That meant, for instance, not teaching students to count for the sake of counting. Instead of doing that, she taught them how to count out change or figure out how much food they needed to bring to get through a work shift. "When's the last time you had to count to five hundred?" she asked. "Never. You never have to sit there and count without a reason. That doesn't come up in your real life. So why would I teach my kids how to rote count? It doesn't help them. But they do need to know to bring the right amount of money for their lunch if they didn't pack one. And they do need to know how many singles to give the cashier at McDonald's if their bill comes to three ninety-five."

This lunch field trip had been a carrot dangled in front of the class for several weeks, a way to encourage students to learn new lessons. It was also a way to get students used to being out in public and for the public to see what wonderful kids Thatcher had. She believed such outings helped break down barriers between her kids and a public that often has little interaction with people with mental disabilities. When the six students qualified, Thatcher gathered them at a table and asked where they would like to dine. The first answers came quick. "McDonald's," they said. But Thatcher sensed that wasn't really where they wanted to go. "It's just that that is all they know," she said. She wanted to help them experience new places, new parts of town, and new restaurants with different expectations of behavior. This was a reward, but it wasn't a field trip just for the sake of having one. It was an opportunity to teach table manners and sharing skills. It was an opportunity to interact with wait staff. It was a chance to tackle a new challenge. The concept behind the lunch was the same one that led her to insist her students work at two different places each year during their time in her program rather than just staying at the same comfortable hardware store or diner for years. She wanted her students to have the opportunity to make a future job choice that best fit their interests and skills, and that meant trying different experiences. She wanted them to see the wide range of possibilities that existed. That meant different employers. And it also meant activities like visiting different restaurants.

Before asking her students for a restaurant suggestion, Thatcher had decided they would benefit from a family-style restaurant, one where they would have to share from plates of food and pass items from person to person. They would have to be courteous and helpful, and hopefully they would walk out of the restaurant with a new feeling of confidence. So she showed them pictures online of several different dining spots in town. They eventually settled on Hollyhock Hill, a restaurant known for its fried chicken and mashed potatoes and its upscale atmosphere. The students liked the name of the restaurant as well as the century-old white farmhouse where the restaurant was housed. Thatcher told them the restaurant was pricey and asked if they were sure they could be on their best behavior. They said they could.

On the morning of the field trip, Justin, a nineteen-year-old with fragile X syndrome (a form of mental impairment) was smiling as he almost always was. He stood with his winter coat bundled and eagerly led his fellow students as they walked out of Manual and across the snow-covered ground to a waiting school bus. He rushed to the back of the bus and happily welcomed the students who followed as they grabbed seats around him. But he grew concerned when he noticed that one of the girls, one of two named Jessica, was standing near the front of the bus. She was hesitant and unsure of where to go. "Come on, slowpoke," Justin said, waving her back. "Come sit back here. It's more fun back here with us."

Justin had finished his schooling a year earlier, earning the certificate that most of Thatcher's students received in lieu of a diploma. But he continued in Thatcher's program and would return the following year thanks to a law allowing students to remain in school until they are twenty-two. Justin had made substantial progress during his time in the program, learning how to cook and balance a checkbook. He worked hard stacking boxes at a local hardware store and had been on the track team. He didn't compete with other students but diligently participated in practices and saw his coordination skills improve dramatically. As we sat on the bus, he told me he hoped to get a full-time job stacking shelves one day. "It gives me a challenge," he said. "Seriously, I need something to challenge me."

He led a cheer as the bus pulled out of the parking lot that cold January morning. As the students waved good-bye to their school, the bus driver headed out through the south-side neighborhoods that surround Manual, passing abandoned homes and shuttered businesses. She drove east of the city's downtown over pothole-scarred streets as the students laughed and talked about what they were going to eat. Thatcher listened and chimed in occasionally, playing the role of mother. "Now remember," she said. "They are going to put bowls and plates of food on the table. So we will have to use our manners and pass the food around carefully and politely."

"Yeah, because it's fancy," said a student named Tony. Tony was eighteen and dreamed of being a video game designer. He talked about the game *Mortal Kombat* frequently and also worked at the hardware store with Justin, unloading trucks and washing the floor. He had been diagnosed with autism, and although he struggled with many of the basics of life, his reading had dramatically improved in three years under Thatcher. He liked to work on computers and was the student Thatcher turned to when she needed someone to hook up the program's Wii system.

An eighteen-year-old girl named Jessica sat on the seat across the aisle from Tony. Her parents suffered from severe learning disabilities and had largely ignored her throughout the years. But in Thatcher's program, Jessica had begun to blossom. In the past two years, she had joined the school choir and held a variety of outside jobs. "Everywhere she goes, people just love her," Thatcher said. It was easy to see why. She had a quiet and sweet nature. As Jessica sat quietly on the bus, I asked her what job she hoped to have as an adult. "I want to be a police," she said almost in a whisper, adding that she liked the show *Law & Order*.

Two rows behind Tony and Jessica, a twenty-year-old student named Ashley sat with Rodney, an eighteen-year-old classmate who was also her boyfriend. Ashley was shy and had spent a full year in Thatcher's program before she finally spoke voluntarily. But now, after five years in the program, she talked frequently, and on this day she spoke about her hope of working with animals. She said she loved all animals. "Even snakes?" Tony asked. "No, no," she said, shaking her head. "No snakes."

Rodney sat with his arm around Ashley's shoulders. He laughed when Justin or Tony laughed but was more serious than the other boys. He had spent many hours loading shelves and stacking boxes at a store and wanted to work for FedEx one day, because he liked planes and thought it would be cool to load and unload them. He was a good worker, his teacher said, and later in the year he and Ashley would go to the prom together. But Rodney had perhaps the most severe problems of anyone in the class. He heard voices and suffered from severe mental illness in addition to his learning disabilities. His mom had adopted him when he was six, after he'd been horribly abused in foster care. He had spent time in state mental hospitals and group homes and over the years had been detained by police after violent outbursts in which he threatened to hurt both himself and his mother. "He has lots of memories I wish he didn't have," his mother said.

The year would end poorly for Rodney. In late May, shortly after the prom, he left home in anger after his mom told him to pick up his clothes. His decision to flee wasn't unusual, but unlike previous incidents, he didn't return home that day. Or the next. Police found him days later in a crime-ridden section of the city, surrounded by drug addicts. He was off his medication and drunk. Police took him to a local hospital for treatment and observation. It was the latest in a long string of troubles. But on the day of the field trip, Rodney sat calmly and happily in the last row of the bus, looking pleased as he and the other students headed toward their destination.

The group arrived at the restaurant forty minutes after leaving the school. The students had grown tired during the long ride but perked up when they pulled into the parking lot; some pointed with excitement at the elegant setting. Tony and Justin high-fived when they saw the restaurant, and most of the others smiled. Rodney and Ashley looked at each other. The two Jessicas calmly walked off the bus.

"Remember, there are other people eating here today," Thatcher told the students. "We're representing Manual, so we're going to be polite and talk softly."

"You got it," Justin said.

The students headed for their feast, pausing only to grant Thatcher a picture in front of the building. They smiled and said "cheese" then walked inside. Tony, the most talkative of the group, rushed to open the door and hold it for the female classmates and staff who had made the trip. "Ladies first," he said. Then he looked at me, smiled, pointed to his head and said, "Smart thinking, right?"

The students walked in and stopped quickly, soaking in the atmosphere. The restaurant was filled with white tablecloths and well-dressed waiters and waitresses. Quiet classical music played, and a group of people at a business lunch sat nearby. "This is kind of fancy," Tony said nervously.

The class was soon seated at a long table overlooking the back lawn. As two waitresses poured water into glasses and began filling the table with appetizers, Tony grabbed his cloth napkin, dramatically fanned it out, and placed it neatly on his lap. The rest of the group followed his example and then sat quietly at the table, still looking around. They had heard a lot about the restaurant and the manners it required. Thatcher had talked endlessly about the need to pass plates politely among themselves. So when Tony wanted sugar for his tea, he politely asked Justin to pass it to him, even though it was only a few inches away and actually closer to Tony. Justin politely reached in front of Tony, picked up the sugar, and handed it to his friend.

"Thank you," Tony said.

"You're welcome."

Rodney then looked over at Tony. "Tony," he said, "would you like some salad?"

"Yes, I would like some."

The other students did the same and peppered their waitresses with constant thank-yous. And a few minutes later, when the main course arrived, they dug in, filling their plates with fried chicken, mashed potatoes, corn, green beans, and biscuits and apple butter. When the boys noticed a spot on their plates had become vacant, they asked another to pass a dish so that they could fill it.

"This is definitely a ten," Justin said.

"It's the bomb," Tony agreed.

"It's, like, better than Subway," Justin added.

For the next hour, they talked about the food and the Indiana Pacers and extreme fighting. Justin and Tony got seconds and then thirds, and Thatcher watched them with pride as they followed all of the rules she had discussed.

This was Thatcher's thirty-sixth year of teaching special education students, and she had no plan to stop. It was tiring work—exhausting, really. But the payoff was worth it. The ability to help give students a chance at real lives in the real world was too rewarding to abandon. She had started at another Indianapolis school in the early 1970s, at a time when nearly all of the district's students with mental disabilities were stuffed into one building. Thankfully, over the years, the special-education philosophy had changed and students had been integrated into neighborhood schools. That was important, Thatcher said, because it gave them exposure to a wide range of students—students they could learn from.

Thatcher was one of the quirkiest characters at Manual. Everything she said deserved an exclamation point because of the excitement and energy that filled her statements. Any visitor to her room was greeted with a shriek. We bonded over our shared devotion to Elvis Presley, whom she strongly argued was still alive. When she left school every afternoon, she went home to take care of her husband, who had survived a massive intracranial bleed fifteen years earlier and often needed assistance.

At the restaurant, the students were slowing. "Stick a fork in me, I'm done," Tony said. Justin was done, too. He laid down his napkin in surrender and turned to Thatcher, giving her a hug. "Thank you, Mrs. Thatcher," he said, as the rest of the class joined in. "Ahh, you know how to get a brownie point," Thatcher said, almost crying. "But you know what? You all earned this. You come to school every day. You come prepared and well groomed. And when you go out into the community, you are fine representatives of Manual High School, just like you were today."

A few minutes later the owner of the restaurant stopped by the table. Forty years earlier, he had been an Indianapolis Public Schools student on the edge. He said he was a sucker for good teachers and good students and told them he'd been reading about their school. He announced that the meal would be on the house. Thatcher began to cry and insisted she'd found room in her budget to pay for the meal. "That's okay," he said. "If it wasn't for you, these kids wouldn't be here. What you do is very important." He looked around the table as the students looked back. "There are great things out there for all of you," he said. "All you have to do is keep working at it."

After lunch the students quietly filed out of the restaurant and walked back to their bus. They looked tired from their long trip and big meal. As the bus pulled out of the parking lot and began heading south, Tony took a nap in his seat. Rodney and Thatcher sang commercial jingles. Ashley talked quietly with one of the classroom assistants, and Justin quietly stared out the window, watching the scenery. "It felt good to get out," he said quietly.

Three hours after leaving, the class arrived back at Manual. The students were still full and tired but proud of their day out. They had learned a lot, but there were more lessons to come. There were always lessons in Linda Thatcher's class.

"Now, remember how we walk through the hallway," she said. "What's the word?"

"Quietly," the six students answered in unison.

"And what do we say to the bus driver?"

"Thank you," they said collectively.

20

★ ★ ★

IT NEVER STOPS AROUND HERE.

Michael Robinson let out a sigh and stared at the smart-aleck freshman standing before him. It was only 8:15 AM, but Robinson already knew this was going to be one of those days that seem to last forever. A special education teacher for more than a decade, he had recently been assigned to work in the discipline dean's office as a backup to Terry Hoover. The office workload—the suspensions, expulsions, arrests, and preemptive strikes—had gotten to be too big for just one person. Robinson had long sought an opportunity to move into administration. On this day, he wondered why that had ever been a goal. In the first forty-five minutes of the school day, he'd already dealt with a handful of class-skipping students and a potential fight between two girls. And now he had to deal with the smart-aleck freshman, a boy named Rrien who had enrolled in Manual at the start of February and in the two weeks since had missed his fourth-period class nearly every day. He stood in Robinson's office wearing a pair of tattered khakis, a red shirt, and a smirk.

Robinson pulled up the boy's class records on his computer and noticed that Rrien's middle name was listed only as the initial P. He tried to make conversation with the student in the hope of relaxing him and figuring out what was causing his problems. It didn't work. "What's the P for?" Robinson asked in a friendly voice.

Rrien waited for a few seconds before finally answering. "I'd rather not say."

Robinson sighed, and the two stared at each other for another second or two. "Okay, well, what's your home number?" Robinson asked. Nothing would be easy with this student.

"It should be on there," Rrien replied.

Robinson gave the freshman a hard look and demanded the number. Rrien gave it after the third request, and Robinson turned back to his computer screen. He noticed that the boy's mother's name was Buffy. "That's an unusual name," he said, sounding friendly again. "I've never met anyone named Buffy."

"You still haven't," Rrien informed him.

That was three smart-alecky comments in a row. But Robinson took it well. He was a mild-mannered guy. He smiled, congratulated the boy on his wit, and put the phone on speaker. He dialed the student's number, and after a few rings an answering machine picked up. A little girl, who sang the message cutely and loudly, delivered the outgoing message. Robinson hung up the phone and laughed. Rrien didn't look happy. He seemed embarrassed and took a seat in a chair along the wall.

"Did I offer you a seat?" Robinson said, knowing he had to keep control of his office.

"No," Rrien said.

"Then stand back up."

"Yes, sir."

Robinson looked over the student's attendance record. The worst problem was fourth period. But he was missing other classes, too. Robinson asked why he didn't like going to his classes.

"Mr. Page is a nice guy," Rrien said. "I went to his class one day."

Robinson then asked specifically about the fourth-period classes the student had missed the previous two days. "Where do you go?" he asked.

"I hang out."

"Where's the hangout?"

"Mickey D's," Rrien said. "I got a Big Mac both days, sir."

He emphasized the "sir," and Robinson sighed again, asking the student what kind of grades he was getting during his short time at Manual.

"Straight Fs, sir."

"You're a smart kid," Robinson said. "That's what bothers me here—a smart kid trying to be dumb. That's like a pretty girl trying to look ugly. It makes no sense. How were your grades at your last school?"

"I flunked a lot there too."

"Was there a McDonald's near there too?" another teacher sitting in the room asked.

"Actually, yes," Rrien said.

This was enough for Robinson. "Look here, dude," he said. "First and foremost, you need to be in class." He told him to stop trying to be dumb, to embrace the fact that he was intelligent, and then sent him back to class with a warning that he'd better make it there. Just to be clear, he announced he would be calling Rrien's mom back. "I want to meet this person named Buffy," Robinson said.

Rrien flung his backpack over his shoulder and left the room, though not before offering one more sarcastic remark. "I'm sure she'll be overzealous to meet you," he said. But the impact of his walk-off statement was diluted, because he had mispronounced the word, saying "over-zee-lous."

"It's *overzealous*," Robinson said. "Now go."

Rrien was barely out the door when another freshman, named Dakota, rushed in. She was a frequent visitor to the dean's office, often in trouble for one minor infraction or another, and recently had been assigned to in-school suspension. She had been sent down by a teacher for a dress code violation and wanted to make clear that the teacher had a vendetta again her. She began racing through her story so quickly that taking down a full record of her statement was impossible. "I was not being disrespectful or threatening or anything," she said so fast there didn't seem to be spaces between her words or sentences or paragraphs. "It's not true. It's just not true."

Robinson's head slumped, and he held up his right arm like a traffic cop. "Hold on!" he said, putting his face in his hands and taking a few deep breaths. "Give me the strength to change what I can and the patience to accept what I cannot," he said slowly and dramatically. "Amen." He smiled and looked up at the girl with the pierced lip standing before him. "How can I help you?"

Dakota went on another speed-talking spree about her science teacher, insisting the teacher didn't like her and was on constant lookout for anything that could be used as the basis for punishment. That day, Dakota had worn a hoodie, a violation of the school dress code. "She keeps coming up with anything just to get me in trouble," Dakota said, dramatically waving her arms and commanding the room like an actress on stage.

As she talked, Robinson started sniffing and made a disgusted face. "Young lady," he said. "You reek of cigarette smoke. Have you been smoking?"

"Why does everyone say that?" Dakota said, before launching into yet another fast-paced defense of herself. "Smoking is disgusting. It causes cancer. My mom smokes all the time. It's so irritating. I tell her, 'You're going to get lung cancer and die.' It's disgusting. I would never do it."

Dakota eventually left with a warning, and a parade of students continued to march through Robinson's office as the morning passed—for dress code violations, not having IDs, eating in class, not going to class, and a few other of the school's less-serious issues. It was a particularly busy stretch for Robinson, because Hoover had spent her morning across town at an expulsion hearing for a student recently arrested for having drugs in the building. The previous day had been just as busy for Robinson, because Hoover had spent part of that day at yet another expulsion hearing for a student who had recently threatened to kill her—the second such threat she'd received that year. "It never stops around here," Robinson said.

The thirty-seven-year-old Robinson was one of two Manual graduates who worked in the building. It had been nineteen years since his final days as a student there, and things had changed dramatically. A school that was once the pride of the near south side had become listless and filled with chronic indifference. "Families were involved and students engaged back in my day," he said. "The school had a vibrancy in those years. There was school spirit." He wondered what had happened to that. He asked why so many in Manual's current generation of students and families seemed to have given up. "Education doesn't mean anything to them," he said. "That is so pervasive here with these students. They're not getting the support they need to reach beyond where they're at in life."

That was particularly frustrating, he said, at a time when the district and the city offered so many alternative programs for students and families looking for a different education atmosphere. The city was dotted with charter schools, and the district itself had recently created a series of magnet programs that were receiving good reviews. "The parents are still thinking they have no options," Robinson said. "That's what makes this difficult. The parents need to advocate for their kids. They have to think about what their kid does best and where they are weakest and then find the program that is best suited for them."

That sounded great. But a bit later I wondered how realistic it was when Robinson called the twenty-nine-year-old mother of a fifteen-year-old student, or when he dealt with another girl whose mother had recently used her to shoplift items from a local Kmart, hoping to keep any criminal charges off of her own record. During my time at Manual, I heard from readers and others who frequently told me that the simple answer to America's education problems was better parenting. The answer, they said, didn't lie in government programs or education reforms or nonprofit organizations. If the students had better parents, they told me, they would perform better. These people seemed to think they'd landed on a miraculous discovery. "But," I often replied, "you've just diagnosed a problem. Finding the cure is the real challenge."

In the waiting area outside Robinson's office, students were always on deck, awaiting their meeting with the dean. One boy sat reading a book titled *Life in Prison*. It was apt; the hallway in one way was like prison: nobody was guilty. "I don't know why I'm down here," a girl said angrily as she sat outside Robinson's office, waiting to lay out her defense.

About noon, I saw a freshman named Dallas, a friendly boy who often approached me hoping to persuade me to write an exposé about one teacher or another he thought was bad. The earnestness with which he made his arguments was entertaining, and I often asked him if he thought the classes might go better if he occasionally studied or did his homework. He waved off my questions and insisted the problem was the teachers. "That's what you should be doing a story on," he told me once. "A story on the list of bad teachers. I'll give them to you." Despite his problems, Dallas didn't seem like the kind of kid who would have been suspended four times already that school year. But he was.

On this day he sat slumped in his green ROTC uniform and waited to find out what discipline he would receive for arguing with a teacher that morning. He had a slight speech impediment and did poorly in school but was nonetheless a smooth talker. It seemed like every time I spotted him in the hallway, he was making moves on one girl or another. I asked him how he was doing. "Better," he said. "My mom's got a job now. She's a bartender." I asked about his father. It was hard to find students in the building who spent much time with their fathers. "He put me through more hell than anybody in the world," he said. "I wouldn't talk to him if he came back."

Meanwhile, a student named Kathy sat in another administrative office with her mom. Kathy was a friendly girl, often laughing and talking with friends, and did well in her choir class. But she rarely went to her other classes and lost her temper easily and often. As such, she was one of the school's biggest and most frustrating headaches. On this day, Principal Grismore dealt with her. "She is skipping classes all the time," he told her mom. "If this behavior continues, if she is not regularly in class, I'm going to file a referral to send her to an alternative school. I think it's a poor decision on her part, but if she's going to just act however she wants, this is the path we're going to take. We can't have this here."

The mom said her daughter was a bundle of frustration. Kathy had even taken steps to make sure calls from school didn't reach her home. She said she had lost the ability to control her daughter. "She won't listen. She won't follow rules. She's endlessly defiant. I can get her here," the mom said, "but once she's on school property, I can't control what she does. If she is not intent on making it work, then what?"

"Then we'll find her an alternative placement," Grismore said, not the slightest bit interested in dancing around the problem. "She'll be somewhere. But not here." He then turned to Kathy and explained to her what it meant to be in one of the district's alternative placement schools. "Small class sizes. A locked-down campus. Group bathroom breaks." In other words, none of the freedom that comes with a typical high school. "Do you want to talk about this?" he asked.

"No," Kathy yelled. "I'm tired of everyone saying they don't trust me."

"She's very defiant," her mom said. "Why won't you go to your classes regularly?"

"Cuz."

"Because why."

"Because I don't want to."

Kathy started yelling louder, not violently but in a way that exposed her as frustrated and feeling picked-on. The yelling was enough for Grismore to end the meeting. He told the student before him she would have to go home and that she was one step from being tossed out of the school. The meeting was over. But Kathy kept protesting. "You'd be well advised to keep your mouth shut," Grismore said.

Shortly after Kathy left with her mom, school police brought in two girls. "We've got a couple fighters," Officer Donnita Miller announced. The girls had been caught fighting in a first-floor hallway. The fight had spilled out of an argument in the cafeteria and stemmed from a yearlong feud that school administrators had spent hours trying to settle. Both of the girls had blonde hair, mild learning disabilities, and a long history of problems. One of them had been kicked out of school during the first week of the year for performing oral sex on a boy in a locker room.

As they were brought in, they seemed inclined to continue their fight, tossing threats at each other. One of the girls had several scratches on her face. The other had sprained her hand. As administrators gathered to discuss the discipline they would be doling out, Miller spoke quietly to one of the girls. "How long have I been working with you on this situation?" she asked.

"A long time," the girl said.

"And still you made a choice to do the opposite of what we've been talking about. You told me all that time I've invested was wasted."

"No, it wasn't," the girl said, looking sad.

"Well, you still went and fought," Miller said, turning away.

The girl sat with her arms folded across her chest and her head slumped. "Who cares about a retarded-girl fight anyway?" she muttered to herself.

The deans, the police, and others in the room turned and nearly leaped at her. Officer Miller rushed over and stopped inches away from the girl. "What?" she shouted. "Don't you ever say that. Never. Do you hear me?"

"I'm sorry," the girl said quietly.

By this point, Hoover had returned from the expulsion hearing. The other girl sat in her office, not seeming nearly as sad. She said her rival deserved what she got, that she had swung at her first and was constantly running her mouth. She wasn't worried about having to miss a few days of school. But over the next hour or so, she grew sad as she talked about a fight she'd had with her mom. Hoover listened and said they could talk more about that problem later. For now, though, she had to be suspended. "Do you have a friend or classmate who lives by you?" Hoover asked, looking for a way to get the girl her homework.

"Yeah," the girl said. "But she's at the hospital for drinking too much."

As the girl left the room, she complained about the things her rival had said about her. Hoover stopped her in mid-sentence. "People are going to talk about you your whole life," she said. "People talk about me. Who cares? There are better ways to deal with it." Hoover paused and stood up. "You know I still care about you, right?"

"Yeah," the girl said.

Back in Robinson's office, the other fighter also wasn't worried about her suspension. It wasn't the first, she said, and it wouldn't be the last. "It's just a suspension," she said. As dispassionate as she now was, the girl did offer a confused reaction when she scanned the suspension form and noticed a C next to a box marked "race."

"C?" she said. "What the hell does that mean?"

"It stands for Caucasian," a teacher in the room said, trying not to laugh.

"I'm not Caucasian," the girl said, puzzled.

Robinson stared at her, forcing her to figure this one out for herself.

"Oh, like white," she finally said. "I get it, it means white."

The deans dealt with a few more brush fires throughout the afternoon, but two hours later the day was finally coming to an end. Not surprisingly, it wouldn't end easily for Robinson. As 2:30 PM approached, he sat in his office dealing with a very angry girl who had cursed out a teacher that afternoon. It was just the latest in a long line of offenses. So as she sat and scowled, Robinson attempted to talk to her about her behavior. He didn't get far.

"I don't want to hear it," the girl said.

"Well, I'm going to make my point," Robinson said. "You want to go to college, and this is how you act? Do you know they put students off campus for this type of behavior? Do you know what would happen if you talked to a professor this way? You'd be gone." She said she didn't care.

Robinson looked up her records on his computer. He noticed she hadn't come to school until midway through the morning that day. "Why were you late?" he asked.

"That's none of your business," she said, scowling some more.

This wasn't going anywhere. The books Robinson had read about dealing with students, as well as the classes he had taken, were doing him no good. So he finished filling out the girl's suspension form and handed it to her. She snatched it out of his hand and stormed out of the room. He sighed once again.

A bit later the day ended. Robinson looked like he'd been through a street fight as he leaned back in his chair. His eyes were tired and his shirt wrinkled. The students were leaving for the day, but he had four hours of paperwork to complete. He was exhausted, and he'd struggled to get through to any of the students who'd wandered in and out of his office. His day was a reminder of the relentless challenges educators and schools across the country face—challenges that stand in the way of progress, challenges that many of the politicians who write education policy laws never experience. It was a reminder, I thought, that this country has to find a way to proactively address the problems facing so many students in its struggling schools. So far it hasn't, and, as such, administrators like Robinson spend their days reacting far too late to issues holding their schools down.

Still, Robinson wasn't going to give up. He remembered Manual being a school filled with hope and the neighborhood around it being filled with engaged parents and economic life. That could return one day. He wanted to believe that. "You deal with a lot of attitudes in here," he said. "But even though they get in trouble, even though they can be a pain in the tush, they're just kids."

21

★ ★ ★

I LIKE TO SOLVE PROBLEMS.

Among the hundreds of students who passed through Manual every day, some were impossible to miss. Students such as Jammyra, who seemed like the student body's elder stateswoman. Or Jeff, the calculus student who walked the halls in his crisp ROTC uniform every Wednesday. Or Melissa, the freshman with the painful home life who seemed to cover it up with a smile and a handshake aimed at every adult she passed. Or Jessica, the special education student who had trouble communicating but had an innocent gaze that was hard to forget. Or, of course, the occasional gangbanger who menaced the neighborhoods around Manual and whom everyone in the school knew to avoid.

And then there was Raymond Rutland. The eighteen-year-old senior was perhaps the most conspicuous student of all. He stood out even when crushed among dozens of other students as he walked through the crowded hallways between classes. He looked like no other student. He wore his khaki pants high above his waist, like an old man would, with his belt pulled tight and his shirt tucked in deep and buttoned to the top. He wore his student ID clipped to his shirt collar at all times and his house key hung from a lanyard around his neck. He walked fast and with determination through the halls, always carrying a stack of books and a calculator. His head jerked to the side occasionally, and he twisted his hand in front of his face frequently. And when someone said hello, as teachers and fellow students constantly did, he was more likely to give them a thumbs-up than a few words.

Raymond had a form of autism that limited his ability to communicate. But he also possessed an inner drive that stood out in his school. That drive had given him a reputation throughout the building as perhaps the school's hardest worker and a grade point average that placed him among the top ten in his graduating class. "You'll assign the work, and he'll do twice as much as you assigned," said Cheryl McManama, one of Raymond's teachers. "I've never seen anything like it." She and Raymond's other teachers repeated the same mantra: if every student at Manual worked half as hard as he did, the school's massive problems would be largely eliminated.

In mid-February Raymond received a letter from the University of Indianapolis. It was a letter he had been anticipating for several weeks and that he had been relentlessly asking his mom and teachers about. His mom opened it on the day it arrived and read it to him. "After a careful evaluation of your academic records we are pleased to inform you that you are eligible for full-time admission to the university," it read. The letter admitted Raymond into a program that was aimed at students with learning disabilities. In a high school where a majority of his class was not graduating, or not graduating on time, Raymond was a welcome success story. The road to this point hadn't been an easy one. That letter was the result of hard work on his part and tremendous resources aimed at him by the school district. But the investment was unquestionably worth it, and Raymond, though not big on conversation, was a student I wanted to get to know.

On a Friday in late February, Raymond was in his U.S. history class. He was sitting up straight and listening as teacher Robert Palmer talked about the recent decision by one of Indiana's senators, Evan Bayh, to not seek another term in office. This wasn't one of Raymond's favorite classes. Because of the occasional essay tests in the class, he struggled to get a B, performing much better in classes in which the answers to tests and homework were more clearly defined. He found abstract questions difficult. So although he could memorize the amendments to the Constitution, he was left at a loss when asked to explain why they were needed.

A school employee named Sylvia Davis sat in a chair a few feet away from Raymond, as she almost always did and as she had for years. Davis was an IPS paraprofessional assigned to Raymond. She traveled from class to class with him, helping him understand the directions given out by the teachers and making sure he was able to communicate when necessary. She was his in-class advocate, charged with letting teachers know when he needed more time and helping him when he grew frustrated. By this point Davis had worked with Raymond for nearly six years, since Raymond had been in middle school. Her assistance had allowed him not only to survive but to thrive in traditional classes. Without her that would have been impossible. Early on, Davis sat right next to Raymond in each class. But now she sat two or three rows away and sometimes even left the class for brief periods of time. "That's because we are working on his independence," she said. "Plus, he has a crush on me."

As the history class wound down and the teacher gave students a few minutes to relax, Davis called Raymond over and introduced me. Then she looked at him and reminded him to properly introduce himself. He reached out his hand. "Hi," he said, his speech impediment slightly blurring the words. "I'm Raymond Rutland." Davis quickly praised him, congratulating him for making eye contact and enunciating. Raymond smiled at the praise, as he often did, and gave me a fist bump. He gave fist bumps often. He then walked back to his desk, smiling broadly the entire way and looking back several times, giving a thumbs-up and holding it in the air until I returned it.

It didn't take long to realize that a column about Raymond wouldn't be full of long quotes. Davis and others at the school said he had trouble expressing what was in his mind. He didn't hold conversations. But he was an inspiring student, an eminently likable teenager, and the type of student I wanted to spend as much time writing about as I could. The school year and my project, after all, were two-thirds of the way completed. There was a long list of compelling students to write about and an increasingly dwindling window of time to do so. Raymond was an example of the obstacles that many students face and of the effort it often takes to get them to the finish line.

After the bell ending his history class rang, I walked with Raymond to his next class. He didn't want to talk while he walked, though. He was too focused on getting to class on time. The building was constantly filled with students who were being scolded for being late to class, and Raymond took the matter seriously—so seriously, in fact, that as a freshman he would sprint across the building between classes. Eventually, school leaders told him he didn't need to run. Still, he never wanted to be late.

Once we arrived at his next classroom, Raymond relaxed a bit. The teacher wasn't there yet and the door was locked. So I asked a question. It was an obvious one: "What's your favorite class?"

"Math," he said, scanning the hall for his teacher.

"Why?" I asked.

"I like to solve problems," he said.

We continued to stand in the doorway as students passed. Raymond continued to look up and down the hall for his missing teacher. He liked to be in his chair when the bell rang. The bell provided a very black-and-white answer to the question of whether a student was or was not late. Even if the teacher was to blame for his not being in his seat, it seemed wrong.

"So what do you want to do after you graduate from college?" I asked.

"Graphic design," he said, quickly answering a question he'd been asked countless times.

"Why?"

"To create pictures," he said.

"What kind of pictures?"

"Like SpongeBob. Okay."

I would soon learn that the word *okay* was Raymond's way of saying he'd answered enough questions and it was time for me to shut up. So I did.

In class Raymond was singularly focused. If there was a quiz at the end of the period, he had trouble focusing on anything else leading up to it. His teachers had learned that he needed frequent affirmation. If he answered a question, he wanted someone to say "good job." When he turned in his homework, he had trouble moving on until he received his grade. He was intelligent and strong in math but had severely underdeveloped social skills. They were on par perhaps with a first-grader, according to Davis and others who worked with him. He liked to eat alone, and he didn't like to be touched. He showed little interest in making friends, though he did sometimes stare intently at girls who showed skin.

Jackie Sababu, who headed the school's special education compliance department, sat in her office one day talking about Raymond. She said he would rather be with adults than students his own age and that he hated to miss school, so much so that he would come even when he was suffering from horrible colds. He got frustrated when things didn't go as he hoped. He was also very literal, so if someone asked to talk with him for a minute, he counted the seconds. He struggled to comprehend reading assignments. "It can be very challenging for the adults in the building to get information out of him, but it's in there," she said. "He knows a lot but has trouble expressing what he knows."

Of late, Raymond was sharply focused on college. Although he didn't talk much, he often stopped by Sababu's office to check on the status of his financial aid application. "He will come and initiate conversations about things he's focused on," she said. "He'll ask about the test waiver he needs to graduate or the class he needs to take. But he has never asked me how I'm doing. It's part of the social-skills issue that he has."

Raymond was three months away from graduating and moving on to college. Everyone from his mom to school administrators agreed that without Davis and other support programs, college would not have been possible for him. But it was happening because of a deep commitment of time and money. It was a wonderful example of what Manual did right. The only disappointing part of the story is that districts can't afford to direct the same amount of effort and resources toward students who don't have learning disabilities but instead have personal problems that put them just as at risk as students who do have learning disabilities.

In a third-period science class Raymond wrote quickly as he took a quiz on the nervous system. Once he and the other students finished, teacher Paul Miller walked through the answers and told the students to come up to his desk and hand in their papers. Raymond was first in line. "How'd you do?" Miller asked.

"Ten," Raymond said. "Ten out of ten." He proudly returned to his seat, looking around the room for someone to give a thumbs-up signal to. But Davis didn't return it; instead, she wanted to talk. She was disappointed that he hadn't done a better job of communicating with Miller. "I want you to use your words when you go up there," she said softly. "Don't just go up there and hand in your work. Okay?" Raymond nodded.

Two classes later, Raymond was in a disaster of a math class, the one I had mentioned in my first column of the series. As usual, the class was noisy and disengaged. Several students spent the period locked in loud conversations with one another. They turned away from the front of the class as they chatted, laughed, and occasionally sent obscenities flying. Some of the other students slept or texted friends. But amid the constant rumble of noise, Raymond sat quietly with his book open, writing down theorems and working on problems that had been assigned. At one point he walked to the front of the room to ask a question. It was the only question asked during the entire period.

At the end of the day, Raymond sat in what had become his most important class: College Summit, a class aimed at helping low-income seniors overcome the obstacles standing in the way of college. Cheryl McManama stood at the front of the classroom, desperately attempting to engage the few students who had stuck around for the last class on the last day of the week. She tried to talk to the students about careers and the need to have a steady paycheck. She grew frustrated as most of them stared blankly ahead waiting for the afternoon bell to ring. "Here's what's going to happen to some of you," she said, frustrated. "August is going to roll around, and some of your friends are going to go off to college, and you're going to have nothing to do." With the exception of Raymond, the students ignored her.

"What are you going to do?" she asked. She looked at one girl in the class, who shrugged and said she didn't really care. "You can't go through life these days without something beyond a high school diploma," McManama said. "Don't you get that? Are you listening to me? You have to do something beyond this building. This isn't nineteen sixty."

More blank looks greeted her as she scanned the room. And then Raymond raised his hand. Something was on his mind. It was often on his mind at this time.

"Financial aid," he said.

"Yes, Raymond, you applied for financial aid," McManama said.

"So I'm all caught up?" he asked. It was a question he had asked repeatedly—to his teachers and others in the building.

"Yes, you're all caught up."

Happy to finally have a student to talk to, McManama asked Raymond what he would be doing that weekend.

"Make my bed up," he said.

"And then what?"

"Start doing homework."

Raymond lived in a Habitat for Humanity home about five miles from Manual with his mother, a 1984 Manual grad, and his older sister and three-year-old nephew. After school, he loved to watch *SpongeBob SquarePants* and other cartoons with the TV's volume turned up loud and the closed-captioning on. In his room, he listened to Michael Jackson and Justin Timberlake music. No matter what the weather, he tried to spend as much time inside as possible. He liked to be by himself, but his young nephew, Eric, was not eager to oblige. So Raymond had grown used to having a little friend trailing behind him and begging him to play. "He's better about it," his sister said. "But sometimes Raymond doesn't want to be bothered and will lock Eric out of his room."

One evening about 6:45 the family had just finished dinner. The others sat in the living room, but Raymond stood about fifteen feet away, smiling and giving a thumbs-up signal, curious about my visit. He continued to smile as his mom walked around the house showing off his artwork. There was a jewelry box and a ceramic coffee jar he'd made. She showed me a statue of two men he'd made in art class. "He's quite an artist," said his mom, Carrie, who worked as a filing clerk for a city agency. A few minutes later Raymond agreed to give me a tour of his room. The blue walls were free of posters or anything else, and a pile of PlayStation games sat on the floor. A Spider-Man cup was filled with colored pencils. I asked about the letter he had recently received from the University of Indianapolis.

"It was great," he said.

"How did you feel when you got it?" I asked

"Transcript," he said.

"But how did you feel?"

"Okay," he said. "It was fine."

Back in the living room, Carrie shared Raymond's story. He was born in 1991 in Indianapolis, and for a while everything was fine. But at eighteen months he stopped talking. The only sound he would make was the occasional squeal. He was first diagnosed with a profound learning disability but later identified as having mild to moderate autism. He began intensive speech therapy but didn't talk again until he was nearly six years old. Along the way Raymond developed a series of curious habits, such as pinching strangers and zipping up their jackets when he could reach them. He liked to smell the furniture. He grew out of those habits. It took Carrie time to realize he wouldn't escape autism. "I would just hope and pray that one day my baby would grow out of it," she said. "But that's not how it is. It's just something we have to live with—him and me."

Carrie smiled often as she talked about her son, who continued to watch us from the doorway of his bedroom. She talked about his math skills and his dedication to school, about his sweet nature and politeness. She said he loved to do dishes and clean up the house. She laughed about his routines and how concerned he got if the school bus didn't arrive by its appointed time of 6:41 AM. At 6:42 he would ask her to call the school to check on the bus. "He's very structured," she said. "He reminds me of that movie *Rain Man*." Along with cartoons, Raymond liked to watch the movie *Mr. Holland's Opus*. Carrie wasn't sure why but suspected it had to do with the relationship Mr. Holland developed at the end of the movie with his son, who could not hear. Raymond hadn't seen his own father in years. That, Carrie said, was his father's loss. "Who wouldn't want to know him?" she asked.

As we talked, Raymond announced from his room that he wanted to take a shower. "That's fine, Raymond," his mom said, offering permission and then turning to me to provide an explanation: "He has to take a shower at exactly seven o'clock every night." She smiled again and then talked about the sadness of not being able to have the type of long conversations that a mom wants to have with her children. "You have to keep asking questions," she said. "Every once in a while you'll get more than one word back. It's challenging at times. You can get down sometimes, thinking about how he doesn't like to interact with people and have fun the way other kids do." But she wasn't complaining. She was a proud mom. She said she hoped he could live independently one day and have his own family. And she laughed loudly when she talked about questions Raymond had raised recently with Sylvia Davis, his helper back at school, about his desire to attend the senior prom. Davis had assured him she would make it happen. "I would never doubt him," his mom said, pointing to a photo of Raymond. "I mean, look at him. A lot of parents with kids with problems might think their kids can't amount to anything. That's not true. No way. Not at all."

Back at school on the following Monday, Raymond walked into a class called Jobs after Graduation, which was aimed at helping students prepare for job interviews and other career and life challenges. On that snowy morning, I asked him how he was as he walked into the room.

"Fine," he said.

I asked how he enjoyed his weekend.

"Fine," he said.

"Did you do something fun?" I asked.

"Yeah," he said.

"What was that?"

"Yeah, okay," he said. The conversation was over. He was focused on getting ready for class and wasn't in the mood to talk.

In his science class later that day, though, I noticed he was looking at me. Davis was next to him, reminding him to communicate clearly. He walked over. "Can I present you with this midterm?" he asked, proudly handing over a progress report that showed four As and three Bs. He smiled, and after I congratulated him he offered a fist bump. Later in the class, he finished an assignment early and got a "good job" from his teacher. He then walked over to one of the room's second-story windows. As other students continued to work on their assignments, he stared ahead as light snow fell on Madison Avenue. I walked over and asked what he was watching. "The flurries," he said.

22

★ ★ ★

I'M THE KID WHO DOESN'T EXIST.

The halls were flooded between periods one morning in early March as I raced up a set of stairs from one classroom to the next, juggling the dozen or so column ideas that were bouncing around in my head. The end of the year was now less than three months away, and I felt an urgency to round out the series I'd spent so many months working on. I wanted to make sure to pick the right columns to work on, the right students to write about, and the right issues to address. There were many more stories to tell and not much time left. Maybe that's why I was moving fast that morning.

As I reached the third floor, a student I had never seen before spotted me and shouted hello. I turned and saw a tall brown-haired young man walking toward me. "I'm Brent Jones," he said as he approached. The look on his face said I should have known who he was. But he didn't look familiar. And I'm horrible with names and didn't recognize his. So he elaborated. "I'm the kid who doesn't exist," he said.

He was smiling when he said that, but his words struck me hard. I had been waiting to meet Brent since Dean Hoover had mentioned him to me a couple of weeks earlier. Providing a broad sketch, she had told me about an eighteen-year-old senior who could not prove his identity. Without the ability to prove who he was, and without a social security number or birth certificate, she said, college, work, driving, and a normal postgraduation life were off-limits. She said he had told her that in the eyes of the government, he simply did not exist.

The story fit into an idea I had been pondering. It was based on the concept that so many students at low-income schools have boulders standing in their way. Some of the boulders are huge, and some are small. But in order for the students to succeed and have the opportunities they deserve, the boulders somehow have to be pushed out of the way. The boulder standing in Brent's way was a huge one.

I had a long list of other column ideas to pursue and a building full of compelling stories to find. But from the moment Hoover had mentioned Brent, his story had sounded like the most promising. Every student faces a world of challenges and obstacles after high school. Many face uncertainty. But Brent faced a black hole of a future. I wanted to know more about him, so I immediately abandoned my plan to sit in on whatever class I was heading toward. I reached out to shake his hand. "How are you?" I asked.

"I'm great," he said, still smiling and offering me a dose of the nonstop optimism I would soon learn was his trademark.

We didn't talk long that morning; he had a class to get to, after all. But I told him I was interested in his story, and we agreed to meet later in the week in the main office so that he could start telling it to me.

It would be quite a story—an amazing, frustrating, and complex story. One that at times would leave me struggling as I wondered what to do with it and how to tell it. But it was also a story that would ultimately give the school year an ending more wonderful than I could have imagined. And it would be yet another example of how much many of the students who walked the halls of Manual High School had to overcome in order to succeed.

Brent was a bright student, sporting a B average and having enough credits to graduate even though he had bounced among four high schools. The only thing left to do to fill out his high school transcript was pass a few required classes. So he went to Manual for half a day of classes in government, economics, and senior English. He left each day as most students were heading to lunch.

We met to talk for the first time just before noon a few days after meeting in the hallway. We sat at a desk just outside Principal Grismore's office and casually talked as he walked me through what he knew of his life story. His final class of the day had just ended. That initial conversation lasted only thirty minutes or so, but I left with the realization that it was going to take a long time to fully report on his story. His tale was filled with confusing questions, uncertainty, and sketchy details, and I had to be extremely careful before putting anything in the newspaper. But getting his story in the paper was my goal from the moment Brent shared it with me.

He believed he was born in the Orlando, Florida, area in 1991 to a woman he'd been told worked as a prostitute. That woman had disappeared when he was a baby, shortly after agreeing to let another woman and her partner raise him. The plan had been for the three women to keep in touch after Brent's birth mother left Florida. But within months the birth mother's phone number was disconnected, and calls to her friends produced no leads to her whereabouts. The women who raised Brent weren't even sure that the name they had for his birth mother—Elizabeth Anne Bennett—was truly hers. She'd had run-ins with the law and had used other names at times. Before long the two women moved to Indianapolis to be near friends and relatives. They broke up shortly after that move, though, and one of the women became Brent's caregiver. Her name was Kim, and she was the woman Brent had long considered his mother. "It's a crazy story, I know," Brent said that first day. "But it's mine."

As we talked, school employees occasionally passed by. Every one of them said hello to Brent, smiling as he charmed them with flattery and jokes. He had been at the school for only two months, but his engaging personality made it seem like he'd been there for years.

Brent told me more. He'd had health problems early in life, some of them appearing when he received immunizations that he'd likely already had but that Kim couldn't verify. They had moved around a bit, and money was always tight. But so were they. "She's my mom," he said simply. "She'll always be my mom. No matter what happens."

His birth's mom disappearance had not been much of a problem during most of his childhood, though it did prevent Kim from claiming a much-needed deduction on her tax returns. She didn't have Brent's birth certificate or any idea of how to find it, which prevented him from getting a social security number. Still, schools had accepted Brent without proof of his identity. And an Indianapolis court had granted Kim legal custody of him when he was four, based on the small number of papers she had from her Florida days.

But problems erupted when Brent turned sixteen. All of his friends were getting driver's licenses and part-time jobs. They were taking the first steps toward adulthood. Without a social security card, he couldn't do any of that. And trips to the social security office produced little but blank stares and disbelieving questions. He earned spare cash by working occasional odd jobs and wondered what the future would bring. "I was livid and really upset after the visits to the social security office," he said. "A lady there told me I was lying and there was no possible way my situation was happening. I couldn't understand how they could deny me. All I wanted to do were the things I need to do—get a job and a car and go to college. I see everyone around me getting cars and jobs. And I just can't do any of that. It crushes your spirit more and more. You have to depend on everyone else to get around and to get money. I feel like a child, and I know I'm not."

When I met him, Brent had recently begged out of the College Summit class that all seniors were required to take. He had received word that he couldn't apply for financial aid without proving his identity, and it was too depressing to sit in class as other students worked to open doors to college that were shut to him. It was particularly frustrating for a student who knew he was capable of succeeding at the next level of education. The school's decision to grant his request to leave College Summit was nothing short of malpractice. How, I thought, could school leaders have not insisted he stick with the class and do everything in their power to help him find the answers he needed? It was another sign of the apathy, low expectations, and assembly-line mentality that too often gripped the school.

Brent had ideas of what he wanted to do with his life. He had spent many of his younger days watching his mom, Kim, wait tables at a local Olive Garden. She couldn't afford babysitters, so he often spent his evenings in a closed-off section of the restaurant, doing his homework, eating, and essentially being adopted by the other staffers who worked there and watched him grow up. Kim spent her breaks and downtime with him, reading and talking. "They were great nights," Brent said. Years later he was dreaming of studying culinary arts at Vincennes University in southern Indiana and eventually owning his own restaurant. "I'm a really good cook," he told me.

I told Brent that newspapers had some pretty effective methods of ferreting out information and that I might have access to records that he did not. He was understandably skeptical, telling me about the lawyer Kim had hired to investigate the matter and the countless hours the two of them had spent on-line searching for his birth mother. They had called West Virginia authorities because Kim remembered hearing Brent's birth mother saying she'd been born there. They had argued unsuccessfully to get information from Florida authorities, knowing that Elizabeth had received public assistance at one point. They had called health departments in numerous states but came up empty every time. "There's nothing out there," Brent said. "We looked everywhere. It's like she's just gone."

Making the situation even more complicated, Kim had left the state for Missouri the previous summer, just after Brent turned eighteen. She faced a mountain of financial and personal problems and thought a fresh start would help. Brent, though, had wanted to finish his high school career in Indiana. So after Kim left he moved into the home of family friends and attended a suburban high school for the first semester of his senior year. Unfortunately he didn't get along with his hosts, and as the second semester of the school year arrived, he moved into a home owned by Kim's former girlfriend. Though the women had broken up shortly after moving to Indiana from Florida, they had kept in touch throughout the years. The old friend welcomed Brent in and happened to live just a few blocks from Manual High School. That became his new school.

Two months later he was doing well in his classes and making friends. Still, he knew that once the year was over, he would have nowhere to go. "I'm very excited about graduation," he said. "But there's this fear that I'm not going to be able to do anything with my life. If I can't go to college, I don't know what to do. I don't want to flip burgers. I want a career and not just a job. I think to better your life you need to go to college. That will take you places." He was at that point in life where opportunities should be plentiful. They weren't. "I can't even get a real job," he said. "I can't mow lawns forever. That's not a life."

I spent the next few days trying to figure out how best to pursue my column about Brent. I spent hours in my office researching online, but searches for "Elizabeth Bennett" were useless. It was a common name and also the name of a character in *Pride and Prejudice* as well as that of a young actress, so my hours were wasted. Calls to government offices in various states resulted in dead ends. I thought a lot about the danger of writing about Brent's story. He was a wonderful young man, full of spirit and energy, and despite his fears he refused to let his obstacles drag him down. He was friendly and polite and had made an army of friends at his new school. I wanted to help him. But as of yet I couldn't prove the accuracy of his story. I'd had to rely on the details he had been given by a woman I had not even talked to and who no longer lived in the same state.

The story was gripping, but I needed to know whether what Brent had been told was true. I hoped it was, because I desperately wanted to write about his situation, and I hoped that a column in the paper would spark one of Indiana's congressional representatives to get involved and help Brent cut through the thick red tape that had been in his way for so long. Colleges had responded well to the Manual series, offering scholarships to other students I'd profiled. Maybe Vincennes would find a way to help one student who couldn't prove his identity.

The next time we talked, Brent was in his typical good mood. He smiled and shook my hand and told me he had spoken with Kim about our first conversation. She had agreed to talk to me and hoped a story in the newspaper might help the situation. She had also given him permission to show me the papers inside a file he kept with him at all times. He had mentioned the file to me earlier, and I was intrigued. It was filled with dental and medical records stretching back to when he was two years old, along with school reports and letters from previous teachers. There was a copy of Kim's birth certificate and awards Brent had won over the years. There was also a letter Kim had written fifteen years earlier when she was first trying to explain their story to the judicial system. The file was his identity. He handed it over as we talked one day. "It feels like it's the only real way to show who I am," he said. "This is proof that I exist. The government might say I don't, but this file proves I do."

It seemed ridiculous that he felt the need to provide written evidence that he was once a baby and an elementary school student and now a teenager. But he did, and once he turned eighteen he insisted on carrying the file nearly everywhere he went. At school it was always in the backpack he carried from class to class. Two years earlier, Kim had given him the letter she had written for the courts. The letter told him a lot of information he had not known about his birth mother and her problems. "I kind of discovered my story by going through it," he said. "I cried when I first went through it. The story is touching. I'm a really happy guy. But it's not a happy story."

A few weeks earlier Brent's frustration had boiled over as he stood in line at a convenience store trying to buy an energy drink. The clerk had asked for his driver's license, because only people eighteen and older could buy it. Brent said he didn't have a driver's license but insisted to the clerk that he was eighteen. "Look at me," he said, "don't I look old enough? I swear I'm eighteen." The clerk didn't budge, and Brent didn't either. He'd had enough of this. And despite the line of customers behind him, he insisted on telling his story. He didn't have a social security card, he said, so he couldn't get a license. He was eighteen but couldn't prove it through normal means. The clerk wasn't interested and said there was nothing he could do.

Years of frustration had led Brent to this point. So as the clerk stared indifferently at him, and as anxious customers waited behind him in line, he pulled out his file. He put Kim's legal guardianship papers on the counter and asked the clerk to do the math. He was four in 1995, he said, so he had to be eighteen in 2009. He showed school records that listed his birth date. "I wanted him to understand I am a person, and I have this paper trail," Brent said. "It's not like I fell out of the sky. They don't understand that this is ridiculous. It's crazy. No matter how much you try to explain, people say, 'There has to be a way.' No. There isn't. I've tried everything." Ultimately a woman standing behind Brent assured him that she believed his story, and she bought the drink for him. That was nice. He thanked her. But he wanted to be able to do such things for himself.

I could tell that Brent believed there was no way of getting his questions answered. So I didn't promise anything other than a column about his situation. As we said good-bye that day, he gave me a copy of the letter Kim had written many years earlier. It answered many of the questions I had. The letter recalled the days in early 1992 when Kim first came across an infant named Brent Jones. She was living in an Orlando apartment complex and was friends with a couple who ran an unofficial day care center in a neighboring apartment. Kim and her girlfriend would visit the couple and spend time with the children they were watching, and Kim was drawn to two of them in particular: Brent and his nearly three-year-old sister. She noticed that the babysitters seemed overburdened and that Brent and his sister were not getting the attention they needed. Brent seemed sickly but was friendly from the first visit. The couple watching him complained that Brent's mom was erratic and sometimes did not pick up her children until two or three in the morning.

Over time Kim got to know Brent's birth mom, a woman named Elizabeth who was pretty and well-spoken but lost. "I found out that she was in serious trouble and had been arrested several times for drugs and prostitution," she wrote. "My heart went out to her because she was only 22, alone and extremely confused. Not being much older myself I didn't know what I could do to help. But being a Christian, I had to try."

Kim was most concerned about the conditions Brent and his sister were living in. Elizabeth's apartment was filthy and sometimes used to entertain clients. The children were being neglected—at home and at their babysitters' apartment. So she offered to begin watching the two children, and the offer was accepted. But there were rules. Elizabeth couldn't pick up the children in the middle of the night. They needed a routine, Kim said. And she had to pay for diapers and food and provide seventy dollars a week. The three women began to spend time together, talking and becoming friends. "We knew that changing Beth's mind about prostitution wouldn't be easy," Kim wrote, "but if she spent more and more time around us, maybe in time we would have a positive influence, and she could straighten out her life before she destroyed herself and her children's."

Over the next couple of months, however, Elizabeth's situation spiraled downward. She was evicted from her apartment, continued to use drugs, and took a job with a sleazy man who ran a sex hotline out of his apartment and refused to pay her for her work. She eventually decided to join a former boyfriend out of state who was her daughter's father but not Brent's. Elizabeth and Kim stayed up through the night on multiple occasions one week, talking through her options. She was thinking about giving Brent up for adoption, and Kim asked if instead she would let her raise the boy, who was now nine months old. She agreed to do so.

Kim and her partner would raise Brent, they decided, and eventually adopt him. They would all stay in touch, and Elizabeth would come back at some point to finalize the legal process. The plan worked for a few weeks. But then Elizabeth disappeared. Her phone number was disconnected, and calls to her friends turned up nothing. Kim and her girlfriend, meanwhile, made their move to Indiana shortly afterward, a move that made a reconnection even less likely. "I realize now that with her instability, I should never have let her leave," Kim wrote. "But I did not think after all I did for her that she would disappear, never to resurface."

I checked with a local juvenile court judge one day to ask about the likelihood that everything I was hearing was true. The judge said there wasn't a doubt in her mind, and that, sadly, she came across similar cases a few times a year. "It is an outrage," she said, "that there is no system in place to help these children. They are left on their own to maneuver through a complicated legal system, and few know how to find the help they need." I also checked with school officials, who said they had no idea what to do for Brent. Many administrators and teachers at many schools over the years had known his story, but nothing had been done to help him.

One day I went to lunch with Brent, the woman he was living with, and a friend of theirs who was a lawyer. The woman Brent lived with, Kim's former partner, didn't like me from the beginning and had no interest in being a part of the story. But at least she provided another layer of verification of the story. And like everyone else who knew Brent, she was a huge fan. "He's one of those very rare people who is genuinely always in a good mood," she said. "He's never down. There isn't anything in life that he doesn't look at in a positive way. That's a gift he has as a person. Considering all the weight he has on his shoulders, he has amazing stature."

The lawyer, meanwhile, told me she was researching an old Indiana law from the late 1800s that was aimed at helping former slaves receive proof of their identity. She said she just wanted to help the boy she'd gotten to know. "He's one of those achievers who is capable of so much but can't do anything because of their circumstances," she said. "They're stuck, and someone has to help them.

I'm going to do whatever I can to do that." That was admirable. But a stamp from a judge didn't seem like enough. If the legal procedure worked—and that wasn't guaranteed—it would indeed help by allowing Brent to get a social security card and apply for college aid. In his words, he would start to exist. But he also wanted answers about his past. He wanted that birth certificate.

At the time, my wife and I were pursuing adoption, and this was becoming a deeply personal column for me. I understood the questions Brent had, and I had to admit that it made me feel better when he told me that while he had questions about his birth, Kim was all the mother he would ever need. "There's always that tickle in the back of your throat," he said of his birth mom. "What's she like as a person? Where did I come from? What stock did I come from? I do want to know what she looks like. I want to know why she did what she did. I don't necessarily want her to be involved in my life. But I would like to talk to her. Just, 'Hey, nice to meet you.'"

Within a few weeks I had gotten to know Brent well. I had watched as other students said hello to him with respect in the hallway. He was an individual, with earrings in each ear and a tattoo on his calf, and he often started classes by sitting alone. But before long other students would surround him. It seemed to happen organically in every class. Teachers loved his exuberance. He paid attention in class and frequently answered questions, unlike so many of his classmates. He had a confidence—not cockiness but rather a mature confidence—that I didn't often see at Manual.

Over numerous conversations we talked about his teachers, friends, and dreams. He shared extremely personal details about his past. I felt like I knew him well. Still, I wanted to make sure I portrayed him accurately, and I understood the difficulty of getting a teenager to express himself to a forty-year-old journalist. So one day I asked him to help me with my column by writing a short essay about himself. "Just answer one question for me," I said: "Who is Brent Jones?" A day later he e-mailed me a few hundred words:

Well, this is actually a more difficult thing to do than I thought. Who is Brent Jones? Hmm. Well, I want to go to college for culinary arts. I have always loved cooking. It's great stress relief. I love to try new things. I really enjoy the occasional party. Video games and computers are my hobbies. I work out daily. I don't really love school. I don't hate it. I just don't love it.

I love to hang out with friends. I find ways to get around the best I can. I love to help out around the house. I helped build a fence in our backyard. Uhhhh. I love to build Legos secretly. I love Star Wars. I can sing, paint and draw. I used to act. I don't consider myself super religious. I am obsessive about my body and hair. I was raised by women so I am very girly. I have a tattoo. I love music and am not super picky about it. I am an all-around nice guy. I can be a dick, but who isn't sometimes? I have moved around a lot but I am still stable. I love dogs. Not a huge cat fan. I am a Leo so prideful and quite egotistical.

In other words, he was a typical American teenager. A really cool one. One who deserved a chance to fulfill his dreams. One who deserved to have that boulder pushed out of his way.

Kim was a crier, and I liked her immediately. She was emotional, especially when the subject was Brent. They talked and texted daily and had been through a lot together. She told me about the work she'd put in trying to find Brent's birth mom and the struggles of dealing with a complicated government system. She cried as she told me what a sweet child Brent was, how he would take food from the family's refrigerator when he was five years old and give it to friends who he worried didn't have enough to eat. They didn't always have health insurance, and some of Brent's youthful health problems had left Kim in poor financial shape. But she said that didn't matter. She just wanted her son to have opportunities. Living a few hundred miles away, she saw him as often as possible and missed him desperately the rest of the time. "Without bursting into tears again, I can't tell you how frustrating this is," she said. "Here is a young man I love, and we go through all of this year after year after year, and we can't get it resolved. It's just crazy."

Kim, who was now waiting tables at an Olive Garden in Missouri, said she had wanted to officially adopt Brent when he was younger. But her finances were always a mess, and she worried she wouldn't have been able to pass muster with those who were making the decision. "When you're in the Bible Belt and you're broke and you're gay, it's tough," she said. Then she cried again. "It was a privilege to raise him as my son, but it's an honor to know him as the man that he is," she said. "His heart is genuinely good."

When Kim was in her early twenties, she had given up a child for adoption. And then, a couple of years later, Brent came along. "We kind of needed each other," she said. "I think that's why God brought us together."

As our conversation ended, Kim asked me to do what I could to help her son. I said I would.

23

★ ★ ★

TROUBLE FOLLOWS ME.

Six weeks before Brent Jones arrived at Manual, another Brent left the school in handcuffs. Brent Walls had been caught dealing drugs in a gym locker room, and school police had found a loaded handgun in his pocket after arresting him. As his dad cried and school administrators breathed sighs of relief that nothing worse had occurred, the seventeen-year-old student was sent to the county's juvenile lockup facility. Within days he'd been shipped to the county jail, charged as an adult with a felony and several misdemeanors.

Walls spent the holidays behind bars. He missed Thanksgiving, Christmas, and New Year's Day. And as hundreds of other Manual students began the spring semester in January, he continued to sit in jail, unable to raise the bail money needed to get out. And he really wanted out—so much so that he signed a quick deal in February with the prosecuting attorney's office, pleading guilty to a felony firearms charge and accepting a two-year prison sentence. It was worth it, he decided. Anything to get the process toward freedom moving. With time served in the county lockup, he would likely spend only about nine months in state prison.

By March, Walls was out of the county jail and an inmate in the maximum-security Wabash Valley Correctional Facility in southwestern Indiana. He was assigned at first to a section of the prison reserved for minors. But he would be transferred to the larger adult section of the complex after his eighteenth birthday in late June. He had agreed to an interview with me early in his stay at the prison largely because he was desperate for visitors—any visitors—and it took longer for family members to win approval to visit the prison than it did journalists. Although I had seen him being arrested and had spent hours with his family, I'd never actually met the former Manual student until I made the 105-mile trip south to do so on a mild March morning.

I pulled onto the prison property as the bright sun beat down upon it. The drab concrete facility was in the middle of thousands of acres of Indiana farmland, miles from any businesses or homes and just off a four-lane highway that connected the Hoosier cities of Terre Haute and Vincennes. Ten-foot-tall fences stretched around the prison grounds. Circular barbed wire decorated the top of the fencing, and several armed guards watched from towers throughout the grounds.

Shortly after arriving, and after going through a metal detector and pat-down search, I sat with a prison employee in a meeting room that doubled as a chapel. I had been in the same building two years earlier while interviewing a twenty-something man who had been convicted of a double murder. Talking with him was heartbreaking. He was smart and funny, and I had written that it was easy to imagine him being a college student or the kid taking your order at Starbucks. How can our city be losing so many kids, I thought at the time.

On this day, Walls walked in a few minutes after I did, a frown on his pimply face. He was skinny and short with buzzed brown hair, and he wore a white T-shirt under a grayish prison-issued shirt. He looked tired; he liked to stay up late into the night and sleep during the day. So this interview was playing havoc on his normal schedule. He wasn't too excited about it anyway. In one of the letters his dad had shown me, he had written he wasn't "a big fan" of mine because of the column I had written about his arrest. But surviving in prison is all about finding distractions and ways to kill time. So here we were.

He had already been convicted and was in prison, so there was little reason to keep secrets about his past or his mistakes. During this conversation and another a week later, Walls laid out a life story that underscored the overwhelming challenges facing America's struggling schools. Here was a teenager who had spent more time in recent years on probation than off of it, whose family life was a dysfunctional mess, who skipped school more often than he showed up, and who had been welcomed back even after previous arrests on campus. Finding a way to educate a kid like him was a colossal task. And although failing schools shouldn't be given a pass, it is worth noting that within those test scores and graduation rates that get so much attention are students like Walls. His story drove home the point I had made countless times: the task of fixing struggling American schools and improving test scores is not a simple one. Anyone who thinks it is has spent little time in such schools.

Leaning back in his chair with his arms crossed, Walls told me about growing up with his mom in a small farm town until deciding to move to his dad's house in Indianapolis several years earlier. He had fought with his mom's boyfriend and was already getting in trouble by the age of ten. He also had been diagnosed with ADHD, bipolar disorder, and schizophrenia. "When I was little," he said, "I was crazy." He moved to Indianapolis while still in elementary school, but as we talked in prison that first morning he couldn't remember which schools he'd attended. He did remember getting into more and more trouble as he got older. He broke into cars and homes, began smoking dope and selling it. For a time he also sold crack, stopping only when he realized how violent the competition was. Along the way he fell in love with guns. By the age of fifteen he'd bought his first, a .357 handgun, on the city streets. Over the years, he bought or stole a few others. "It was crazy," he said of moving to the city. "I fell right into hanging out with the wrong crowd. There was gang activity. Everything. It was pretty bad. I experienced new stuff. It was nothing like living in the country. When I got to the city, everything got worse."

He estimated he had been in the juvenile lockup more than thirty times over the years, for offenses ranging from battery to drugs to theft. A recent probation report noted his "progression toward more severe and involved activities." He also landed with routine frequency in psychiatric hospitals and other treatment facilities. "When they asked me what medications I've been on," he said, "I said 'every one.' I was on just like everything when I was younger. I used to have so much anger it was unbelievable. People would say something to me, and I'd go right off. It was unbelievable. It ain't like that now. I can walk away from words. I didn't used to be able to do that. If someone's pushing me I can walk away from that. I can feel myself getting better in life. I'm learning. It's a learning process. That's what my dad says too."

It's easy to say such things in prison. But little in Walls's life to that point suggested he was ready to change. Even while he was in the county jail, he picked up an additional charge for fighting with another inmate and then a guard. That day, as he sat in prison, he talked nonchalantly and without regret about the time he slugged a female teacher at Manual in the face when she tried to break up a fight he was in. "She didn't have no training breaking up a fight, and I didn't like her," he said. "I went off on her. That's when I had a lot of anger."

As we talked, with his scowl and sour attitude, I couldn't help but think what an unlikable young man he was. Still, he was only seventeen and had come from a household that essentially guaranteed problems. And now he had a life ahead of him that was going to be filled with huge obstacles because of the felony on his record. He was a lesson for other students who dance on the edge of trouble. But he was also in need of tools that would give him a fighting chance once he was free and once he joined the roughly five thousand felons released into Indianapolis each year.

The felony had been heading his way for years, and he'd been on a particularly fierce collision course with it in the days leading up to his arrest. He said if he hadn't been arrested at Manual that November morning, he probably would have been arrested for something even worse in the days or weeks to follow. His life had become about little more than drugs and his obsession with guns. By the day he was busted, he said, he'd been arranging drug deals at Manual daily for about three weeks. Sometimes he would make the sale in a school bathroom. Often the actual transactions would take place in one of the ratty apartment complexes near the school. As the holidays approached, he was working hard, eager to earn money because he wanted to buy back a gun he'd sold to a friend. He had stolen the gun from his grandfather and had received a mountain of grief for doing so from his family. "I just had got off probation," he said. "I was doing good. I made a mistake, stole a rifle. I wanted it back. I wanted my grandpa's trust back, and I knew I couldn't get it without that rifle."

He continued telling a story that was frustratingly inconsistent. "I didn't want to get in trouble," he said. "I didn't want to at all. But trouble follows me. I ain't gonna lie. I was smoking weed. But I don't see nothing wrong with smoking weed. I see more people on the news crashing and killing people because of alcohol. I ain't addicted. I don't see it as a drug. I can just say no." He said he was one of several dealers at the school, and Manual's arrest records appear to back that up. In a school stained by poverty and occasional crime, word got around to others that he had drugs and money in his pocket. That, he said, is why he brought the gun to school that morning. He had heard that another student planned to rob him.

He woke up on the morning of his arrest still hazy from smoking too much weed the previous night. He threw on some clothes, stuffed a .25 caliber handgun he'd recently bought in his back pocket, and asked his dad for a ride to school. His initial plan was to have breakfast with a friend in the cafeteria and then head into the neighborhood to sell his product on the streets. That changed when he decided his first two classes would offer a good chance to catch up on sleep. He and his friend ultimately stayed for a third class, gym, so that they could work out.

But before long, they were in the locker room selling drugs. They had talked openly about it in the gym, so openly that another student overheard them and informed the teacher. Without much trouble, police found Walls and, soon afterward, his gun. He hadn't enjoyed a minute of freedom in the three months since. "That day I didn't want to take the gun," Walls said, sounding sincere but conflicted. "At the same time I did. I was reaching for it in my bedroom, and everything went through my head about what could happen. Should I take it?" He paused and then answered his question. "I took it. Honestly I don't know why. I was scared. The day before everybody was like, 'You're gonna get burned. This guy is serious.' Well, no one is going to take my stuff and hurt me. They'd get shot."

On the way to school he sat in his dad's backseat, his younger brother in the front. Thoughts raced through his head. Memories of a lifetime of mistakes and lockups hadn't yet persuaded him to straighten up. But they made him think. "On the way there I was thinking, 'I need to put this in the car,'" he said. "I just don't know why I didn't do it. I had all these thoughts about things going wrong."

I then asked the most important question: "Were you going to use it?"

"If I had to," he said. "I believe it protected me. I do believe God, or whoever, did this for a reason, got me in trouble for a reason. It just helped me, that's all it did. Opened my eyes. I just got off probation, and now I'm back in. What the fuck was I thinking? It's pretty bad. Not even three months free after five or six years on probation, and now I'm back on. I was pretty upset, so I think it opened my eyes."

He talked for the next thirty minutes about his plan to get a GED and then, hopefully, return to Manual after his prison stay to get a real diploma. It was a fantasy. He would be six months past his eighteenth birthday on his release date, and he had only three high school credits out of forty-two needed to graduate. A normal high school life wasn't a realistic option. He also talked of his lifelong dream of joining the army and his belief that a felony firearms conviction wouldn't get in the way. "That's all I want to do," he said. Later his dad told me his son still didn't seem to understand the gravity of his situation. That was hard to imagine as I watched Walls sit in his prison outfit in a maximum-security lockup in the middle of Nowhere, Indiana. He spent much of his days in a cell that was all of eighty square feet and that he shared with a roommate. But dreams are necessary in prison.

He said he thought about having a girlfriend and a baby someday, a kid who would look at him without judging him and who would offer him a chance to make amends for his life. A kid that wasn't like him, he quickly added. He talked about moving out of the big city and settling someplace quiet, somewhere like the farm town he once lived in with his mom, a woman he hadn't seen in years.

I asked about his sentence. "Ain't nothing," he said. "People in here got eighty. It ain't nothing. I can do this and get myself together. Just keep your head on straight, don't get into nothing." He said the key was staying out of trouble and finding ways to kill time. Television was good for that. So was working out. He could do more pushups than he thought was possible, he said. And he was looking forward to taking GED classes, though ultimately he never did. "It's not going to be easy," he said. "I'm not smart at all—that's from skipping, not going to school, being high at school, and doing all that dumb stuff. It really affects you. I don't know a lot at all. So hopefully I can pass it. It's gonna be hard. Everybody says it's easy. It's not easy for someone who doesn't know much."

As our meeting went on, Walls relaxed and occasionally even smiled and seemed more like the seventeen-year-old boy that he was. I actually started to like him, despite his past and his lack of remorse for the victims of his many crimes. He helped me understand the hole that some students dig themselves into at such a young age and the inability of some to see a world beyond their neighborhood. When he talked about earning two hundred dollars a week selling drugs—and that was during an extremely good week—I asked why he didn't just get a normal job, one that offered a stable paycheck and little danger. "Everybody is like, 'Why didn't you fill out applications?'" he said. "I did that for months. Nobody was hiring. I wouldn't do this stuff if I had a job. I never had that opportunity. I filled out hundreds of applications. Kroger. CVS. Popeye's. Every fast-food place. I did it for months, and they couldn't see I was trying. So I ain't gonna keep trying—that was my mind-set back then."

That excuse was hard to buy. Manual was filled with students who worked at the many nearby fast-food joints. But that was Walls's excuse. He just couldn't get a break, he said. Sitting there in prison, he did what many prisoners do: he made promises. "I plan on getting one of those jobs when I get out, though," he said. "Anywhere. I don't care if I have to scrub toilets. I'll do it—save up and get my life together. Quit hanging around with the wrong crowd. I have to earn everything. Show people. You can't just do it for months and say, 'I've changed.' It takes time. I ain't changed all the way yet, I can admit it. It's going to be hard for me to go home and if someone walks up and says, 'Let's go smoke a blunt.' What am I going to say to that? If I'm on parole, I'm not going to do that. But if they're offering it for free it's going to be hard. I love doing that stuff. But I got my mind set to say no."

We said good-bye a few minutes later, and Walls asked me to visit again sometime to help kill time. I said I would, shook his hand, and began to make my way out of the maximum-security prison.

Back at Manual, Raymond Rutland was continuing to race to his classes, set on never being late. Jammyra Weekly was talking with a classmate about the possibility of rooming together as freshmen in the fall at Indiana University, determined to move past the circumstances of her childhood. Brent Jones was wondering whether his identity problem would be resolved but was intent on studying and working hard in the meantime. There were many more students who had overcome tough circumstances and were heading toward better things.

Back in prison, Brent Walls left our interview and was taken by guards to another room, where he was strip-searched before returning to his tiny cell. He spent his days writing letters to his dad, asking him to visit and put money on his commissary account so that he could buy things such as soap and stamps. In those letters he promised he would have a brighter future. "Prison is big, Dad," he wrote in one letter. "Never been somewhere so bad that's so big. I can't wait till I get to hug you."

During the drive back to Indianapolis, I thought of what it would have taken to prevent Walls from making the decisions that eventually landed him in prison. I wondered whether he had a chance of doing something with life once he was out. It was noon, and he should have been in the Manual High School cafeteria, eating lunch with friends and complaining about teachers and homework. Instead he was spending the day in a cell.

24

★ ★ ★

I'M WILLING TO RUN THESE SCHOOLS.

Manual seemed to be in a leaderless rut by April. Principal Grismore was out of the school often and was frequently distracted by his new duties at district headquarters when he actually was in the high school building. Vice principal Elizabeth Owens had been selected to replace him as the school's top boss. But she was a low-key, behind-the-scenes type of administrator, who would not ascend to her new role until summer and who spent the semester hobbled by a nasty back injury.

This was particularly disturbing because schools like Manual desperately need strong and vigilant leaders. Paul Pastorek, who as Louisiana's superintendent of education led New Orleans schools through a dramatic post-Katrina transformation, insists that strong school leadership—leadership freed from district bureaucracy—is key to success. Manual not only lacked strong leaders but also was hampered by a suffocating top-down approach within the district. "What has to happen in public education," Pastorek said when we talked in 2011, "is that principals have to run the school. The future has to be about pushing responsibility, accountability, and autonomy to the principals. There has to be a person who can bring a team of people together around a shared mission." There was no such person at Manual High School.

A large part of the problem was the absence of Sergeant Barrow. The man who in many ways was the adult face of the school, the man every student knew and many turned to for help, the man who was a constant larger-than-life presence in the hallways, had collapsed on the hard tile floor just outside of his office in late February. He would be out for months, with major injuries to his face and a long recovery from an emergency surgery to remove a mass from his lungs. Although he would return in time for the next school year, healthier and as energetic as ever, his absence in the spring of 2010 was deeply felt. No other police officer and no other administrator possessed his ability to manage the hallways and work so well with so many teenagers. The building seemed even more lifeless without him, as if a big chunk of Manual's soul had been sucked out.

Meanwhile, an effort to get more students into their classes had fizzled from lack of effort. That initiative had begun in the fall as a group of teachers and other staffers joined together to conduct several hall sweeps each week after the start of class. With each sweep, dozens of students were corralled into an auditorium with threats of punishment ranging from in-school detention to out-of-school suspension. The students complained, but the effort temporarily helped with the problem and provided a spark to the best teachers in the school, the ones who participated in the sweeps and had pushed for them. They had desperately wanted to see expectations set at a higher level, and they knew their jobs would be more manageable if students knew there were consequences to their actions.

The problem was that the parents of the students most likely to be caught didn't seem to care, so the punishments carried little weight. Like many initiatives at Manual, this one faded away eventually. It was a lot of work, and Grismore was already trying to do two jobs. Thus, by spring the halls were more of a crowded mess than ever during class periods. On one typical spring morning I counted seventeen students trolling a second-floor hall ten minutes after second period began. Four other students stood just inside a bathroom. On the first floor at least ten more students meandered, missing whatever classes were on their schedules. There were five more students on the third floor. The funny thing was that these were students who actually showed up for school that day.

I asked one who often wandered the halls why he skipped so many classes. He told me he would think about that, and I asked him again when I spotted him skipping class later in the day. "I thought about that a long time," he said. "I have no idea." I asked about his grades. The answer wasn't surprising. "Rock bottom," he said. Another student, named Austin, stood laughing with friends near a stairway. "Right now, I'm one of the leading skippers in the building," he said, proudly. "I'm really smart. I just don't go to class." Other students complained about boring teachers and annoying assignments. They said they often didn't come to school at all because the day started too early and lasted too long. Most said they weren't sure they would graduate one day. Their words were depressing but not surprising; such apathy was a hallmark of the school and was also coming from the top of the hierarchy. Administrators had surrendered on the hall sweeps. They did little to lure missing students to school and clearly accepted the problem of students who didn't go to class or didn't show up on time.

I had long ago noticed a curious event that underscored the administration's indifference. Each morning one of the school's leaders would roll a cart into the hall just inside the school's main doors. The cart was covered with passes and a stamping machine. For ten or fifteen minutes after the first-period bell rang, the administrator would stand there, stamping and initialing passes that allowed late students to go to class. One morning I watched as Grismore handled the chore, handing passes to dozens of students. "Ladies, ladies," he said to a group of slow-moving and chatty students at 7:40 A M. "It's not time to conversate. You're late already." "Why are you always late?" he asked another student, receiving a shrug in return. At 7:45 a boy showed up with his shirt untucked. Grismore handed him a pass and told him to tuck the shirt in. The boy tossed down a textbook in frustration, tucked his shirt in, and walked away after picking up the book. "That boy would be out of school constantly if I suspended him for tardiness," Grismore said.

He blamed the teachers once again, saying students with engaging first-period teachers tended to show up on time with more regularity than other students. The teachers, on the other hand, blamed Grismore for not cracking down. They asked why so many students who showed up late were given free passes day after day. Both arguments had truth in them.

But at least those students who got passes showed up to school. Many others did not. Attendance was worse than ever. During the nineteen school days in February, only 12 percent of Manual's students had perfect attendance, and the school had not suffered a flu outbreak or other health epidemic that would explain the huge amount of absenteeism. The problem of missing students continued, largely without being addressed, into March and April. One day in April, as Vice Principal Owens sat at her desk, she read off the number of students who had missed one or more classes without an excuse during the course of a recent week. On that Monday, she said, 44 percent of the school's student population was absent at one point or another. The number jumped to 50 percent on Tuesday. It hung in the 45 percent range on Wednesday and Thursday before jumping to 56 percent on the last day of the week. "It's Friday," she said, explaining the late-week jump.

Manual had a tremendous list of problems and challenges. But getting students to class was its most fundamental. The lack of urgency on the issue was incomprehensible. How, I thought, could a school allow so many students to miss so many days of school, knowing those students, in many cases, were also the most likely to join the huge list of dropouts? When I asked Grismore about the class-skipping, he told me the school didn't have the manpower "to cover all the nooks and crannies" in the building. When I asked Owens about the poor attendance, she said, "Attendance is a complex issue." Both said they struggled to get parents to take the issue seriously, telling me about calls to parents who essentially told them, "Sorry, but my kid just doesn't like getting up in the morning."

They were lackluster excuses, and they were yet more examples of the apathy I so often thought about and wrote about during my year at Manual. I had gotten tired of saying and writing that word, but it defined so many aspects of Manual High School. It was standing like a razor-wired prison fence between Manual and improvement. And it explained a meeting that occurred about four miles north of Manual on another spring morning.

The meeting involved arguably the two most important men in Indiana's public education system: Tony Bennett, the second-year state education superintendent, and Eugene White, the superintendent of Indianapolis Public Schools. The meeting was set so that the two men and their aides could discuss the looming possibility that the state government would seize control of Manual High School and nearly two dozen of the state's other worst-performing schools. That dramatic and unprecedented threat had hung over Manual all year, and it had led to the visit by a state assessment team in the fall, that group's scathing report, and constant questions from teachers and staff about the future of their school.

There was no guarantee that a state takeover would bring vast improvement to the affected schools. There was no quick fix and no easy way to increase the participation of parents or to make up for the academic struggles of high school students that stretched back to their youngest years. The lack of such a guarantee, though, couldn't be an excuse to sit back and watch another generation of students fail and drop out. As the latest school year at Manual approached its conclusion, it was clear that its current and future students deserved big and dramatic changes to the way their school was run.

The meeting between Bennett and White was intended to see if the district was capable of putting a serious plan in place to implement such changes. It took place in a sixth-floor conference room in the school district's downtown headquarters. Twenty other state and district officials would sit around a table debating the issue. Ultimately, though, this meeting was about White and Bennett—two big personalities who would be sitting at opposite ends of the table.

White was in his fifth year in the district. Tall and known for his bold suits and blunt talk, he had disappointed many in the city with his unwillingness to clean house in a district known for inefficiency and mismanagement. But he was an engaging figure, and he had brought some positive changes to the district's long-established acceptance of low standards. At graduation ceremonies, he had angered many in the city for kicking out loud parents. He had irritated students, parents, and some faculty for insisting on a strict dress code aimed both at making the schools look better and ridding them of obvious signs of gangs. He had created magnet programs and closed schools because of continuing budget cuts. He created alternative programs for students who couldn't behave in traditional settings. And he had scolded bad parents and at times ordered busloads of students sent home when he spotted them misbehaving.

Bennett, meanwhile, was a southern Indiana Republican whose blunt talk on behalf of reform had sparked a series of controversies within the state's education community. Teachers despised him, arguing that he blamed them for the shortcomings of Indiana's schools. Superintendents and school boards complained that he was too tough on their schools. He fought with opponents who didn't like his push for more charter schools, performance-based pay for teachers, and sweeping changes to the way teachers are licensed. His battles with teachers unions were the fiercest, earning severe reprimands from union leaders. And he loved it. A former high school coach and local superintendent, Bennett had won the state superintendent's election on a vow to radically redefine education in the state. He had promised to dramatically increase the state's graduation rate within four years. He claimed allegiance to the reform-minded message of Arne Duncan, Democratic president Barack Obama's education secretary. He loved the idea of leaving a big mark on the state's education landscape. Taking over a group of schools would leave quite a mark.

As 9:00 A M approached on the morning of the meeting, fifteen school district employees hovered around a long wooden table waiting for the state officials to arrive. White sat calmly in his checked suit, strategically directing his employees where to sit. He told one staffer to sit in the chair that would be just to Bennett's left. "Slap him if he gets out of hand," White said with a smile.

Word came that the state officials had arrived and were in the lobby downstairs. One of White's employees offered to go down to guide them to the conference room. "No," White said. "Let them find their way up."

A few minutes later Superintendent Bennett was the first state official to walk in. His constantly bubbly personality quickly filled the room as he shook hands and offered greetings in his southern Indiana twang. White stood to shake Bennett's hand. He towered over him but knew Bennett had the upper hand in this meeting.

The greetings didn't last long. Within a minute, Bennett was seated, and the meeting had officially begun. His opening message was blunt. "We need to emphasize the seriousness of this issue," Bennett said, his smile gone. "And I want you to be able to have every discussion you have going forward with a framework. And that framework is this: who do we want to run these schools? I know who I want to run these schools. That's the guy sitting at the other end of the table." He pointed toward White, then continued. "But I'm willing to run these schools," he said. "And we need to have a serious discussion about what this district is willing to do differently, because if we don't get to where we need to be, the state will be taking over these schools." White didn't react, and Bennett continued to talk. "My goal is to be a resource, either a teammate or adversary for you," he said. "I'm either for you or against you. Whatever helps the most."

By that, Bennett meant White could blame the state for unpopular decisions he would have to make to truly turn around his schools. Or they could work together on changes to state law that would give the district more power over the teachers union. I had often thought that White and Bennett could be an unstoppable force if they worked together. Bennett, the white Republican from rural Indiana, and White, the black Democrat from the big city. Both had big personalities and strong support from the general public. They would be a force. But on this day they appeared to simply be feeling each other out. They were not teammates.

The prospect of a state takeover stemmed from a 1999 Indiana law aimed at better monitoring the performance of the state's public schools. Through a long series of steps, evaluations, and studies, the law could result in the first round of state takeovers beginning in the summer of 2011. The takeovers would allow dramatic and immediate changes. Union rules at the affected schools would be tossed out. Lackluster teachers could be displaced immediately without regard to seniority, and the new school leaders could replace them in any way they chose, rather than having to use the rules mandated by a union contract. The school days and school years could be expanded. There would be increased curriculum flexibility, allowing the school, for instance, to give students three hours of language arts a day to improve their reading skills if that was needed. New administrations would be brought in. The buildings could be run like charter schools. "The intent," Bennett said, "would be intense structural reform of the school."

Sitting at the table, he told White the state wanted to see the district turn around the schools on its own. That was the best possible scenario. But he was tired of tweaks and baby steps that sounded good but had given Manual and other schools yet another generation of lousy test scores and graduation rates. This meeting was a call for big changes, he said. "The last thing I want to do is make a recommendation to the state board of education that we should take over these schools," Bennett said. "But I will, and I won't flinch. And I don't think the state board will flinch before accepting my recommendation."

As Bennett and White talked, both had in front of them copies of the devastating state report documenting conditions at Manual. The report blasted the school's leadership and learning culture, as well as everything from its outreach to parents to its communication with students. There were similar reports with similar findings for several other Indianapolis high schools. As the state officials outlined them, White didn't argue. He had been complaining about the caliber of his high schools since he arrived five years earlier. But he did emphasize that the state takeover would put the new school leaders at an advantage, because they would not be bound by the strict union rules that he blamed in part for keeping bad teachers in his schools. "That's a great advantage for you and a great disadvantage for me," White said. "I don't see the teacher contracts being put to sleep, so I think your conversation should begin with the teachers union. I want to see what you can make them do."

With that, a state aide asked White to identify the percentage of ineffective teachers at the various schools the state was threatening to take over. White's answers provided the most stunning moment of the meeting and underscored the chronic problems in the district.

The state aide started with the teachers at Arlington Community High School on the city's north side. "I would say sixty percent of them would be questionable," White said.

The state aide moved next to Manual. "Again, sixty percent," White said.

Northwest High School? "Sixty percent," White said.

The state official then asked about two middle schools. In both cases White said, "I would say forty percent."

Howe Community High School? "We'll give them sixty percent."

George Washington High? "Definitely you have to put them in the sixty percent category," White said.

Only one high school, which had just been transformed into a magnet school, escaped such low marks. Even there, though, White said one in ten teachers were not up to par.

The superintendent then acknowledged a glaring self-inflicted problem in the district: despite so many poor-performing teachers, the district had done little until recently to hold them accountable. Firing even the worst teachers, a complicated process filled with union contract obstacles, can take eighteen months or longer. And although White said there were many poor teachers in his district's classrooms, he added that a serious teacher evaluation system had just begun that school year. He said leaders were finally in the process of tackling the problem more diligently but that it would take at least three to five more years before significant results could be recorded. "We have a bunch of people who are pedestrian or below that," White said. "They have twenty-five or thirty years of service, and they aren't going anywhere unless we push them out. That's a reality for us."

The state officials appeared stunned by White's candor. They had been in meetings in other districts across the state in which local officials had greeted them with animosity and brushed off their criticism. That wasn't happening here. White was a realist. He knew changes were needed. He was also a better politician than most local school bosses. He knew what to say and when to say it.

Still, the Indianapolis school leader did not yet have a comprehensive turn-around plan. All he had done was point fingers of blame at the teachers and ask for more time. That wasn't enough. After White finished talking, Bennett emphasized that he wasn't inclined to let three or four or five more years slip by without noticeable improvements in the schools. As for the union rules, he reminded everyone in the room that those rules would be completely wiped out under state control. Such a threat, he said, should give White leverage in his talks with the unions.

That was enough for a pair of union officials sitting in the middle of the room. "You guys believe we protect bad teachers, and we don't," Ann Wilkins, president of the local teachers union, angrily told Bennett. "We protect the process. If you don't respect the process, I'm coming after you." Everyone listened quietly as Wilkins talked. "We don't want bad teachers out there," she said. "I don't appreciate the argument that we want bad teachers in the classroom."

Bennett wasn't the least bit swayed. "Here's the reality," he said. "If you've protected one bad teacher, you protect bad teachers, period."

"I don't protect bad teachers," Wilkins said, sounding even angrier. "I protect the process."

"That particular argument is an argument for protecting bad teachers," Bennett replied.

A few days after the meeting between White and Bennett, I sat in the Manual principal's office. Grismore sat behind his desk, agreeing with White's assessment that 60 percent of his teachers were underperforming. He also acknowledged that he had done little to address the problem. He didn't have time to deal with the time-consuming process of firing a bad teacher, even though he knew there were several in his building. Teachers told me of going a year or more without having an administrator sit in their classroom.

In the weeks that followed, Grismore and Owens would begin the process of laying out a district turnaround plan to their teachers. At the heart of it would be a requirement that at least half of the school's staff would be replaced after the next school year. Everyone in the building would have to interview for their job. In a sign of the district's infuriating lack of big thinking, though, the staff who left Manual would likely be replaced by those kicked out of other district schools that were going through similar turnaround processes. And those who were kicked out of Manual would likely be placed in other district schools. "They're just shuffling the deck," history teacher Sean Marcum told me one day.

He was right. It was another tweak in a school that had seen many of them over the years. Ultimately, few imagined that would be enough to deter Bennett from taking over at least some of the city's schools. He wanted to see major reforms, the type that America's struggling schools desperately need, and it didn't appear that Manual was capable of such things.

25

★ ★ ★

NOW I KNOW WHY I'M TALL.

I continued to talk to Brent Jones as often as I could as the spring progressed and the end of the school year drew closer. His story had to be written. But for some reason I found myself struggling to write a column about him. I had started to write it several times only to be repeatedly disappointed with what I'd produced. Each time, I would temporarily push it aside and write a column on another subject. That wasn't surprising. I had long found that the columns I cared the most about were the ones I had the most trouble writing.

Meanwhile, I had run into nothing but dead ends during my research about Brent's birth mother, and I continued to worry about writing a column full of unanswered questions. I also wondered how readers would react. Most people are kindhearted, and the Manual series in particular had generated a wonderfully positive response. But some people can be horribly brutal toward the subjects of newspaper profiles these days, and there would undoubtedly be questions raised about whether Kim had done enough over the years or whether the story was even true. Others would hurl homophobic comments her way on online forums. I had warned Brent and Kim about this, but they both said they weren't worried. Still, I struggled as I looked for the best way to tell their story.

One day toward the middle of April, I decided I simply had to write the column. I couldn't worry about having a perfect ending or all the answers. The story was so compelling that it alone would grab readers. Brent deserved to have his story told, and he was excited by the prospect that a column might inspire others dealing with the same problem to come forward. "I know there are a lot more cases like mine," he said. "So I hope it will help people in my situation who are afraid to come out because they are scared of what might happen. Plus," he added, "if nothing changes, I'll be graduating in a few weeks with no options." As I prepared to write the column, I spent a few more days going to Brent's classes, watching him interact with other students and teachers. Danese Kenon, the photographer I worked with, joined me and took dozens of candid photos of Brent. Later I noticed there were few shots in which Brent wasn't smiling.

One morning Brent and a few dozen classmates attended a meeting in the auditorium. The goal of the meeting was to help teenage boys—the most at-risk students—navigate the many landmines in their paths. That morning, Bruce Shadiow, a veteran teacher who helped organize the meeting, talked for a few minutes before introducing the day's speaker. "Guys, you never know when your opportunities in life are going to come up," he said. "When they do, you need to take advantage of them." Brent sat in the front row, listening intently. He deserves to have opportunities to take advantage of, I thought.

I left my office on a Friday afternoon in April planning to begin writing the column about Brent the following Monday. No more delays. The column was slated to run April 25, roughly a month before his graduation. The timing was perfect—it would underscore the urgency of Brent's situation. I couldn't wait to get it in the newspaper.

Although it might seem silly, the movie choice my wife and I made that weekend dramatically changed the angle of the column. That Sunday evening, as the warm weekend faded away, we paid $3.99 to watch *The Blind Side* on pay-per-view. The movie is based on the true story of a gifted high school football player, Michael Oher, who was adopted by a wealthy Southern family. Sandra Bullock won an Oscar for her portrayal of the film's heroine, Leigh Anne Tuohy, the woman who took the young man in and fought hardest for his future. It was a fine movie, but one scene in particular struck me. In it, Bullock traveled to one of the worst housing projects in Memphis to track down the boy's mother and hopefully find the birth certificate he needed to get a driver's license and move on with his life. During her trip to the other side of town, she met the boy's mother and emerged from her apartment with the answers and documents he needed.

As I watched the movie I thought about Brent. The stories were different. In the movie, the boy at the center of the story knew who his mom was and generally where she lived. Sandra Bullock's character only had to track her down. But Brent's birth mother was a mystery. Additionally, Brent had grown up in safe environments in Indianapolis, not the violent neighborhoods of Memphis. And unlike the young man in the movie, he'd had loving adults around him from the beginning who watched over him and kept him safe.

But there was a familiar missing piece in the lives of the two young men. They both were in search of answers and futures and opportunities. When the movie ended, I knew I had to try harder to find Brent's birth certificate. Simply telling his story wasn't enough. As a soon-to-be adoptive dad, I knew the importance of filling in the missing pieces of an adopted child's past and having answers about his or her birth family. My son would have those answers. And Brent, I thought, should too.

I talked to Brent at school on Monday. I wanted to make sure he was comfortable with my attempt to locate his birth mom. I had asked before, but I'd read a lot about adoption in recent months and didn't want to force information on him that he wasn't ready to receive. As always, though, he was calm and relaxed and said he wasn't worried. "I want to know anything I can know," he said. "Who wouldn't want to know where they're from?"

When I returned to the newspaper from school early that afternoon, I walked straight over to Cathy Knapp, one of the paper's librarians. She had worked at the *Star* for forty years at that point but remained one of the most optimistic and hardest-working employees in the building. I wasn't surprised when she agreed to help me on my quest to find the elusive Elizabeth Anne Bennett, or when she took a nearly obsessive approach to the task. I gave her everything I had learned from Kim: Elizabeth's name, the estimate that she was forty years old, that she had lived in Florida in the early 1990s and might be from West Virginia originally. I told Cathy that Elizabeth had at times danced in strip clubs in Florida and likely had an arrest record. Cathy planned to run a comprehensive report on Elizabeth, a search that would look for all names associated with her, as well as addresses, liens, lawsuits, professional licenses, relatives, neighbors, and just about any other public record imaginable.

As Cathy got to work, digging through public records and other databases, I went to my office and did the same. Although Kim believed Brent was born in June 1991, she said she couldn't be sure of that. So I spent two hours going through the *Orlando Sentinel*'s online archives, searching birth records for a Brent born to an Elizabeth sometime in 1991. And then I went to a Florida government website and paid forty-eight dollars to find arrest records from that time period for an Elizabeth Anne Bennett. That produced our first clue. My heart beat fast as I read the reports, which detailed arrests for shoplifting and drug possession and a few other crimes in the late 1980s and early 1990s. I rushed to Cathy. Her early searches had turned up a world of bad and confusing information. But we now had a birth date and partial social security number to use, and one police report listed Elizabeth's birth state as North Carolina. Those were crucial pieces of evidence that would help us target our search.

A bit later, Cathy hit a home run. She had mixed into a public records search the last name Jones, Brent's last name, with the name Elizabeth Bennett and some of our other new information. After doing so, she found another potentially affiliated name: Elizabeth Jones-Gati. The woman's age seemed correct. And she had worked in Florida in the 1990s. Two of the employers listed were strip clubs. "This has to be her," I said. These reports, though, are typically filled with mistakes and information that will send searchers on maddening wild goose chases. The list of potential phone numbers and relatives are often incorrect. Still, the information was helpful. We had something to go with and phone numbers to try. According to the report, Jones-Gati was currently living, or recently had lived in, a tiny South Carolina city.

Cathy printed off the roughly fifty-page report, and I retreated with it to my office. It was a little after 5:00 PM as I started dialing the dozens of phone numbers listed on the report. Time and again the people I reached said they'd never heard of Elizabeth. Other numbers were disconnected or went unanswered. But as the phone rang during one call, I typed "Elizabeth Jones-Gati" into a simple Google search. And there it was: a Facebook page for a woman of that name, whose picture looked like that of a forty-something woman, and who lived in South Carolina. That's got to be her, I thought. But could it really be this easy?

To be sure, I copied the woman's photo and e-mailed it to Kim, the woman who raised Brent. I reached her on her cell phone as she waited tables at the Missouri Olive Garden and asked her to check her e-mail when she had a break. She took one almost immediately, borrowing her boss's computer. She called back a few minutes later. "Oh, my God, Matt," she said. "That's her. There's no doubt in my mind. That's her. She's older. But, my God, it's been twenty years. How did you find her?"

Amazingly, I told her, it hadn't been that hard. And although I didn't say it, the lawyer she had hired a couple of years earlier should have been able to turn up the same information. And the schools Brent had gone to for thirteen years should have been able to find a social services agency capable of getting his questions answered. But that wasn't important now. I told Kim there was more work to be done and I would call her when I had more information. I suggested she not tell Brent what I had found until we were certain. She hung up the phone and returned to waiting tables.

I sat at my desk tossing a baseball in the air and pondering my next move. I could have sent Elizabeth a direct message on Facebook, but that seemed risky. How would a woman react to a strange man writing her to say he was a journalist who had met her long-lost son? She might not believe it, and even if she did, I worried that an e-mail could simply be ignored. I had no way of knowing whether she wanted to know anything about her son.

So instead of e-mailing, I dialed the one phone number listed on the comprehensive report under her name. I had called it several times throughout that day, but it had gone unanswered each time. That was still happening. I wasn't sure the number was even hers, but I called it every twenty minutes or so as 6:00 PM and 7:00 PM passed, hoping it would be answered at some point. Meanwhile, Elizabeth's name had turned up a few other bits of information online. She had gone online recently to sign on as a 1987 graduate of a high school in Florida for troubled teens. The fact that she was in Florida at that time seemed to reinforce the belief that we had found the right person.

After another unanswered phone call at about 8:30 PM, I scanned yet again through the long comprehensive report Cathy had given me and spotted something I hadn't noticed before. It listed a potential employer as a polo farm in South Carolina. "Yes!" I shouted to myself. Elizabeth's Facebook page had included a picture of her on a horse. I Googled the farm and found its website; it was located in the same city in which Elizabeth lived.

I called the farm's office number, but it was, of course, closed by that time of night. Fortunately there was another number for the horse barn listed on the website. Hoping it would be answered after hours, I dialed it, and a friendly woman answered. I casually asked for Elizabeth but was told that nobody by that name worked at the farm. Before hanging up, I asked if an Elizabeth Jones-Gati had ever worked there. She had, the woman said. Great, I thought. I finally had a person on the phone who knew Elizabeth. I wasn't going to waste the opportunity, and I knew that dealing with a person in the barn after hours was likely to be easier than dealing with someone in the main office in the morning. I asked the woman on the phone if she knew how I could reach Elizabeth. "We're not really allowed to give out that kind of information," she said. I understood and asked the woman if she was friends with Elizabeth. She said she was. I paused and thought about what to do next. Then I decided to go for it.

"This is going to sound crazy," I said. "But I'm a newspaper columnist in Indianapolis, and I'm writing about a boy I believe Elizabeth gave up when he was a baby. I hate to bother her, but her son is having trouble getting into college because he can't find his birth certificate. We really need to talk to Elizabeth." There was dead air. "Can you help me?" I asked. The woman sweetly said that she shouldn't give out Elizabeth's number but would call her and relay the message and my phone number. She promised to call me back regardless of what Elizabeth said. "Thank you," I said.

I sat in my office, pacing the room and wishing there was someone around to talk to. But my pacing didn't last long. The phone rang two minutes or so after I had hung up. It was the woman from the barn. "I talked to Elizabeth," she said. "I'm sorry, but she said she doesn't have a son."

My jubilant mood immediately sank. And as the woman continued to talk, saying she wished she could help and that she wished Brent well, my other phone line rang. It was coming from the same South Carolina area code. It was Elizabeth. "I've got to take this," I said, apologizing for cutting the conversation short.

Elizabeth had a soft voice, and it trembled as she asked for me. I told her who I was and why I'd been looking for her. I reached for a yellow legal pad and a pen as I talked. And before I got very far into my explanation, she asked for the name of the boy I had met.

"Brent Jones," I said.

"Oh, my God," she said, breaking into tears. "I can't believe you found me. I've never known how to reach him."

"He's been looking for you for several years," I said.

"I didn't know," she said.

Immediately, as she sobbed, she asked if he was healthy. I said he was.

"What's he like?" she asked quietly.

"He's one of the most impressive kids I've ever met," I said. "He's really friendly and optimistic. He's very bright."

"Oh, my God," she said again. "What does he look like?"

"He's a really good-looking young man," I said. "He's tall with brown hair."

As Elizabeth stopped crying she told me she had long wanted to talk to her son. Her friend from the horse farm had confused her, she said, apologizing. She said she'd lived so long without a son that she didn't understand the woman's call at first. It was only after they hung up that she realized I was calling about the son she had given up.

I told her again why I was calling, about Brent's struggle to prove his identity. And she began to fill in the holes. Brent had been born in Fairfax, Virginia, not in Florida. That explained many of the dead ends Kim had run into. And she'd left Florida with her daughter in 1992 for Virginia, not West Virginia, as Kim had long believed. She had changed her name with marriages over the years. Jones had been her maiden name. She verified Brent's name and birth date and told me his sister was living in the Southwest. She said she gave up Brent because "I was really young and on drugs and not able to take care of him." She hadn't done it the right way. But she'd done the right thing, I said. She wasn't capable of giving her son the life he deserved, and Kim had raised Brent with love and affection. The two were really close, and he was graduating from high school. He'd had a better life because of Elizabeth's decision.

Elizabeth told me that her life had begun to take a positive turn in the past several years. She had given up dancing awhile back—"Age catches up with you," she said—and had been sober for seven years. She had a longtime boyfriend who she said was a strong and stable influence. She loved horses and worked as a groomer at another farm. She lived paycheck to paycheck but was getting by. "I'm doing good," she said. "It was bad for a long, long time. But I'm doing good now. A good man saved me and helped get me away from all the drama and all my drug problems." She was born in North Carolina but told me she'd grown up both in England and the States after being adopted by an English couple. They had kicked her out of their house when she got pregnant with Brent's older sister while in high school, and she ended up at the boarding school in Florida. Before long she was a young single mother with a world of problems.

We talked for a while longer, and when we said our good-byes I told her I would give Kim her phone number the next day. It was well past 9:00 PM, and I was in uncharted territory as a journalist. I wanted to talk with my boss before taking the next step, just to be safe and certain that I had considered all of the potential ramifications of what was happening. I asked Elizabeth if we could talk again, and she said that would be fine.

"Thank you for finding me," Elizabeth said before we hung up. "And thank you for helping Brent."

"It was an honor," I said.

I went to Manual the next day and found Brent in his chemistry class. He and his classmates were boiling cabbage in a Bunsen burner as part of an experiment. Brent started at his own table, but before long three students had joined him. I didn't tell him about the events of the previous night but instead asked again whether he was sure he was comfortable with my looking for his birth mother. "No sweat," he told me with a smile.

Back at my office a bit later, my boss, Tim Swarens, was excited by the development. As the father of adopted children himself, his only suggestion was that I check with an adoption expert to see if there was anything I should consider before helping Kim, Brent, and Elizabeth reunite. I took the advice and called the adoption agency with which my wife and I had been working. The head of the agency assured me that everything sounded good and offered to talk to Brent if he wanted to work through the emotions of meeting his birth mom. She also expressed frustration with the situation. If someone had called her office or another agency, she said, they could have easily helped Brent maneuver through the legal issues standing in his way. Ultimately, it turned out that all the preparation was not necessary. Elizabeth had been so excited by the news that she had "friended" Kim on Facebook shortly after we talked, and the two of them had shared a long, tear-filled talk overnight.

At about 2:00 PM on Tuesday, Brent called me. He had just had his first conversation with his birth mom. "I was nine pounds, twelve ounces at birth!" he said. "Can you believe that?" He laughed and told me he'd learned he had family in Australia and that there was a statue to an old relative of his in some town there. "And now I know why I'm tall," he said, telling me that Elizabeth was five feet, ten inches. He said Elizabeth had already ordered a copy of Brent's birth certificate from Virginia and that he would likely have it in his hands by the end of the week. We talked about what that meant. A car. A job. And most important, college.

Kim called later to cry and laugh about the development, and I talked to Elizabeth that evening. "I just think he's an awesome kid," she said. "He's willing to give me his love. I'm willing to give him whatever he wants. I just want what's best for Brent."

The three of them were hundreds of miles apart. So they turned, not surprisingly, to Facebook. "Having the best day ever," Elizabeth wrote. "Just spoke with my son."

"Everything has come full circle," Kim wrote. "The sun is a little brighter today. The storm has passed. I love you, Brent. Welcome back, Beth."

"I just talked to my biological mom," Brent wrote shortly after their first conversation. An hour later, he was writing more. "My emotions are off the freaking charts."

"I feel the same way," Elizabeth replied.

My column ran that Sunday under the headline "Kid Who Doesn't Exist Looks to Future." The reaction was unlike anything I had experienced in my career. I checked my e-mail after a Sunday morning run and found dozens of messages already. My voice mailbox quickly filled up. The messages continued to pour in every minute and were filled with beautiful words of hope and kindness. Readers offered Brent jobs and financial assistance. They thanked him for being such a great young man. Many sent him cards and gifts at school. The president and a trustee from Vincennes University were among the first to write, promising to do whatever it took to find money for Brent. They did, and he was soon admitted under a full scholarship.

The following week, Brent went to the social security office with his birth certificate. Unlike previous visits, during which his story was dismissed, the manager of the local office rushed to the counter to help him. He had heard about Brent and promised to oversee the application personally. By summer Brent had his long-awaited social security card.

Brent, Kim, and Elizabeth were in constant contact in the days after their reunion. Kim repeatedly thanked her old friend for giving her a son; Elizabeth thanked Kim for raising such a good young man. They agreed they would all meet in Indianapolis for Brent's graduation in just a few weeks.

When I saw Brent in school in the days after the column ran, he told me about the constant text messages he and his birth mom were sharing. He jokingly called her his "bio-mom." He became something of a local celebrity. A TV news crew followed him around, and he was invited to be in a south-side parade. At school a visitor asked for his autograph. But he handled it well. "Hey, I'm eighteen," he said. "I might be getting a big head, but I'm trying to make sure it doesn't get too big."

26

★ ★ ★

WOW, THIS IS AMAZING!

Students walked through the front doors early one morning late in the school year, filling the hallways with noisy conversation. They laughed and argued and shouted on their way to the start of the day. But even the collective voices of hundreds of students could not drown out the mighty voice of English teacher Roslyn Stradford. Stradford was one of Manual's most dedicated and energetic teachers, with a high-pitched voice that spilled through the closed door of her classroom every day. She was known for taking students in need of a formal outfit shopping and for answering e-mail questions from students late into the evening. She is one of the thousands of dedicated teachers who fill American schools. On this day, her advanced placement students would be taking their end-of-the-year standardized tests. She had spent months preparing them, engaging them in classroom conversations and hoping to help them earn scores that would allow them to move on to college. Her voice that morning, though, was louder and pitched even higher than usual as she nearly screamed into her mobile phone. She was talking to a student who hadn't yet shown up, a student she'd worked with for countless hours during the past several months. She had told him the day before to be at school by 7:15 AM, and not a minute later, just to be sure he was sitting at his desk and relaxed and ready for the 7:30 AM test.

But it was now five minutes before the start of the school day, and the student was nowhere to be found. Stradford wasn't surprised, but she was frantic as she dialed his number. Her voice got even louder, providing an early morning comedic moment, when he told her he had overslept and was still a few blocks away. "You have five minutes to get across the street and get to room one thirty-one so you can take that test," she shrieked, her voice filling the hallway. Then she reminded him of the school's cost of handling the test. "If you don't make it, you're going to owe me eighty-five dollars. I'm serious." She was indeed serious, and within a minute the boy was sprinting across Madison Avenue so that he could be in class before the bell rang. The moment, while funny, was also a shining example of what a great teacher can mean to a student.

All around the building, students and teachers were making similar final pushes as the school year came to an end. It had been a long one. But the conclusion of an academic year is naturally a celebratory time. There are graduation ceremonies, the much-anticipated release into summer vacation, and, despite all of Manual's problems and headaches, the ability to at least claim that another year had been survived. For some students the end of the year was a time to relax a bit, knowing they had done the work necessary to guarantee good grades and graduation. There were final tests to take, but most of the work was done. Others, though, still had to push. And they had to push until the final minutes. Michael Canner was one of those students.

With long brown hair and a likable lackadaisical style, Michael had veered from school in past years. He had missed weeks at a time during some semesters, because he was more interested in playing his guitar or his piano—or, yes, watching TV or sleeping in—than going to class. But now graduation was approaching—it was less than two weeks away—and Michael realized what he'd done. He wanted to graduate. He had decided that a few months earlier. But Manual administrators had informed him that he was four credits short. His only option was a credit recovery program that would allow him to take the English and history classes he needed online, racing through dozens of assignments and tests, working day and night, so that he could complete the work by May 19.

I had talked to Michael several times throughout the year in his band class. He spoke of his plan to try out for *American Idol* one day and possibly go to a local community college to study music. At the band and choir department's spring concert, he had wowed the crowd with a whirlwind of a rock piano solo he'd written himself. Another day in April we talked after he played with the school band at Conseco Fieldhouse before an Indiana Pacers game. The team had declared the night Manual Night. "I loved it, playing for all the people here," he said. "I think it gets our name out so people don't think we're the ghetto kids. We're really doing good things."

In May he was trying to do the basic things necessary to graduate. Like many of his fellow students, he was finding that past mistakes can come back to haunt you. "I started coming back to school, but I waited a little long," he said sheepishly in the hallway one morning. "I have to start from scratch. I should have been here earlier. Now I realize I might not graduate. It would break my mom's heart."

His mom, Kim, was at home dealing with various health problems and wondering why her very bright son struggled so much in school. He had gotten top grades in the years leading up to high school and even did well as a freshman—so well, in fact, that he'd collected extra credits that first year. Those credits made up for some of the ones he missed as a sophomore and junior. If not for that freshman year, this mad dash at the end of his senior year wouldn't be enough, his mom said, adding that school just wasn't for him. "He doesn't like classes and being around other people," she said. "He is so smart, but he just stopped going to school. He said the classes were so boring he was melting in his seat. It wasn't a challenge for him at Manual, and once it wasn't a challenge, he stopped coming."

Kim said her son complained about other students being disruptive and about riding the school bus. He grew irritated with the problems that were always in the halls at Manual and didn't like people his own age. He grew restless and nervous around them. On the other hand, he did well on standardized tests and was a standout in band—the class that actually persuaded him to give school another try as a senior.

His biggest problem was one that got in the way of success for many students at Manual: the lack of belief in the value of education. He had repeatedly told his mom over the years that he didn't consider a diploma important. "It's just a piece of paper," he argued, saying that shouldn't define his intelligence. "I've had to deal with this forever," his mom said. "It's so frustrating. I always thought he'd get all As and go to college. But he'd rather just sit around and play music. He was a good student for a long time, but then he just fizzled out."

He was interested in school now, though. At least for a couple of weeks. And so he was staying up through the nights, working harder than he had ever worked at school with the hope of cruising through a series of online classes and graduating with his class May 19. "I'm going to do everything I can to get the work done," he said.

Upstairs in the classroom that was called the Opportunity Center, the program for students who had fallen woefully behind in high school, three other students were completing work as graduation day approached. The three would be the first graduates to come out of the three-year-old program. Joyce Cook, who was in her fortieth year as a teacher at the school, was a bundle of excited energy at the thought of her three graduates. She had seen them arrive in her classroom after years of discipline problems and academic struggles. She had watched them grow, mature, and work hard. She said their upcoming graduation would provide hope to the other thirty students in the program. Not all of them, or even most, would follow in the footsteps of the three students. But they would learn key life skills while in the program, in areas such as interviewing, communication, and self-esteem. And regardless of how much they achieved academically, their participation in the program meant they at least received more schooling than they otherwise would have.

Cook was a reminder that the best teachers can also be the most veteran. She served as an argument for making sure teachers have different options within their field even if they decline to switch schools or move into administrative positions. She was no longer interested in the life of a standard teacher, one charged with standing in front of several classes a day and working methodically through lesson plans. She wanted variety, and the Opportunity Center offered plenty of that. The students in this program also offered her the type of challenge she wanted at that point in her career. Her own children were grown. She had more time. And she enjoyed the chance to help her students deal with the drama in their lives. And they had plenty of drama. Some had been in trouble throughout their school years. Many needed special attention. Many had learning disabilities or troubles at home. Some had their own children.

"We have the time to get to know these kids on a very personal level," Cook said. "That's really what every kid in this building needs. But we have the ability to do it. All kids are worth getting to know, and you can make progress with them if you just have the time. They just need someone to love them and care about them. I sometimes wonder how many times these kids have heard 'good job' or 'we're proud of you.' They need to hear that. We make sure they do." Cook continued to talk as her students worked at their computers. "I've always believed that you can't teach them until you get to know them," she said. "I feel like I'm everyone's mother. It's perfect for where I am in my career. These kids have problems. They need to have someone to talk to. And I love listening."

Georgeann Niarchos, who had been teaching for thirty-seven years, walked into the room as Cook talked. The two had led the Opportunity Center program since its first days. "We're like their grandmothers," Niarchos said. "Or their mothers." Many of her students came from homes in which communication consisted of little more than yelling or bickering. Many of them had been largely ignored as children. As such, some just weren't suited for typical classroom environments. They needed attention and guidance, and they got it in this room. Because of that, three students who likely otherwise would have been dropouts were on the verge of graduating. They had a little more work to do but were largely finished.

Michael O'Harra was one of them. He was shy and preferred to be left to himself. The self-paced, computer-based program worked for him. "His feeling," Cook said, "is, 'Tell me what to do, let me do it, and leave me alone.'" As he sat in Cook's office, O'Harra talked about his struggles with school, about getting in trouble frequently when he was younger and missing so much school that only now, at the age of twenty, was he set to graduate. "I'll be the first one in my family to graduate," he said. "My sister and brother dropped out. So did my mom." He didn't know anything about his dad. But he did know plenty of other people who had dropped out, and he had realized that leaving school meant heading down a road toward few opportunities. "Seeing everyone around the neighborhood and their failure," he said, "I just wanted to make something better out of myself." O'Harra was understated and rarely smiled. He said he was happy to graduate but didn't particularly show it.

Jessica Goodman, another soon-to-be graduate, said she hoped her diploma would help her move up at her job at a local hotel. She didn't know exactly what she would do next but knew it would be easier as a graduate.

So did Shkayla Spradley, an eighteen-year-old who had moved to Indiana from Georgia to live with her dad six months earlier. She had fallen behind and was racing to catch up, a chore that was slowed at times because she was eight months pregnant. She was trying to rush through the work she had remaining, but as graduation day approached she'd realized she wasn't going to make it. She wasn't giving up, however. After a short break to have her baby, she would return to her schoolwork and finish over the summer. "I feel like I can be different than most of the people in my family," she said. "All my little brothers and sisters are looking up to me and want to see me do it." Once she graduated she hoped to get a job at Walmart and an apartment for her and her baby. The father wasn't interested in being a part of that experience, but she hoped he would change his mind one day. Either way, she planned to make it. "I'm balancing everything," she said. "I think I can do it. I believe in myself."

Meanwhile, Rachel Tucker, whom I had met on that first day of school in the gymnasium, was ecstatic. She couldn't suppress the wide smile that crossed her face when we talked about the upcoming graduation ceremony that would come after two years of hard catch-up work. "I'm so happy," Rachel said. "For a long time I thought school was not for me, but now I sit back and say, 'Wow, this is amazing!' I get to walk across the stage in my cap and gown and wave to all my friends, and say, 'I made it. I stuck with it and made it.'"

Rachel and the other eligible graduates were called to a senior meeting in the auditorium one morning shortly before graduation day. About 130 students filed in and filled most of the first eight rows of the auditorium. If every student from the class of 2010 who had arrived as freshmen four years earlier were graduating, sixteen more rows would have been filled. Principal Grismore and the other administrators had called the seniors in to talk about the graduation ceremony. But, as usual, this event wasn't filled with inspiring talk. It was filled with the same assembly-line mentality and the same concern about answering to the district bosses that so often dominated life at Manual.

Grismore told the students that top officials from the school district would be observing the graduation rehearsal on the morning of the big day. So they'd better be in their school uniforms that morning, he warned, even though they would not be going to classes. He said the same officials would be at the ceremony that night, checking carefully to make sure students were wearing the proper clothes under their gowns. If they weren't, he told the students, they wouldn't be able to participate in the ceremony. He said Superintendent White had made that clear to school principals and district leaders. "We had a cabinet meeting last night," Grismore said, "and Dr. White said he is going to be looking at your shoes, ladies." Then he reminded the students that many of them had not yet paid various bills owed to the school. That had to be rectified by graduation day, he said, and he reminded the students that checks would not be accepted. Not after all the ones that had bounced in past years. "Dr. White will not let you walk if your bills are unpaid," he said.

White had made a point of trying to eliminate the district's recent tradition of raucous graduation ceremonies. The sight of screaming parents and loud cheers from the stands embarrassed him. He angered some when he said graduation should be seen as the norm and not some sort of miracle. He demanded decorum, and his principals received tremendous grief if White was not satisfied with the crowd's behavior. "The last four years, we've had the best commencement in town," Grismore said. "I want to make sure my fifth commencement is better than the four before it. I want to go out on top. Just do it. Be right."

The students stared at him blankly. And as the meeting ended a bit later, it seemed like another opportunity lost. These were students who in many cases had overcome tremendous obstacles on their way through high school. They had done the work and were now days away from one of the biggest moments in their lives. But there was no celebration and no joy in the room. There was no talk about the future or the many opportunities the students would now have. Instead the moment was focused on pleasing the district boss. It was yet another example of the failure of some schools to instill a spirit of engagement and community into their students. The meeting should have been filled with inspiring words. The students should have been uplifted. Instead they were scolded about unpaid bills and lectured about their shoes.

Fortunately, most of the graduating seniors didn't seem to mind. They were used to the way the district did business. As they walked out, they smiled and talked with one another. They had survived Manual High School.

27

★ ★ ★

WE'VE ACTED LIKE THIS IS OKAY.

The final weeks of the school year raced by quickly. I spent my days trying to file a few final columns I'd been meaning to write while continuing to deal with the avalanche of a response that my column on Brent Jones had generated. But as the days grew warmer and longer and the last day of the school year approached, I knew the series was largely complete.

What an experience it had been. In this one building I had met many of the most interesting people I'd ever come across. I had watched dramatic everyday scenes unfold that would stick with me longer than any of the congressional debates or political conventions I'd covered. I had walked into the building back in August contemplating the conclusion of a career in newspapers that I'd first thought about pursuing when I was five. Now, as Manual students prepared for graduation day, I found myself more energized by the world of journalism than ever. I would be leaving this school with a stronger belief in the unique power of newspapers and the role they can play in their communities. I didn't know what the future would bring, but I did know this school on the south side of Indianapolis had ultimately reminded me that there was nothing else I wanted to do for a living.

I had also learned a lot. I had seen the impact that a strong and engaged teacher can have on a student, and I remained stunned by the refusal of school leaders and city residents to demand that every child spend every possible class with such a teacher. I had seen the heartbreaking effect that apathy—among parents, staff, and the district—can have on the future of students. I had learned that Manual was filled with students who had daunting obstacles standing in their way. In response the school should be filled with volunteers—and they would not be hard to find—whose job it is to help clear away those obstacles. I had been struck by the negative impact of bureaucratic systems that rob school leaders and teachers of their autonomy, flexibility, creativity and, it seemed, passion. I'd become an even stronger advocate of charter schools and other efforts to make sure students can find the education that most fits their needs, rather than being limited to the school, however good or bad it is, that just happens to be closest to their home. Most important, I had learned that something must be done to address the cruel gap in early childhood learning between children born into poverty and those born into wealth or even middle-class environments. Many of the academic problems that devastate Manual can be traced to years before students even started their schooling.

I had come to wonder how this country could allow so many children to go to schools that don't offer the range and quality of opportunities found in wealthier districts, or how we could tolerate assembly-line mentalities that doom schools like Manual to failure. In an interview after my time at Manual ended, Diane Ravitch, an education historian and former assistant U.S. secretary of education, blasted the increasing emphasis on testing in America's schools. "The focus," she said, "has turned schools into factories and killed the ability of schools to address their unique circumstances. Every school has a different profile. You have to send people in and figure out what the issues are in that school. You can't treat every school like it's a pancake going into the frying pan." The apathy I so often wrote about, Ravitch insisted, is a result of the nation's obsession with standardized testing. "Children don't come to school eager to engage in test prep or to take another test," she said. "We need to rethink the ways we try to engage students in schools where there is intense poverty. We have to have more arts programs and other programs that draw students to school. Teachers have to have the freedom to tap into their students' imaginations and creativity and use those things to teach them what they need to know."

I had seen far too few creative solutions to Manual's big problems during my year at the school. That was disappointing because the instances of it that I had seen—in Spencer Lloyd's choir room, for instance, or in Linda Thatcher's program for learning-disabled students—were working well. Still, I didn't fully agree with Ravitch. If done right, testing can provide invaluable data and help schools drive instruction. The problem at Manual was not testing. It was the lack of urgency and expectations. It was indeed, as Ravitch said, the tendency for these schools to have an uninspired one-size-fits-all mentality. And that, Arne Duncan, the U.S. education secretary, told me in a 2011 interview, is killing schools across the nation. "For decades we've acted like this is okay," he said. "We've said that this is the norm and this is what we expect poor kids to do. The lack of urgency has been stunning. Or staggering or disturbing—whatever the word is that you want to use. But it's just stunning how little the country has done about this. It's been a stain on our country, and it's been devastating not only for children but also for communities."

One morning in May I drove to Manual without a specific agenda. I had already written my most recent Sunday column and was doing what I often did: heading south on Madison Avenue just to check in and see if there was anything I was missing. The school was mid-morning quiet when I arrived. It was one of those days that made it easy to forget the fundamental problems the school endures. There were few kids trolling the first-floor hallways, and there was little drama in the dean's office. I stopped and said hello to Dean Hoover, who had recently been told she was being transferred over the summer to another district school. She was already starting to clean out the many plants and pieces of art that decorated her office. Classic rock continued to pour out of her radio, though. "I'll be okay over there," she said, but I wondered what Manual would do without her.

There was nothing going on in the main office, so I left and began wandering the building. As I did, I found myself noticing how special the inside of a high school can seem. I walked past Spencer Lloyd's classroom and heard his choir students singing loudly and preparing for the upcoming spring concert, which would draw about four hundred people without much publicity. I looked inside Linda Thatcher's class and saw her smiling and talking at a table with several of her special-education students. A few minutes later I saw a few students working on computers in the library.

I had often noted the lack of school spirit at Manual—the absence of signs and decorations on the walls and in many of the built-in cases throughout the building. The walls, I had argued, should be filled with pictures of students who, as Kelly and Allison had said early in the school year, were doing the right thing and who were providing Manual with the type of success stories that needed to be more common. But as I walked the halls that morning, I took the closest look I'd taken at the artwork that hung on some of the first floor's white concrete walls. The artwork was part of the school district's wonderful and exhaustive collection of paintings by Indiana artists.

Outside the auditorium there was a decades-old landscape painting, with a horse and buggy in the foreground. There was a painting of an old Indiana barn by T. C. Steele, Indiana's most famous painter, near the office and another by him of Charles Emmerich, the first principal of Manual High School. I had often walked by the paintings and thought that although they were nice, they weren't the best fit for an urban high school, circa 2010. But on this melancholy morning, as I realized I would soon have to move on from a school and a story I had come to love, the beauty of the paintings stuck me. They were part of the school's long and once-proud history, and that history was something that needed to be embraced. Somehow school leaders and teachers had to find a way to draw students into the school experience. For Manual to succeed, its students had to be filled with the same type of pride that can easily be found among students of suburban schools. I stopped and stared quietly in front of painting after painting as if I were walking through an art museum.

I continued to wander the school. A secretary had lent me a key to the alumni office, a room in the back of the building in which I'd spent hours studying the history of the school. I walked in and browsed through the photographs and old books, stopping at a yearbook from 1956, one of the first years that Manual was based in its current building. Dozens of pages were filled with pictures of school groups and clubs overflowing with members. The stories were filled with pride. Students talked of being honored to attend the school. "Manual prepares us for tomorrow," one headline read, adding in smaller text, "A beautiful modern building, set in a picturesque campus and furnished with the finest equipment, makes our school days enjoyable and rewarding." Enjoyable and rewarding. That's not a bad goal for a school.

One class ended and another began while I sat and studied the yearbook. When I returned to the halls they were quiet once again. I walked slowly toward the main office but stopped when I reached a set of doors heading to the outdoor courtyard that the school had closed to most student traffic because of past fights. I pushed one of the doors open and stepped outside, noticing yet again the beauty of my surroundings and the same picturesque campus some student had written about in that yearbook fifty-four years earlier. Two dozen trees decorated the courtyard, and the welding class had planted a large metal sculpture of a blue butterfly in the middle of the yard. The May morning weather was ideal, with just a few clouds overhead and temperatures in the seventies. Leaves had bloomed, and the spring grass was covered with a slight mist.

The courtyard was empty and quiet, and for the first time I noticed a golden-colored plaque on the red brick wall just outside the doors. Its text said the plaque had been donated by the class of 1922 at the time of its graduation and was dedicated to the students who had gone through the school a few years before them, in time to go off to fight in World War I. It had been transferred from the original Manual building to this one when it was built in 1954. "In honor of our schoolmates who answered their country's call," the plaque read, "and, golden-starred, who gave their merry youth away for country and for God."

Not far away sat a small gray memorial stone. Teachers and students had dedicated it just a year earlier in memory of Paschal Robinson, a popular student and star basketball player who everyone in the school had called P. J. The Manual senior had been fatally shot at a party the previous school year, a horrific incident that still left many in the school with raw emotions. "Role model, athlete and friend," the stone's inscription read. "The world is a better place because of the joy you gave us." The plaque rested under the most freshly planted tree in the courtyard.

28

★ ★ ★

YOU ARE SURVIVORS.

Graduation week was a big one for the seniors at Manual. But for Brent Jones it was life-changing. Like the rest of his classmates, his last day of school was the day before the May 19 commencement ceremony. Like the others, he said good-bye to his teachers and his books and the classrooms he'd spent so many hours in. Unlike the other students, he would be meeting his birth mother for the first time on the evening before graduation. But he had so much else on his mind that the meeting wasn't causing him much stress. He insisted it was nothing to get worked up over. After all, he said, his years-long mission to find Elizabeth had centered on his simple desire to find his birth certificate. He hadn't spent his youth pining for a reunion with his birth mom. His fears leading up to the end of high school had to do with uncertainty about his future and not questions about his family history.

He was calm at school that Tuesday. "Meeting her is nice but not necessary," he said, telling me he was a happy young man and that his birth mother's absence hadn't left an emptiness in his life. "Don't get me wrong, it's going to be nice to meet her. But to be honest, what I'm really stressed about is graduation. I want to meet her, but I don't expect to cry tonight or anything."

Part of his calm was no doubt due to the whirlwind that had been his life for the past few weeks. He'd had so many big experiences that yet another wasn't going to knock him off stride. In addition to wrapping up his high school days, he had been on the front page of the newspaper—with his picture above the fold and his name in a bold font. He had visited Vincennes University and gotten word of a scholarship the school would provide. He had received his birth certificate and taken the steps necessary to get a social security card. He had talked to his birth mom. A driver's license and job would be coming soon. "What everyone else here did over three years, I did over three weeks," he said.

Dean Hoover, who had first mentioned Brent's story to me, stood next to him as he talked in the hallway that Tuesday. She smiled and put her arm around him. "It's like the whole world is open to him," she said.

Brent smiled slyly. "The world is my oyster," he said.

Six hours later Brent walked out of his house just a few blocks from Manual and stepped into my Honda. He would be meeting Kim, the woman who'd raised him, and Elizabeth, his birth mom, at 6:30 PM at an Olive Garden in a suburb just west of the city limits. Since Kim had worked at the restaurant for years before leaving for Missouri, and Brent had spent many of his youthful nights at the restaurant, they had many friends there, and Kim had decided it would be the perfect location for a family reunion. She and Elizabeth had met earlier in the day, after Elizabeth's long drive from South Carolina and Kim's from Missouri. They had gotten reacquainted, crying and laughing at times, and would be driving to the restaurant together. Kim asked me if I could drive Brent over to meet them.

I agreed to do so. And with a TV camera crew in my backseat, Brent and I made the thirty-minute drive from his house to the restaurant. He joked along the way, talking about "my mom and bio-mom," a duo he said sounded like the name of a comic book. He pointed to apartment complexes and neighborhoods in which he and Kim had lived over the years. As we approached the strip of chain stores and restaurants that housed the Olive Garden, he smiled and said, "This is my old stomping ground." He shook his head when I asked if he was nervous. "I'm calm, very calm," he said.

He had dressed up for the night, wearing a neatly pressed light blue button-down shirt and black slacks. He wore two earrings and looked like any other American teenager on the verge of graduation. It was hard to believe how much he had gone through on the way to adulthood—just as it is with so many of the students at schools such as Manual. But he wasn't worried about the past. And he wasn't worried about the immediate future, either. "This is going to be fun," he said at one point.

We pulled into the restaurant's parking lot as the sun was setting and walked toward the front doors. Despite the busy afternoon commuter traffic, we were a few minutes early. So we stood and waited. As we did, the TV crew set up near Brent, leading to curious looks from the suburban diners who were walking into and out of the restaurant. Meanwhile, a stream of Olive Garden employees walked outside to see Brent, a young man they'd known for years and who many had watched grow up.

"Hi, handsome," one young waitress said, giving Brent a long hug. He told her he was graduating the following day. "I'm so proud of you," she said.

"Mr. Brent," the manager of the restaurant said a few seconds later, offering a handshake. "How are you?"

Brent chatted with the group for a few minutes but then stopped suddenly, looking past me and looking nervous for the first time. "Here they are," he said, taking a deep breath. Kim and Elizabeth were approaching.

Kim was already near tears, as she would be for much of the night. Elizabeth looked nervous. They were both dressed up in black, looking like a pair of forty-something friends on the town. Kim slowed as they arrived, letting Elizabeth meet up with Brent first. "Hi," Brent said to his birth mom. "How are you?" They hugged for several seconds as Kim looked on, and then they whispered a few words to each other. Elizabeth told Brent she loved him. He returned her words.

Kim walked up after the hug ended and gave Brent one of her own. They had been through a lot over the years. Kim acknowledged in phone conversations that her life was often a sea of drama. But they'd been a duo all those years. "You look awesome," Kim said.

The three of them began to walk into the restaurant. Kim let the other two walk ahead, selflessly giving Brent and Elizabeth time to get to know each other. "This is a good thing," she said as she walked in behind them. "It's been a long time coming. You tell the same story for years and years, and you beg for help. And now, all of a sudden, this is happening."

A few other friends joined the group at a long corner table, and before long everyone was laughing and talking, with Brent calmly in the middle of both the table and the conversation. They had been at the table for only a minute when Brent reached into his pocket and pulled out a ticket to the following night's graduation ceremony, handing it to Elizabeth.

"I'm trying to see a resemblance here," one of Kim's oldest friends said, staring hard at Brent and Elizabeth, bouncing her eyes between them as if she were watching a tennis match. "I think I see it. It's the eyes."

Another one of the friends leaned toward Elizabeth and said it must have been painful to live without her son for so many years. Then she added that it must have been hard waiting to see him for the past three weeks, since the day of their first conversation. "It was," Elizabeth said. "But it's been worth it. My head is spinning, but it's fantastic."

The table was alive with nonstop chatter and activity. Old friends talked and laughed as restaurant employees continued to stop by to say hello. Brent ordered a few appetizers for the group, and at one point I noticed Elizabeth sitting quietly as the others talked. She was the stranger at the table. I moved in and asked how she felt, noticing how pretty she was despite so many years of hard living. "He's a good-looking boy," she said. "I can't believe how big he is."

She had brought with her pictures of Brent's sister and her christening necklace, mementos for him to keep. She had also bought a silver baby rattle and had it monogrammed with Brent's birth date and initials. "Since I wasn't able to give him stuff when he was a baby, I thought I'd give him this now," she said. "He can give this to his child. I couldn't figure out what to give him for graduation. I figured sentimental was better."

The previous three weeks had been surreal, she said, like a dream. It wasn't until she began packing the day before that it felt real. As she talked, Brent sat at the table telling jokes, and I thought how much easier he had made this moment for her. He had been open and friendly and not worried about the past. He was happy to have another friend in his life.

"I'm excited to have a second chance," Elizabeth said. "I want to be in his life as much as I can without being overbearing. I'll take it as slow as we need to. I just want to be in his life."

Brent noticed that Elizabeth hadn't been a part of the broader conversation, so he moved over and began talking to her. He asked about her drive and her hotel. They talked about graduation and Vincennes University and South Carolina. At one point, she told him that his middle name, Patrick, had come from her mother's name, Patricia. They talked, and Kim watched with more tears. "There's a lot of different emotions," she said. "This has put me on a little bit of a roller coaster, but not a bad one. What a story this is. It's a remarkable story. But he's a remarkable kid."

I stayed for only a few more minutes. This was a family event, and they didn't need a journalist there all night. Brent, Kim, and Elizabeth had allowed me to tell their story on the front page of the newspaper, and I'd already gotten enough material to write a follow-up column. Elizabeth had opened her life to me even though she knew it would result in her past demons and mistakes being read by thousands of people. She had agreed to do so because she hoped it would help Brent. Kim had spent hours on the phone talking to me with the hope that her son would finally get the answers and the opportunities he deserved. Brent had given me permission to tell his story in part because he hoped it would help others in a similar situation.

Just before I left, Brent asked a question about the menu, addressing it to "Mom." He was referring to Kim. But he had room in his life for Elizabeth. The next day, the three posted photos of the evening on their Facebook pages. Kim titled her photo gallery, "A new beginning." That perfectly summed up the evening. Even though Brent was ending his high school career, he was beginning a new chapter of his life that was filled with hope and opportunity.

He wasn't alone. The morning after his reunion, Manual's graduating seniors met in the school auditorium for a meeting about that night's ceremony. Before long they would be walking from the auditorium to the school gymnasium, where their friends and families would be waiting on the wooden bleachers. Four years of hard work, and even longer periods of time for some, had led to this evening. The auditorium was filled with students who had been through childhoods filled with poverty, crime-ridden neighborhoods, absentee parents, and, in some cases, personal mistakes that had threatened their futures. But now they were on the verge of an important night in the life of any teenager.

Michael Canner, the young musician, was in the auditorium. He had spent the morning nervously waiting to learn if he had adequately completed the work necessary to pass the online courses he'd spent day and night working on during the previous week. "Are you graduating?" I had asked him earlier in the day as he stood in the hallway biting his fingernails. "That's what I'm trying to find out," he said. Before long, a school counselor walked up to him and, with about seven hours to spare, handed him his tickets for that night's ceremony. "We're okay," she said as Michael smiled. "I made it," he said.

As the hour of the ceremony approached, I thought of the many students I had gotten to know during the year. Students like Jammyra, who had been a good student since her kindergarten year and was as driven as anyone in high school. She had won permission to head down to Indiana University early to take a summer class. That was not only good for her education, but it would also separate her from the family issues that had forced her to bounce among the homes of relatives for the past several years. She had been talking to her mom as graduation approached, but their relationship remained strained. "This has been a long year for me," she said. "I've been through a lot. But I'm just really excited." Then she offered an example of the eighteen-year-old wisdom that had allowed her to overcome obstacles that would have slowed many others. "I can't dwell on the small stuff," she said. "You just have to make sure you take advantage of every opportunity you have and don't let anything get in your way." She certainly hadn't.

Neither had Tricia, the cheerleading calculus student who'd spent her high school years working at a pizza joint and dealing with her sometimes-troubled home life. She was on her way to the University of Indianapolis to study criminal justice and hopefully have four years away from the home and family issues that add to the struggles of so many Manual students. "I don't want to leave," she said, tearing up. "I'm so close to my teachers."

Allison and Kelly, who had sent my series on a wonderful path thanks to their outspoken ways early in the year, smiled and laughed as they stood in the auditorium. They had spent their final weeks of high school plotting their impending departure for southern Indiana, where they would attend Vincennes University and study social work.

Raymond Rutland walked over to me at one point, smiling and giving me a thumbs-up. He'd had a good spring. His grades remained high enough to place him in the top five of his class. And a senior named Tiffany, a tough-talking smoker with a tendency to get in fights with other girls, had invited him to the prom after hearing he was hoping to go. His autism hadn't kept him from succeeding. I said hello to Raymond as he approached.

"I'm going to the University of Indianapolis," he announced, smiling as broadly as possible.

"I know," I said. "Everyone here is so proud of you."

"Okay," he said.

In the back row of the auditorium, far from the graduates, eighteen-year-old Dillon McKee sat watching. He held an infant in his lap. McKee was watching his girlfriend, Rachel, as she prepared to graduate. The two had arrived at Manual as freshmen, but McKee hadn't made it any farther. He came from a family in which few had graduated, and school had always been difficult for him. He gave up before his freshman year was over. Now, four years later, he realized what a mistake he'd made. He worked as a telemarketer, unable to get anything better because of his lack of education. He was only eighteen but said he knew he faced the prospect of one awful job after another. "I quit for some reason," he said of high school. "It was a stupid idea." Still, he was proud that Rachel had made it, even while giving birth during her last semester in school. He bounced his child on his lap and pointed to her mom.

At the front of the auditorium, the graduates-to-be listened as a district official once again warned them about the commencement ceremony's rules—the dress code, for instance, and the requirement that audience members not clap when a friend or relative's name is called. "You know what's expected," the official said. "Please make sure that the people you give tickets to understand the rules."

It was another lackluster way to end a meeting. But the students left the auditorium in smiles. Principal Grismore stood to the side as they filed out of the room. "This is my last graduation," he said. "It's always hard to say good-bye to kids. It's going to be particularly hard to do tonight." As the last kids left the room, he quietly offered one more thought. "It's a hell of a group of kids," he said.

A few hours later that group of kids headed from the auditorium to the school gymnasium. The boys wore red caps and gowns while the girls wore white. They walked quietly through the halls, passing the main office and their lockers and classrooms. Raucous cheers and waves and applause greeted them when they stepped onto the gym's wood floors. Few flinched as they continued walking, moving past the ROTC color guard and school police officers on their way to the red plastic chairs that awaited them. They stood in front of those chairs during the Pledge of Allegiance and the school band's playing of the national anthem. They sat as Spencer Lloyd led two dozen of his best choir students—the boys wore black tuxedos and the girls black gowns—through "Irish Blessing," a quiet song filled with inspiration. "May the sun shine warm upon your face," they sang softly, "and the rains fall soft upon your fields."

Superintendent White was on hand to deliver the commencement address, receiving a mild welcome from the crowd when he was introduced. "It's been a long time coming," he told the students. "No one gave you this. You earned the right to be here tonight. You should feel proud that you are here. So many others started with you but aren't here tonight. You are survivors." The students sat silently as White talked. "Tonight is your beginning," he said. "All along the way you had so many things going against you. Despite those setbacks, those obstructions in your way, you have proven that you are going to make it."

In the crowd, friends and relatives took pictures of their graduates. Some cried. Many smiled. Police kicked out two people in the audience for shouting a graduate's name. "Get on up," Officer Donnita Miller told the two, dismissing their appeals. "Go. Now!"

On stage, White finished his speech. "These are some of the best young people in this country," he said. "And they are destined to do great things."

The audience applauded. One of those doing so was the soon-to-be retired math teacher I'd seen lead so many lackluster classes. She watched the students quietly on this evening, one of a minority of teachers at Manual who had taken the time to attend the ceremony. I had often noted that in her classes the teacher seemed burned out and disinterested and that her room was frequently in chaos. But on that night she dabbed tears from her eyes. I didn't know what to make of that.

Once White concluded his speech, the graduates walked across the stage. They received a handshake and diploma from the superintendent as Principal Grismore read short statements of thanks the students had written. They thanked family members, friends, and teachers. A boy named Sammy thanked his wife, and several girls thanked their children.

"Thanks to God, my family, and my baby," one girl's statement said. "They all pushed me to succeed."

"I would like to thank my parents, who are resting in peace," another said. "This is for you."

"Much love," a boy named Newton had written. "Thanks to all."

In the audience Tamika Johnson waved her arms energetically and covered her mouth, trying desperately not to violate the rules against cheering when her niece and nephew walked across the stage. "They're just the fourth graduates in our whole family in four generations," she said later. "I'm just so excited."

Back on stage Grismore read the words of the last graduates before finally allowing the audience to cheer. Then he turned to the students before him. "On behalf of the Emmerich Manual High School faculty and alumni, we welcome the class of 2010 into the fellowship of those who have been privileged to graduate from this institution," he said.

As I stood and watched the students file out of the room, I spotted Vickie Winslow, the great English teacher who once told me about the regularity with which students cursed at her and whose frankness had led to a public rebuke from Superintendent White. She received a steady stream of hugs from her now-former students. She told them she would miss them and asked them to keep in touch. "Do good things," she added.

It had been a long, hard year at Manual High School. Many of her students had disappeared during the school year. Others had been arrested, expelled, or were the source of headaches in the classroom. She was tired. She was ready for summer. But as she watched the graduates gather in the courtyard to toss their caps in the air triumphantly, Winslow smiled. "The school year can drain a person," she said. "But this makes me want to do it all again."

★ ★ ★

EPILOGUE

On a hot afternoon in the summer of 2011, roughly a year after I ended my series on Manual High School, I walked into the Indiana Statehouse and headed toward the offices of the Department of Education. In a cavernous room there, Superintendent of Public Instruction Tony Bennett was huddled with his five top staffers and advisors. The question they were pondering that day was whether to launch a state takeover of up to six Indianapolis schools—a collection of schools that according to the data and a series of investigations had long ranked as the worst-performing in Indiana.

Manual High School, of course, was on that list. The threat of such a takeover had hung like a dark cloud over the school during the entire year I spent there. Teachers would routinely ask me about the confusing decision-making process and whether I thought Bennett was serious about the idea, and the issue was at the center of the infamous 2010 meeting between local and state officials at which IPS Superintendent Eugene White estimated that 60 percent of the teachers at his worst schools were downright ineffective. Now, after years of failure, Manual's fate that afternoon was in the hands of a small group of state officials.

What struck me most about the meeting, which Bennett had agreed to let me observe, was how quickly the group made its decision regarding Manual. Unlike with some of the other schools, there was no real debate. The idea that radical state intervention at the school was warranted was a foregone conclusion. There was no reason, the group declared, to believe Manual in its current form and with its current leadership could be salvaged. There was no driving force pushing the type of reform the school needed and even if there had been, the dysfunctional school district would likely get in the way. Thus, the group agreed that a private firm would be brought in to run the school beginning in the summer of 2012, ending more than a century of local control at one of Indianapolis's most historic schools.

A few weeks later, after the state officials decided to take over Manual and three of the other city schools, the local school district announced plans to challenge the decision in court. But that challenge would be limited to two of the other schools. White would not dispute the state's declaration that Manual was failing or fight its decision to seize control of the once-great school. Local control of Manual would end with a whimper.

I couldn't help but feel sad about the state's decision, even though I supported it. I'd grown to love the troubled school, and the drastic move served as a reminder of its tragic decline. I felt for many of the teachers, those who cared so much about their students and who would now enter a long period of uncertainty, as many months would pass before they would learn if they still had jobs. Shortly after the announcement, I grabbed a beer with welding teacher Jason Wiley, who had become a friend during my time at the school. In recent years, he had singlehandedly persuaded many at-risk students to stay in school by talking to them daily about the need to have a diploma to go along with their welding certificates, by convincing them of the comfortable life a welding career could offer, and by making his class a lure that kept them coming back to school and going to their other classes. Now, his future was uncertain.

"Those kids need that program," he said. "I'll be fine if I lose my job. I can get another one. But I want to be there for those kids."

Unfortunately, the dedication and passion found in Wiley has not been the norm at Manual for many years. And as much as I felt for him and the others who had refused to give up, it had long ago become clear to me that radical change was needed. Still, a forced intervention is no guarantee of success.

From disengaged parents to the emotional baggage so many students carry to school, the challenges facing Manual will remain. The state's move is at its core an experiment and, in a way, Manual is a guinea pig. Bennett promised dynamic new school leadership teams, better teachers, and a more flexible curriculum that better suits the needs of individual students. With the takeover, the school will be free of the dysfunctional district bureaucracy and contract rules that have long made it hard to get rid of burned-out teachers. But in the end, it's an experiment.

I can only hope it works. The hard-hit neighborhood surrounding Manual desperately needs a good school. And while many of the students I got to know will be gone by the time the new operator moves in, generations of students with similar faces and similar stories will follow them. They deserve better.

The year I spent at Manual has become a major part of my life. Rarely does a day pass without someone talking to me about my series or asking about the students who starred in it. And few days have passed without my thinking about the time I spent there, the people I met, and the role the school played in reminding me of my love for journalism. I don't go back to the school often, but every time I drive by the red-brick building I quietly think about a year filled with both heartbreaking scenes and inspiring moments. It feels like driving by a house I once lived in; it's not mine any longer, but it is so full of memories.

I still don't completely understand why the series connected so deeply with so many people. But I'm pretty sure it is because many readers for the first time got to know, through the paper, the people who spend their days in the struggling schools they hear so much about. In many ways, I've since realized, my job was easy. All I had to do was step away from legislative hearings and policy papers and head to the epicenter of the nation's education debate. Once there, I just wrote down what I saw—the good and the bad—and quoted the voices of the students, parents, and teachers I met. Their stories and words taught me daily lessons about the power of education, the cost of failure, and the challenges facing those who want to improve our schools. Most importantly, I learned more about the students whose futures are on the line.

Most often, people ask me about Brent Jones, the boy who went far too long with lingering questions about his identity. I tell them that Brent has grown into a fine young man. He completed one year at Vincennes University and then moved back to Indianapolis, where he plans to continue his culinary education at one of the many schools in the city. He talks occasionally to his birth mom and almost daily to Kim, the woman who raised him. We get together for lunch or dinner sometimes and whenever we meet I remind him of how much he talked about wanting a college degree during our many conversations at Manual. I have no doubt he'll eventually earn such a degree.

People also often ask about Kelly and Allison, the two seniors who set my series on a wonderful path with the tough questions they aimed in my direction early in the school year. The two young women are thriving, getting great grades at Vincennes, where they are both studying to become social workers. When we caught up over pizza in the summer of 2011, they still laughed as much as ever, but their worlds are now bigger. Allison talked about her hope to study overseas, and they both talked about continuing their educations after Vincennes and eventually building successful careers.

"I loved Manual," Kelly told me. "But kids need to realize there is so much more out there."

Raymond Rutland, meanwhile, continues to overcome challenges placed in his way by autism. He earned good grades during his first year at the University of Indianapolis and is continuing toward his goal of becoming a graphic artist. I stopped by Raymond's house one day to drop off a package of books and pictures that the producers of *SpongeBob SquarePants* had sent to my office after reading of his love of the show in one of my columns. He smiled and, when I asked, said his favorite thing about college life was the cafeteria.

Another memorable student, Brent Walls, continues to struggle. I drove home from prison with Brent on the day before Thanksgiving in 2010. He had just finished a nearly year-long sentence for bringing a loaded handgun to Manual one morning and, as we drove, he promised to stay clean and out of trouble. He talked about the Indianapolis Colts, and his hope to get a job and spend as much time as possible with his family. But major obstacles, internal and external, face an eighteen-year-old ex-con. Before long, Brent was involved in a minor scrape with the law, centering around a neighborhood fight. It wasn't much, but it was enough to land him back in prison, where he finished the final five months of his probation.

"I'm really trying," he said when we met at a Wendy's one afternoon after his second stint in prison ended. "But it's hard."

One of the most interesting reunions I had with a student came in the fall of 2010 as I worked on a column at another Indianapolis high school. As I walked through the campus that afternoon, I crossed paths with a student who stopped and stared at me. "Zach," I said, recognizing the former Manual student who had once so desperately wanted to beat me up for writing about his brother's drug arrest. On this day, though, old grudges had clearly been forgotten. Zach reached out to shake my hand and we talked for a few minutes about his plan to graduate and, at seventeen, about his impending fatherhood. I wished him well as we said our good-byes.

The school those students once attended is now a much different place. Even before the state takeover was announced, the district had transferred roughly half of the staff, haphazardly hoping to show that it was serious about reform. The move cost Manual some of its best teachers, however, teachers such as Vickie Winslow and Jill Haughawout. And the effort was too little, too late. Too many kids had gone through a building filled with apathy and low expectations. Too many years and classes have passed without sufficient effort. Too much potential has gone untapped. Another round of tweaks didn't impress state officials, and they didn't impress me.

People often ask me if I think the state takeover will lead to a real turnaround. It's the toughest question I receive. I honestly don't know the answer. But I do know it will only happen if the school's new leaders can somehow change the building's ingrained culture of apathy and connect with the parents who too often are absent from their children's education. It will only happen if they do a better job of addressing the social problems that hobble so many students and find ways to connect the school with its community. It will only happen if students on each school day enter a building filled with energy and high expectations.

That said, the state's unwillingness to accept the status quo is heartening. And if you walk into the school, there are still signs of hope. Sergeant Barrow continues to patrol the halls with his undying energy. And then there is Spencer Lloyd's choir room. Hopefully, Spencer will remain at the school for many years to come and have a chance to build his choir into the powerhouse program he envisions.

One day, as I sat in my office at the newspaper, I received an e-mail from a concert organizer in New York City. His company had read about Spencer's music program and had invited it to join a handful of other school choirs at a concert at Carnegie Hall in early 2012. It would be a wonderful opportunity for the program and for a group of students who, for the most part, have never traveled far from Indianapolis. There was only one problem: The trip would cost Manual $30,000, and that wasn't in the budget.

One afternoon, I met Spencer at a downtown coffee shop to talk about the trip. I brought along my infant son, Reid, whom my wife and I had adopted at birth eight months after my series on Manual ended. My son's arrival had only intensified my belief in the urgent need to improve this nation's schools and make sure every child has a chance to thrive. As we talked, Spencer held Reid, making silly faces and lifting him in the air.

"You're going to study hard and go to a good school, right?" Spencer said at one point, as Reid and I smiled.

I'd already decided to write about the Carnegie Hall trip and to once again challenge the people of Indianapolis to help out a teacher and a group of students who deserved it. Would it work? I didn't know. The school had been out of the spotlight for months. But I wrote the column anyway, hoping it would at least help Spencer raise the few thousand dollars needed to make a down payment on the travel costs. I filled the column with more scenes of Spencer's engaging class and the words of his hard-working students.

The column ran on a Sunday in the spring of 2011, under a headline that read, "Manual choir needs more than practice to get to Carnegie Hall." Once again, the community responded. By the end of the week, Spencer's classroom was filled with hundreds of cards and letters. People who had been inspired by his work and his students wrote words of encouragement and support and included checks large and small. By the time Spencer was done counting, his choir had collected more than $90,000. The ManualAires would be going to New York to sing on one of the world's most famous stages.

The community reaction was a reminder of the deep concern so many people have for the students who fill America's struggling schools. It was an example of the deep well of support for such students that this country's education leaders must find a way to harness. For me, it was a reminder of how lucky I was to have somewhat blindly walked through the front doors of the school nearly two years earlier. And, as I wondered what would happen to Manual under its new leadership structure, it was yet another reason to have hope.

MATTHEW TULLY is an award-winning journalist who has written a popular column for the *Indianapolis Star* since 2005. Raised in northwest Indiana, Tully is a 1992 graduate of Indiana University. His commentary has appeared in the *Wall Street Journal* and *Education Week*. He has appeared on MSNBC, NPR, CNN, and numerous other national media outlets. Tully lives in Indianapolis with his wife, Valerie, and their son, Reid.

★ ★ ★